SOCIALISM

SOCIALISM

Edited by

**Ellen Frankel Paul, Fred D. Miller Jr,
Jeffrey Paul and Dan Greenberg**

BASIL BLACKWELL
for the
Social Philosophy and Policy Center
Bowling Green State University

Typeset in 10 on 12 pt Ehrhardt
by SB Datagraphics Ltd, Colchester
Printed in Great Britain by Whitstable Litho, Kent.

Contents

INTRODUCTION

One of the most bitterly argued debates of our time is the ongoing dispute over the nature of socialism. What, exactly, is it? Is it primarily authoritarian or democratic? What is the moral theory which underlies it? Can it be merged with a market system? Is it compatible with individual rights? Does it supply freedom or slavery to those under it? And what does the historical performance of societies proclaiming themselves to be socialist have to do with the nature of socialism?

These questions are particularly relevant in light of the changes that are sweeping the world today. While the political and economic course of the Soviet Union is the subject of debate both within and beyond that country, socialist ideas and ideals continue to animate many of the inhabitants of what is called the Third World. In many Western industrialized countries, large numbers of people are favorably disposed towards some form or other of socialism. The following essays in this volume explore several of the many important questions about the nature of socialism, as well as the consequences of certain answers.

The first three essays are concerned primarily with the normative foundations of socialism; they each offer an account of a moral theory which might support a socialist society. Daniel Little, in "Socialist Morality: Towards a Political Philosophy for Democratic Socialism," argues that there is a coherent moral foundation for democratic socialism. Little's democratic socialism is based on the values of human freedom, self-determination, social cooperation based on equality, and confidence in the possible universality (and the resulting electoral feasibility) of socialist arrangements. On his view, socialist political actors (both in their pursuit of political power and after its attainment) must respect conventional democratic institutions of decision-making and policy implementation. Several implications follow from these constraints: the politics of democratic socialism require that socialist political measures be supported by majorities, as well as that an effective set of decision-making institutions be created which both respect individuals' rights and embrace universal suffrage. The use of force for socialist ends is thus prohibited in a free and democratic society; a socialist party may use force in an effort to gain political power only if legal and democratic means do not exist.

Joshua Cohen's "The Economic Basis of Deliberative Democracy" is also concerned with democratic socialism. His essay proposes a philosophical account of socialism that proceeds from the idea that socialism represents an extension of democratic ideals. To characterize those ideals, Cohen develops the notion of a deliberative democracy, an association in which the justification of the terms of association is based upon the free deliberation of the members of that association. He explores the connections between this deliberative conception and notions of autonomy and the common good. He then shows how this conception, in conjunction with several arguments about the ways that capitalism constrains free deliberation among equals, provides the basis for democratic socialism. He pays particular attention to the way that socialist concerns about workplace democracy and public control of investment are intimately tied to the deliberative ideal.

David Miller is more concerned with the "quality of life" aspect of the socialist critique of capitalism, asking "In What Sense Must Socialism Be Communitarian?" In contrast to the tendency of many other contemporary socialist theorists, he wants to emphasize the question of what sort of good life will be lived under socialism, rather than the question of the way goods will be distributed in that system. He argues that a socialism based on justice cannot entirely dispense with communitarian ideals, as it requires social relationships that embody an appropriate conception of distributive justice. The interpretations of community offered by Alasdair MacIntyre, Charles Taylor, and Michael Sandel are examined and found inadequate for this purpose. Miller finds that a socialist conception of community must be spelled out in terms of citizenship, and therefore directs socialists to come to terms with nationality as a source of communal identity.

The next two essays suggest that capitalist solutions to two different economic problems are inherently problematic. John E. Roemer challenges the conventional wisdom on the "tragedy of the commons": the idea that the inefficiency and waste produced by common access to a scarce resource is best resolved by privatization. In "A Public Ownership Resolution of the Tragedy of the Commons," he argues that public ownership can resolve inefficiency as well as realize distributional goals that privatization ignores. Four resource allocation rules are offered as suggestions to a planner who wishes to resolve the "tragedy of the commons" and retain public ownership of the common resource. Roemer then investigates whether these methods can be decentralized in an economy where the planner lacks knowledge about the preferences and skills of the agents, and finds that some of them can be. Roemer is also interested in whether there is an efficient procedure for privatizing the commons which also satisfies Robert Nozick's version of the Lockean proviso (namely, that privatization by one must leave all others at least as well off as they were when the resource was used in common); he

finds that society cannot devise a laissez-faire rule for resource allocation that
satisfies the demands of both Nozick's Lockean proviso and Pareto-
optimality.

Jon Elster's essay is an attempt to answer the following question: why are
there so few cooperative enterprises in capitalist economies? In "From Here
to There; or, If Cooperative Ownership Is So Desirable, Why Are There So
Few Cooperatives?" he begins by describing two sorts of answers. The first is
that cooperatives are inherently inefficient relative to capitalist firms, even
when accounting for the additional benefits derived from cooperation; the
second is that cooperatives are worse performers when they are isolated
enclaves in a capitalist economy than when they are part of an all-cooperative
economy. Elster discusses several varieties of the second answer, including
endogenous preference formation, adverse selection, discrimination, and
externalities. He then discusses several historical examples of cooperatives
and the resulting implications for political action.

Loren Lomasky takes a rather different tack in a paper entitled "Socialism
as Classical Political Philosophy." He begins by noting an oddity: socialism
has managed to retain its luster in many quarters despite a general eclipse of
the Marxian economic theory on which it was constructed. In his paper, he
provides a possible explanation for socialism's continuing appeal. Arguing
that socialism's perceived advantages are primarily political and not
economic, he suggests that those political advantages have a distinctly
classical flavor. That is, socialism's underpinnings hew to ideals that
dominated the political thought of Athens and the medieval world; those
ideals were jettisoned by Machiavelli, Hobbes, and their successors. Lomasky
identifies classical motifs that shape the politics of Marx and other leading
socialist figures – a politics of deliberation, hierarchy, and the remaking of
the character of citizens. He argues that the persistent attractiveness of these
ideals renders socialism largely impervious to disconfirmation by developments within the theory and practice of economics.

The next three essays are all concerned, in one way or another, with the
socialist calculation debate. This debate – at least as it was perceived by F.A.
Hayek, Oskar Lange, Ludwig von Mises, and other leading participants –
was primarily about whether or not central planners would be able to make
the calculations needed to run a socialist economy with any appreciable
degree of efficiency or, indeed, to run it at all. Daniel Shapiro's essay,
"Reviving the Socialist Calculation Debate: A Defense of Hayek against
Lange," offers a critique of Allen Buchanan's account of the debate in *Ethics,
Efficiency, and the Market*. In this book, it is argued that Hayek failed to show
that the absence of a producer goods market in Lange's version of market
socialism would produce serious inefficiencies. This argument rests on the
claim that a central planning board – which would fix prices and plan

investment – could mimic a perfectly competitive market; since a perfectly competitive market is Pareto-optimal and therefore efficient, Lange has allegedly refuted Hayek's claim of the superiority of market capitalism. Shapiro suggests that Buchanan's defense of Lange fails because of a misunderstanding of Hayek. Since Hayek argued that economic problems arise primarily because of the nature of economic information (it's scattered, scarce, and constantly changing), models of perfect information or perfect competition are irrelevant. Hayek's standard was plan coordination: the completion and coordination of as many different plans as possible. Shapiro argues that the coordinating processes such as price and product competition that are found in real markets would be crippled in Lange's system, and suggests that the ultimate winner of the socialist calculation debate is, therefore, Hayek.

N. Scott Arnold's paper, "Marx, Central Planning, and Utopian Socialism," is also, in part, an exploration of the socialist calculation debate. Arnold's primary emphasis is on Marx's vision of the economic system of post-capitalist society. He argues that Marx thought post-capitalist society would necessarily have a planned economy. Since the economic results of central planning have not been promising, this creates a problem for Marxists which can be evaded only by denying that Marx favored central planning or affirming the value of this practice. The first half of Arnold's essay documents and provides the motivation for this account of Marx's support of central planning; the second half explores the normative and theoretical problems that a defense of central planning creates for Marx and his defenders. The key to this second half is a reconstructed version of the argument of Hayek and Mises that, as compared to market economies, central planning must be grossly inefficient.

John O'Neill, on the other hand, suggests in "Markets, Socialism, and Information: Reformulation of a Marxian Objection to the Market" that recent theorists tend to ignore crucial problems endemic to markets. O'Neill notes that proponents of market socialism have attempted to argue that the only defensible form of socialism is some version of market socialism. These arguments have involved a rejection of Marx's account of economic crises in capitalism, and an acceptance of some features of the Austrian model of the market. O'Neill then claims that proponents of market socialism misrepresent the Marxian critique of the market, and he reformulates some of Marx's central claims through a criticism of Hayek's account of the Austrian model of the market. He argues that an important claim of Hayek's – that the price mechanism provides all information relevant to the coordination of economic actors – is false, and therefore that his implicit assumption that the communication of relevant information is a sufficient condition for such coordination must be rejected. In this way, the Marxian analysis of economic crises in capitalism as coordination failures can be sustained. O'Neill concludes by suggesting that recent work by defenders of market socialism fails to address the coordination problems inherent in market economies.

The last two essays raise questions about more concrete aspects of socialism. Williamson M. Evers, in "Liberty of the Press under Socialism," investigates what sort of liberty of the press is possible in a socialist society. According to one influential model of socialism, the sole employer and the sole owner of resources is the state. In a society of this sort, is liberty of the press likely? Some socialist theorists contend that this is a basically empirical question, while others draw on socialist theory for a response. Evers critically analyzes the plans that have been proposed by various socialist theorists to ensure liberty of the press where resources have been nationalized. He also sketches a history of the newspapers in the Soviet Union in order to show the effect of Soviet economic structure and economic policy on liberty of the press.

Finally, Alec Nove raises the question of the significance of the historical experience of the Soviet Union for the success or failure of socialism. In "Socialism, Capitalism, and the Soviet Experience," Nove examines the deficiencies of the Soviet model of centralized economic planning, and then discusses in what ways these deficiencies are indicative of problems inherent in socialism. Since it is not analytically correct to equate the deficiencies of the real Soviet economy with smoothly functioning neoclassical economic models, Nove describes a variety of ways that meaningful comparisons can be made between real socialist and real capitalist economies. He concludes with an examination of whether the Gorbachev reforms can find ways to overcome the defects of centralized planning while retaining an economic system which could fairly be termed socialist.

Questions about the nature of socialism will continue to be of primary importance in the continuing search by intellectuals, politicians, and the public for the best ways to order our collective affairs. These essays, along with those in our companion volume, *Capitalism*, should be of aid in resolving some of the issues crucial to a complete understanding of these competing models of a good society.

CONTRIBUTORS

Daniel Little is an Associate Professor of Philosophy at Colgate University. He is the author of *The Scientific Marx* (University of Minnesota, 1986), *Explaining Agrarian Change* (Yale University Press, forthcoming), and articles on Marxism, rational choice, and the philosophy of social science. His current research interests involve the study of various theories of collective action in application to processes of social change in China.

Joshua Cohen is an Associate Professor of Philosophy and Political Science at MIT. He is the co-author (with Joel Rogers) of *On Democracy* (Penguin, 1983), *Inequity and Intervention* (South End, 1986), and *Rules of the Game* (South End, 1986), and his articles on issues of political philosophy and social theory have appeared in the *Journal of Philosophy*, *Philosophy and Public Affairs*, and *Ethics*. He is currently working on issues of democratic theory and on problems at the intersection of ethics and historical sociology, in particular on the connections between the injustice of slavery and its demise.

David Miller is Official Fellow in Social and Political Theory at Nuffield College, Oxford. His books include *Social Justice* (Clarendon Press, 1976), *Philosophy and Ideology in Hume's Political Thought* (Clarendon Press, 1981), and *Anarchism* (Dent, 1984). He has a long-standing research interest in the theoretical foundations of market socialism; his book on this subject, entitled *Market, State and Community*, will be published by the Clarendon Press in 1989.

John E. Roemer is Professor of Economics at the University of California at Davis. His latest book, *Free to Lose: An Introduction to Marxist Economic Philosophy* (Harvard University Press, 1988), uses elementary microeconomic models to study the relationship between exploitation, class, and wealth. In recent work, he has applied methods of mathematical economics to study questions of political philosophy in a formal way, as in, for example, "Egalitarianism, Reponsibility, and Information," in *Economics and Philosophy* (1987). Currently, he is working on problems having to do with public ownership.

Jon Elster is a Professor of Political Science at the University of Chicago and Research Director at the Institute for Social Research, Oslo. Among his publications are: *Leibniz et la Formation de l'Esprit Capitaliste* (1975), *Logic and Society* (1978), *Ulysses and the Sirens* (1979), *Explaining Technical Change* (1983), *Sour Grapes* (1983), and *Making Sense of Marx* (1985). *Solomonic Judgments, The Cement of Society*, and *Nuts and Bolts for the Social Sciences* will be published by Cambridge University Press in the fall of 1989.

Loren E. Lomasky is Professor of Philosophy at the University of Minnesota, Duluth and has been a visiting scholar at Virginia Polytechnic Institute, Australian National University, and the Social Philosophy and Policy Center. Lomasky's research interests include ethics, political philosophy, and the philosophy of religion. He is the author of *Persons, Rights, and the Moral Community* (Oxford University Press, 1987) and, with Geoffrey Brennan, *Democracy and Decision* (Cambridge University Press, forthcoming).

Daniel Shapiro is Assistant Professor of Philosophy at West Virginia University. He received his Ph.D. from the University of Minnesota in 1984 and has previously taught at Rice University, the University of North Carolina at Chapel Hill, and Bowling Green State University. Among his areas of interest are rights theory and Marxism. His articles have appeared in *Canadian Journal of Philosophy*, *Public Affairs Quarterly*, and *Philosophical Studies*.

N. Scott Arnold is an Associate Professor of Philosophy at the University of Alabama at Birmingham. He has written extensively on the ethics and economics of capitalism and socialism. In the summers of 1987 and 1988 he was a visiting scholar at the Social Philosophy and Policy Center. His book, *Marx's Radical Critique of Capitalist Society*, will be published by Oxford University Press in the fall of 1989.

John O'Neill is a Lecturer in Philosophy at the University College of North Wales, Bangor. After receiving his Ph.D. in philosophy from Lancaster University in 1984, he was a Lecturer in Philosophy and Politics in Beijing, China (1984–85), and then in 1986–88 was Research Fellow in the Philosophy Department at Lancaster University. His publications include papers in *Inquiry*, *Studies in History and Philosophy of Science*, *The British Journal for the Philosophy of Science*, and *Philosophy of the Social Sciences*. In addition, a play of his was produced by *BBC Radio 3*.

Williamson M. Evers is a National Fellow at the Hoover Institution at Stanford University. He was a Visiting Assistant Professor of Political Science at Emory University during 1987–88, after having received his Ph.D. from Stanford University in 1987. He has published articles on the history of political thought, on political philosophy and public policy, and on legal philosophy. He is currently writing a book on the bioethics of aspects of human genetic engineering.

CONTRIBUTORS

Alec Nove is Professor Emeritus of Economics and former Director of the Institute of Soviet and East European Studies at the University of Glasgow. He is a Fellow of the British Academy, a Fellow of the Royal Society of Edinburgh, and an Honorary Fellow of the London School of Economics. He has held numerous visiting appointments, including ones at Kansas, Columbia, Pennsylvania, U.C.L.A., Paris, Rennes, Santiago (Chile), and Montreal. His publications include *The Soviet Economic System*, *Economic History of the USSR*, *Stalinism and After*, *Political Economy and Soviet Socialism*, *Socialism, Economics and Development*, and *"Glasnost" in Action* (forthcoming).

ACKNOWLEDGMENTS

The editors wish to acknowledge several individuals at the Social Philosophy and Policy Center, Bowling Green State University, who provided invaluable assistance in the preparation of this volume. They include Mary Dilsaver, Terrie Weaver, Cameron Webster and Kim Kohut.

We wish to thank Executive Manager Kory Tilgner, for his tireless administrative support; Publication Specialist Tamara Sharp, for her patient attention to detail; and Managing Editor Dan Greenberg, for editorial assistance above and beyond the call of duty.

SOCIALIST MORALITY: TOWARDS A POLITICAL PHILOSOPHY FOR DEMOCRATIC SOCIALISM*

BY DANIEL LITTLE

There has been much discussion in recent years of the role of moral ideas within Marxism.[1] Marx's stringent criticisms of purely philosophical inquiry impose rather narrow limits on the form which a Marxian moral philosophy might take. For Marx often holds that moral ideas and moral theorizing are irremediably ideological. By this Marx appears to mean that moral ideas are part and parcel of a system of class domination, a way of preserving class domination through internalized norms.[2] As many recent commentators have shown, however, these criticisms of moral reasoning, though present in Marx's system, cannot be the beginning and end of his stance on moral matters. For Marx himself is committed to making normative judgments about capitalism and socialism, and there is a richly textured set of normative ideas that run through his writings from early to late.[3] Further, and perhaps more compellingly, there is a pressing need internal to Marxism for discussion of moral ideas in order to steer the course towards the attainment of socialism. Marx's approach to socialism is a distinctly rationalist one; he regards revolution and socialism as objects of rational, strategic deliberation among both leaders and workers. In order to make out such a view, it is necessary to provide for rational consideration both of goals and of means,

[1] George Brenkert, *Marx's Ethics of Freedom* (London: Routledge & Kegan Paul, 1983); Allen Wood, *Karl Marx* (London: Routledge & Kegan Paul, 1981); Steven Lukes, *Marxism and Morality* (Oxford: Oxford University Press, 1985); Richard Miller, *Analyzing Marx* (Princeton: Princeton University Press, 1984); Adam Przeworski, *Capitalism and Social Democracy* (Cambridge: Cambridge University Press, 1985); John Roemer, ed., *Analytical Marxism* (Cambridge: Cambridge University Press, 1986).

[2] Allen Wood, *Karl Marx*, pp. 141–45; Richard Miller, *Analyzing Marx*, pp. 45–50; George Brenkert, *Marx's Ethics of Freedom*, ch. 3; and Steven Lukes, *Marxism and Morality*, pp. 5–10.

[3] George Brenkert provides the most extensive arguments in support of this view. "Marx's views on ideology and the justification of moral judgments also allow for a Marxist morality. This morality is not simply relativistic but one which is applicable to communist society as well as to previous societies" (*Marx's Ethics of Freedom*, p. 81). See also Daniel Little, "Rationality, Ideology, and Morality in Marx's Social Theory," *Social Praxis*, vol. 8 (1981), pp. 73–88.

* I am grateful for comments received on earlier versions of this paper from Kenneth Winkler, Gerald Doppelt, Charles Beitz, and an anonymous reader for this journal.

and this requires moral deliberation.[4] It is therefore legitimate to hold – from a Marxian point of view – that it is both possible and desirable to attempt to work out the implications of the set of normative commitments (e.g., freedom, autonomy, democracy, solidarity, etc.) which lie at the heart of Marxism.

A variety of authors have shown that Marx's own writings contain substantial resources upon which to construct a socialist morality. First, Marx's corpus contains a set of ideas about fundamental human values: freedom, self-actualization, community, democracy, emancipation, and the like. George Brenkert has given an extensive treatment of the idea of freedom in Marx; Allen Wood, despite his anti-moralist conclusions, gives a clear exposition of the role of the idea of self-actualization in Marx's system;[5] and Alan Gilbert analyzes some of the Aristotelian features of Marx's moral ideas.[6] These ideas are expressed throughout Marx's writings, from the *Economic and Philosophic Manuscripts* to *Capital*. This set of ideas is complex and developed; it changes through the course of Marx's writings; and it unavoidably points to a normative system within classical Marxism. Jointly these ideas contribute to a theory of the good for human beings.

Second, Marx's normative system contains a framework of social criticism which is grounded in these values. This framework includes the theory of alienation, the idea of exploitation, Marx's criticisms of the division of labor in *Capital*, and the like. Different social arrangements are faulted on the ground that they undermine or subvert various of the values identified in the theory of the good; thus the theory of alienation depends on the idea of freedom,[7] and Marx's criticisms of the division of labor in *Capital* presuppose the value of self-actualization as a human good.[8]

These points show that there is a rich and structured basis for a normative political theory within Marxism. But what sort of normative inquiry is

---

[4] It should be noted that Wood and Miller dissent from this conclusion. Thus Wood writes, "Marx sees historical materialism as 'breaking the staff of all morality' by showing people the real reason why moral ideologies appeal to them" (*Karl Marx*, p. 156). Miller's dissent, however, appears to be semantic rather than substantive; he allows that Marxism needs a normative context, but denies that this context is a *moral* one because it is not universal, general, or neutral (*Analyzing Marx*, pp. 15–18).

[5] Allen Wood, *Karl Marx*, pp. 22ff.

[6] "Marx's Moral Realism: Eudaimonism and Moral Progress," Ball and Farr, eds., *After Marx*, pp. 154–83.

[7] Karl Marx, "Economic and Philosophic Manuscripts," ed. Quintin Hoare, *Karl Marx: Early Writings* (New York: Vintage, 1975), pp. 322–34. Brenkert discusses this conception of freedom as self-determination at length in *Marx's Ethics of Freedom*, pp. 90–116, as does Kevin M. Brien in *Marx, Reason, and the Art of Freedom* (Philadelphia: Temple University Press, 1987).

[8] *Capital I* (New York: Vintage, 1976), pp. 470–91. "[The capitalist division of labor] converts the worker into a crippled monstrosity by furthering his particular skill as in a forcing-house, through the suppression of a whole world of productive drives and inclinations" (p. 481). See also similar criticisms in Marx's "Economic and Philosophic Manuscripts," p. 285.

appropriate for Marxism? This question requires that we recall Marx's criticisms of philosophy more generally. As a materialist, Marx criticizes a purely philosophical stance toward intellectual problems: a stance which is wholly abstract and non-historical, one which is unrelated to practical activity, or one which is primarily speculative and universal. And he insists that abstract thought must be oriented to practical purposes and activities. These comments suggest that if philosophical consideration of moral issues has a place within Marxism, the problems considered and the methods employed should have certain features. First, moral problems should be considered in a concrete historical and social context. Second, the primary focus of discussion of morality ought not be meta-ethical – e.g., discovering the epistemic basis of moral judgment – but, rather, substantive: working out a set of principles in terms of which to address practical problems of action and policy. Finally, moral discourse within Marxism ought to be practical, and this means that it should be primarily concerned with the sorts of problems which are likely to be confronted by a socialist movement in its pursuit of a transition to socialism.

I. A PROGRAM FOR SOCIALIST MORALITY

These considerations suggest a coherent program for socialist morality: to formulate and develop moral principles which are concretely related to the historical circumstances of the transition to socialism, and which promise to provide insight into concrete problems of socialist action and policy. Socialist actors – revolutionary party leaders, socialist policy makers, or rank-and-file followers – will be confronted with choices: more or less coercion, more or less mass involvement, more or less rapid reform, etc. A pressing problem for a socialist morality is to determine whether there are values and commitments within the moral culture of Marxism which ought, on socialist grounds, to guide such choices. The practical problems for a socialist political morality which arise from this point of view fall in two broad areas: revolution and the pursuit of power, and the process of socialist reform.

Consider first problems of revolution. Socialism can only emerge as the result of a political process of change – organized parties, mass collective action, alliances with other political groups, and so forth. Further, given the conflict of interests between a socialist economic program and the dominant classes in existing society – abolition of private property, fundamental land reform, and destruction of the political power of previous elites – one may expect that socialist political action will meet with determined resistance from powerful groups in existing society. Is there a socialist morality of revolution? What are the role and limits in the use of force in the pursuit of socialist ends? What value attaches to political honesty, loyalty, and commitment to allies?[9] What is the role of intra-party democracy, dissent, and competing political activity?[10]

Turn now to problems of socialist reform. Once in place, a socialist regime must use its political power to transform society in the direction of socialism. How should a socialist state, once in power, conduct policy, resolve conflicts of interest, respect political liberties, and so forth, in the transition to socialism? The process of transition is certain to be a lengthy one (witness the experience of Chinese communism: land reform, collectivization, production responsibility systems, etc.).[11] Given that these changes cannot be enacted instantaneously, a socialist regime must govern effectively through an extended period of transition: it must remain in power, it must effectively design and implement policies of reform, it must raise revenues to fund its policies, and it must be capable of controlling social conflicts as they arise as the result of dislocations caused by new policies.[12] What principles should govern the form and pace of land reform? How should intergenerational issues be resolved? How should the interests of town and country be accommodated and resolved? What sorts of political liberties should a socialist state protect and respect? Problems of socialist reform are particularly important because they may be expected to be hard and intractable, they do not have obvious "socialist" solutions, and in fact some of the most troubling aspects of socialist policy in this century have arisen in this context – e.g., the Great Leap Forward, Stalin's war on the kulaks, Soviet and Chinese restrictions on dissent, etc.[13]

[9] Consider, for example, Stalin's betrayal of Spanish communists, Chinese communists, etc., under the banner of "Socialism in one country." Baruch Knei-Paz offers an extensive description of this doctrine in *The Social and Political Thought of Leon Trotsky* (Oxford: Oxford University Press, 1978), pp. 340–48. E.H. Carr treats the self-serving policies which the Comintern imposed upon Spanish Communists in *The Comintern & the Spanish Civil War* (New York: Pantheon, 1984).

[10] Isaac Deutscher illustrates some of these problems in the context of the early development of Bolshevism in his biography of Trotsky: *The Prophet Unarmed* (Oxford: Oxford University Press, 1959). Arthur Koestler's recollections of the European Communist movement in the 1930s is of interest in this context as well: *The Invisible Writing* (New York: Stein and Day, 1984).

[11] Vivienne Shue provides a careful survey of the early part of this process in *Peasant China in Transition: The Dynamics of Development toward Socialism, 1949–1956* (Berkeley: University of California, 1980).

[12] Elizabeth Perry provides a glimpse of some of the political problems in the countryside which confront the current Chinese regime in "Rural Collective Violence: The Fruits of Recent Reforms," eds. Elizabeth Perry and Christine Wong, *The Political Economy of Reform in Post-Mao China* (Cambridge: Harvard University Press, 1985).

[13] For an extensive discussion of some of the problems inherent in designing and pursuing a feasible socialism, see Alec Nove, *The Economics of Feasible Socialism* (London: George Allen & Unwin, 1983). "I should like to include in my own definition of 'feasible socialism' the notion that *it should be conceivable within the lifespan of one generation* – say, in the next fifty years.... I would add that for a society to be regarded as socialist one requires the dominance of social ownership in the economy, together with political and economic democracy" (p. 11). Nove's discussion makes extensive use of comparative examples of socialist programs: the Soviet model, Hungarian and Yugoslav models of socialist organization, and Allende's Chile.

These observations suggest that Marxism both needs and can provide a practical political morality – a set of goals to guide political activity and a set of principles, guidelines, or rules to constrain the choice of means on the road to socialism. In the following I will single out several prominent moral problems that arise within the pursuit of socialism and offer a treatment of these problems on the basis of the moral resources of democratic socialism. The problems I will consider include socialist exploitation, political rivalries within socialism, and the role and scope of force within socialist political movements and regimes.[14]

II. SOCIALISM AND DEMOCRACY

Much of the following analysis depends upon the core idea that socialism requires democracy. Let us pose the prior question, then: do Marx's own writings support the idea that socialism requires democracy? There are two somewhat contradictory lines of thought in Marx, one supporting democracy and the other undermining it. On the positive side we have Marx's many discussions of the importance of free human beings managing their social institutions consciously and autonomously. Thus Marx gives special prominence to some of the central values of democracy – the idea that a society ought to be self-regulating, that its fundamental political and economic institutions ought to be subject to popular control, and that true human freedom requires that people have rational, deliberate control over their social arrangements. These ideas provide the basis for the view, to which most western Marxists now subscribe, that socialism presupposes democracy – that true socialism is unavoidably *democratic* socialism.

This commitment to democracy is manifest in several distinct strands of Marx's thought. First, Marx makes plain his commitment to the value of self-determination for individuals and groups. In his critique of Hegel's *Philosophy of Right*, he writes of the importance of "true democracy";[15] in the *Economic and Philosophic Manuscripts*, he writes of the alienation implicit in the fact that the economic institutions of capitalism are imposed on the worker as an external power;[16] and he emphasizes the value of the masses of workers determining their own future in the *Communist Manifesto*. Socialism is *true*

---

[14] It should be noted at the outset that this investigation is not intended to be a faithful explication of Marx's own moral views, but rather an effort to handle certain important normative problems making use of some of the guiding values of Marxian socialism. I no more presuppose that Marx's own writings unambiguously imply a resolution to the current problems of socialism than would a contemporary political philosopher working with the political theories of Kant or Locke. The aim is simply to offer credible and workable suggestions for socialist morality within a Marxian framework.

[15] Karl Marx, "Critique of Hegel's Doctrine of the State," ed. Quintin Hoare, *Karl Marx: Early Writings*, pp. 86–91. "In a democracy the constitution, the law, i.e. the political state, is itself only a self-determination of the people and a determinate content of the people" (p. 89).

[16] Karl Marx, "Economic and Philosophic Manuscripts," ed. Quintin Hoare, *Karl Marx: Early Writings*, pp. 326–33.

democracy – an economic form within which the masses rationally direct their own economic and social arrangements. Second, socialism is intimately connected with freedom, in Marx's view; it is the system in which individuals can throw off the constraints imposed on them by authoritarian political arrangements and coercive economic institutions. Finally, socialism is fundamentally compatible with majoritarianism because it represents the objective interests of the great majority of society.[17] Therefore, the attainment of socialism should meet with the approval of the majority. These considerations all suggest that socialism is intended to embody the ideas of true freedom, self-regulation, and cooperative social life that may be said to express genuine democracy.

On the other hand, however, we find Marx's many criticisms of 'bourgeois' democracy. This line of thought finds its clearest expression in the "Critique of the Gotha Programme."[18] There Marx criticizes the democratic utterances of the leadership of the German Social-Democratic Workers' Party.

> There is nothing in its political demands beyond the old and generally familiar democratic litany: universal suffrage, direct legislation, popular justice, a people's army, etc. . . . All these demands, unless exaggerated into fantastic dreams, have already been *realized*. It is just that the state to which they belong does not lie within the borders of the German Reich but in Switzerland, the United States, etc.[19]

These points add up, in Marx's view, to a demand for a *democratic republic* – a political form that already existed in the United States. And Marx appears to hold that this political form is the one most well-suited to contemporary capitalist society – a state form within which the bourgeoisie is well-positioned to defend its class interests.[20] It is possible to construe this view as maintaining that democratic institutions within capitalist society are a sham;

[17] Karl Marx and Frederick Engels, "The Communist Manifesto," ed. David Fernbach, *Karl Marx: The Revolutions of 1848* (New York: Vintage, 1974), pp. 75–79. The same assumption about the universal interests of the proletariat may be found in the closing pages of *Capital*; Karl Marx, *Capital I* (New York: Vintage, 1977), p. 929.

[18] Karl Marx, "Critique of the Gotha Programme," ed. David Fernbach, *Karl Marx: The First International & After* (New York: Vintage, 1974), pp. 354–55.

[19] ibid., p. 355.

[20] Recall Marx's similar comments about political emancipation and human emancipation in "On the Jewish Question," ed. Quintin Hoare, *Karl Marx: Early Writings*, pp. 215–33. And in the *Communist Manifesto* he writes of the modern state in the following terms: "The executive of the modern [representative] state is but a committee for managing the common affairs of the whole bourgeoisie" (Karl Marx, "The Communist Manifesto," ed. David Fernbach, *Karl Marx: The Revolutions of 1848*, p. 69).

they function effectively to secure the interests of the bourgeoisie. This impression is further enhanced by the following passage:

> Between capitalist and communist society lies a period of revolutionary transformation from one to the other. There is a corresponding period of transition in the political sphere and in this period the state can only take the form of a *revolutionary dictatorship of the proletariat.*[21]

Some interpreters have construed this passage to mean that Marx believes that the transition to socialism *must* occur through an anti-democratic process. However, Elster argues persuasively (citing Hal Draper and Richard Hunt) that the concept of a dictatorship of the proletariat ought not to be understood as an authoritarian, anti-democratic regime. Instead, Elster argues, "the dictatorship of the proletariat . . . is characterized by majority rule, extra-legality, dismantling of the state apparatus, and revocability of the representatives."[22] There is thus good reason to interpret Marx's position, even in the "Critique of the Gotha Programme," as requiring that a socialist regime must embody democratic institutions. Socialism is to be attained through a process in which the proletarian majority achieves political power and directs the reorganization of the property relations of capitalist society.

These considerations suggest that Marx's own values dictate adherence to democratic socialism. But whatever position history ultimately assigns to Marx himself on the possibility of a democratic process of socialist reform, it appears clear from the socialist experience of the twentieth century that contemporary socialists *must* accept this commitment. The anti-democratic route to socialism has all too often led, not to socialism, but to an authoritarian, heavily coercive regime that lacks popular support. The values of majoritarianism, freedom, and self-determination are among the most fundamental value commitments that underlie the appeal of socialism. And if socialism is not attainable within a process that pays due heed to the importance of these commitments, then it loses much of its appeal. Much of the following, then, will be premised on the requirement that socialist politics and socialist reform must be designed in such a way as to be compatible with democratic political institutions.[23]

---

[21] Marx, "Critique of the Gotha Programme," p. 355.

[22] Jon Elster, *Making Sense of Marx* (Cambridge: Cambridge University Press, 1985), p. 448.

[23] Though it is not my purpose to develop a theory of democratic socialism in this paper, I assume that such a system requires at least the following: universal suffrage; effective protections of the political rights of all citizens – the rights of free speech and association, the right to hold office, and protection from arbitrary punishment; and stable, predictable political institutions that embody universal suffrage and that subordinate policy formation to an electoral process.

III. SOCIALIST EXPLOITATION

Let us now turn to several specific problems of socialist morality. An historically important issue in the context of socialist reform concerns the control of economic surpluses. A socialist regime will have at its disposal a variety of mechanisms for influencing the disposition of such surpluses: tax policies, grain quotas, mandatory grain prices, etc.[24] This means that the regime is in a position to extract surpluses from rural producers for a variety of purposes. Should such surpluses be used to fund urban development, build agricultural infrastructure, or subsidize higher consumption levels for rural workers? If rural incomes are kept low and surpluses transferred to urban projects (industrial development), then one might regard this as exploitation of peasants on behalf of workers.[25]

The concept of exploitation plays a central role in Marx's critique of capitalism. Exploitation may be defined in terms of coercion and surplus extraction; it describes a transfer of wealth, labor time, or products from one group or individual to another through "unfree" (coercive) mechanisms. Marx's primary use of this concept is in his critique of the capitalist economy. But exploitation is also relevant to the forward-looking problems of socialist morality. For once the formal structure of exploitation has been analyzed, it is possible to ask whether, and in what circumstances, socialist exploitation might occur, and it may be possible to use some of these ideas in order to provide principled solutions to some of the knotty problems of transition to socialism.

In order to begin to develop our intuitions about socialist exploitation, consider the following hypothetical cases:

1. *Inequalities between peasants and workers.* Suppose that a socialist regime imposes a taxation policy on its rural population which extracts one–third of the net rural product, and a settlement policy which prohibits farmers from moving to the cities. Half of the tax revenues are used for normal costs of government and rural development (i.e., projects which directly benefit rural residents), and the other half are used to support a rapid process of urban industrial development (investments which immediately benefit urban dwellers through expanded employment, and indirectly benefit all members of society in fifty years through greater economic prosperity). Is this an example of exploitation? And if so, should that finding lead a socialist regime to avoid such a policy?

---

[24] Examples of all of these mechanisms may be found in the history of Chinese rural policies since 1949. See Dwight Perkins and Shahid Yusuf, *Rural Development in China* (Baltimore: Johns Hopkins University Press, 1984) for details.

[25] Similar questions arise in connection with long-term investment policies and inequalities among regions. Pranab Bradhan briefly considers these problems in "Marxist Ideas in Development Economics," ed. John Roemer, *Analytical Marxism*, pp. 64–77, as does Jon Elster's "Historical Materialism and Economic Backwardness," eds. Terence Ball and James Farr, *After Marx* (Cambridge: Cambridge University Press, 1984), pp. 36–58.

2. *Intergenerational inequalities.* Suppose that policy-makers have decided to leave incomes of peasants and workers at roughly the subsistence level in order to use the economic surplus to fund rapid industrial development. That is, the division of the surplus between increasing present consumption and increasing current investments in productive assets is largely in favor of the latter. Is this a form of exploitation of the present generation for the sake of future generations?

3. *Regional differences.* Gansu and Hunan are Chinese provinces with sharply different *per capita* incomes. Suppose that the explanation of these differences is this: both are primarily agricultural areas, but Gansu possesses soils of low fertility, while Hunan has high fertility soils.[26] The affluence of Hunan and the poverty of Gansu, then, stems from differences in natural endowments. Does this represent a case of exploitation? Are Gansu rural workers exploited by Hunanese rural workers? Does this sort of inequality represent a situation which a socialist regime ought to try to modify?

4. *Equal incomes based on unequal contributions.* Suppose that Chu is a collective farm which employs 100 workers. Workers earn work points based on the number of days they work, and the net income of the farm is distributed to workers in proportion to work points. Half the workers are slackers and work only at 60% of a normal rate of intensity for agricultural work, while the other half are hard workers and work at 100%. Each worker works the same number of days; therefore each worker receives the same wage. Finally, suppose that a normal day's work under these technical conditions would generate N yuan net income. Total income on the farm per day may now be computed:

$$50 * .6 * N + 50 * 1.0 * N = 80N$$

Per capita income may be determined as well; each worker receives $.8N$ yuan. In this case we have equal wages but unequal contribution. May it be said that slackers exploit hard workers? If slackers were to take their *per capita* share of productive assets and work at the same intensity, their incomes would be $.6N$ yuan, while hard workers would receive $1N$. Thus hard workers receive lower incomes in order to subsidize slackers.[27] This seems to be reason to conclude that hard workers are being exploited.[28]

---

[26] Dwight Perkins and Shahid Yusuf, *Rural Development in China*, pp. 115–19.

[27] This is a problem with practical significance in cooperative farms, and Chinese policy makers have addressed it by trying to make estimates of the value of a given worker's day of work, including intensity, skill, strength, etc. For empirical discussion of this problem, see Louis Putterman, "The Restoration of the Peasant Household as Farm Production Units in China," eds. Elizabeth Perry and Christine Wong, *The Political Economy of Reform in Post-Mao China*, pp. 63–82.

[28] But briefly consider a slightly different case: strong and weak workers. The strong worker generates more output than the weak though well-motivated worker. Would we want to say that the weak exploits the strong in such a case?

5. *Bureaucratic exploitation.* Suppose that all producers earn the same income, but that all officials earn an income deriving from tax revenues which is five times that of workers' income. Is this a form of exploitation by officials of the rest of the population?[29]

Which, if any, of these cases represents features of socialist exploitation?[30] And are there reasons for socialist policy-makers to avoid a set of arrangements because they are exploitative? John Roemer's theory of exploitation has shaped discussion of this issue in recent years.[31] Roemer's theory is intended to be general in the respect that historical forms of exploitation – feudal exploitation, capitalist exploitation, socialist exploitation – may be seen to be special cases of the general theory. Roemer introduces a preliminary definition of exploitation in terms of socially necessary labor time for subsistence. *A* exploits *B* just in case *A* works less than the socially necessary amount of labor time, while *B* works more, and *A*'s advantage depends upon *B*'s disadvantage.[32] Roemer's general theory of exploitation takes the form of an analysis of the production process in a given society in terms of hypothetical alternative arrangements. "A group [will] be conceived of as exploited if it has some *conditionally feasible alternative* under which its members would be better off."[33] This criterion is intended to capture the connection between exploitation, coercion, and alternative production arrangements. That is, if there is an alternative form of production which some class in society could adopt by withdrawing its share of the productive resources which would leave its members better off, then that class is being exploited by other classes in existing production

---

[29] This is a particularly obvious case: officials are using the coercive powers of the state to extract part of the economic surplus for their own luxury consumption. Roemer treats this type of case under the heading of status exploitation: the enrichment of the class of officials at the expense of the producers through the power of the state to tax. "New Directions in the Marxian Theory of Exploitation and Class," pp. 109–10.

[30] In comments on this paper, Chinese and Soviet academics have both rejected the premise that there can be such a thing as socialist exploitation. Igor Rogov, a philosopher at the Leningrad Polytechnic Institute, argues that there can be no socialist exploitation because the workers and peasants own the means of production (personal communication). And Xi Wang, a senior economist at Fudan University, takes a similar line: "It is argued that under the socialist system, all the means of production are nationalized and the output of these nationalized means of production (including land) eventually benefit the people as a whole. The 'exploitation' only exists under a capitalist system where private ownership prevails" (personal communication). It is my position, however, that the state's capacity to employ coercive means to dispose of surplus product makes a *prima facie* case for the possibility of socialist exploitation.

[31] Roemer's theory is presented in *A General Theory of Exploitation and Class* (Cambridge: Harvard University Press, 1982). The main ideas of this theory are summarized in "New Directions in the Marxian Theory of Exploitation and Class," ed. John Roemer, *Analytical Marxism*, pp. 81–113. Note also his arguments to the effect that exploitation is *not* the central moral issue in Marxism in "Should Marxists be Interested in Exploitation?", ed. John Roemer, *Analytical Marxism*, pp. 260–82.

[32] Roemer, "New Directions in the Marxian Theory of Exploitation and Class," p. 86.

[33] *ibid.*, p. 103.

arrangements. On this criterion, capitalist society is exploitative because it depends on a coercively-enforced system of property arrangements in productive assets through which a minority class derives a higher than average income at the expense of the majority class of workers. Capitalist exploitation may be overcome by distributing productive assets on the basis of equal shares to each person.

Roemer applies this framework to the problem of socialist exploitation as well. "A coalition is socialistically exploited if it could improve its lot by withdrawing with its *per capita* share of society's assets, once alienable assets are distributed equally."[34] In applying this criterion, we are to imagine that capitalist exploitation has been abolished through equal distribution of alienable assets (land, factories, mines, and other forms of capital), but that inequalities of income still persist because of inequalities of talent, skill, and the like. This remaining inequality is what Roemer calls socialist exploitation.

As it stands, this criterion is unsatisfactory. First, it is unclear why these remaining inequalities should be counted as *exploitative*; it might reasonably be held that inequalities based on skill or talent do *not* represent a form of surplus extraction by the skilled from the unskilled. More fundamentally, however, this criterion is flawed because it is only concerned with arrangements within a finished socialist society; it assumes that the process of socialist reform has already been carried out by assuming that alienable assets have been distributed equally. The remaining inequalities which it addresses are those which derive from skills, talents, and other inalienable assets of individuals. This principle thus provides no guidance for the process of transition to full socialism from class society.[35]

It is not at all simple to formulate a conception of exploitation which *is* applicable to the process of socialist reform. Coercion and inequalities would appear to be virtually unavoidable within this process (e.g., through expropriation of landlords). Moreover, there are a great many inequalities which might emerge within socialism which might be considered undesirable but not exploitative. As no more than a first approximation loosely based on Roemer's insightful ideas, then, consider the following. A group[36] is socialistically exploited if and only if:

(1) the group's *per capita* income is lower than the social average,

[34] *ibid.*, p. 109.

[35] Roemer gives a more developed treatment of socialist exploitation in *A General Theory of Exploitation and Class*, chs. 7 and 8, but the discussion there too largely overlooks the process of socialist reform.

[36] I restrict my attention to groups defined by economic criteria: principally occupation and region. This account is thus not intended to provide a basis for analysis of relations between ethnic or religious groups – let alone arbitrarily defined groups (e.g., members of sports clubs or subscribers to *Newsweek*).

(2) the group's *per capita* income is lower than its *per capita* contribution to the net national product (NNP), discounted by the rate of investment,

(3) its material disadvantage is the result of state policies, coercively enforced, which extract part of the surplus produced by that group to be used for purposes which largely benefit other groups, and

(4) it could improve its lot by withdrawing with its *per capita* share of society's assets.

This set of conditions is somewhat ungainly, but it embodies the central ideas of the traditional concept of exploitation as coercive surplus extraction. Condition (2) excludes cases of inequality which stem from poor natural endowment of assets (e.g., soils or weather conditions – inequalities which are undesirable but not exploitative (as in the case of Gansu and Hunan above). Condition (1) excludes cases in which groups with superior natural endowments (e.g., highly fertile soil) are taxed down to the social average income levels. (That is, it is not exploitative for the state to create policies which reduce rich peasant incomes in order to raise poor peasant incomes, generate additional investment funds, etc.) Condition (3) asserts the causal requirement that exploitation can only be said to occur if it is imposed on a group or individual against its will, and imposed for the sake of benefiting some other person or group; for socialist exploitation, the primary agent of coercion is the state. Finally, condition (4) embodies Roemer's intuition that certain forms of inequality may be unavoidable: there may be no other feasible set of production arrangements in which the exploited group would do better.[37]

A central idea in this account is the notion of *per capita* assets. A *per capita* share of productive assets may be defined as an average share of each type of productive asset – industrial capacity of various types, crop land of various fertilities, transportation and communication assets, etc. This analysis can be converted into *per capita* income terms quite simply; each type of asset generates an average amount of income per unit of labor in current technical conditions of production.[38] The basket of *per capita* assets then generates a *per capita* income which is the sum of the incomes generated by a share of each type of asset.

On these assumptions, reference to *per capita* assets can be replaced by reference to *per capita* income. Thus socialist exploitation reduces to certain types of inequalities of *per capita* incomes among groups. The qualification required here concerns the *causes* of these income inequalities. In order for inequalities to count as exploitative, it is necessary to show that the higher incomes flowing to one group depend upon the productive activity and lower

---

[37] John Roemer, "New Directions in the Marxian Theory of Exploitation and Class," p. 110.

[38] Note the formal parallel between this concept and Marx's analysis of concrete and abstract labor in *Capital*.

incomes of the other group. (This captures the idea of surplus extraction in a more general way.) And it is necessary to show that these inequalities are brought about through a coercive process.

Let us now apply these conditions to cases (1) and (3) above. In order to assess the first case described above, we need to ask where peasant income stands after this policy: at, above, or below *per capita* income. If the resulting peasant income is at or above national *per capita* income, then this might be a reason to hold that this policy is not exploitative, since it involves compensating the urban sector for the rural sector's having direct access to a disproportionate share of national productive assets (land). Accordingly, let us suppose that peasant incomes were 10% above the social average prior to the policy, and dropped to 10% below average as a result of the policy.

It is now possible to assess the arrangements described in case (1); under these circumstances, peasants are being exploited. The group's average income is below the social average, and is below its net contribution to the economy. (This follows from the fact that part of the rural surplus is being converted into investment funds.) Further, farmers' incomes are depressed through the deliberate policy of the state. The state uses its coercive powers in two relevant ways: it collects revenues, and it prevents farmers from moving to the cities. Part of the surplus which is extracted, however, is being used to benefit the affected group; this part of the arrangement is therefore not exploitative. The other portion, however (one-sixth of the net rural product), is being used to benefit urban dwellers and future members of society. This part of the development policy may be classified as exploitative. Further, there is a feasible alternative arrangement in which the peasantry would be better off in these circumstances: one in which some of the surplus is retained within the rural economy in order to keep rural incomes at the social average. The peasantry is therefore being exploited by these arrangements. Intuitively, these arrangements represent a process through which the state squeezes the peasantry to fund the process of industrialization.

Consider now case (3), regional inequalities based on unequal natural endowments. Gansu incomes are lower than the social average. However, these incomes are not lower than the group's contribution to the net national product; given low soil fertility, Gansu is a small producer as well as a small consumer. Moreover, the cause of Gansu's disadvantage is *not* state policy; the state is not extracting a surplus from Gansu for the benefit of other groups. (Though if there are limits on internal migration, one might hold that the state is using coercion to confine Gansu peasants within their poverty.) Finally, there are no alternative arrangements which would improve the material circumstances of Gansu farmers *if* their income is limited to the capacity of the Gansu rural economy to produce; it is not feasible to transfer fertility from Hunan to Gansu. On this set of conditions, therefore, Gansu's lower-than-average incomes do not represent a form of exploitation.[39]

Exploitation and socialist democracy. What implications does an analysis of socialist exploitation have for socialist development plans? Should socialist policy-makers refrain from development schemes that are exploitative on these criteria? I hold that it is reasonable to regard Marxism as being committed to the view that exploitation is a bad thing, in that it represents coercion by one group of another, and represents an offensively unequal distribution of the burdens of socialist development. This finding suggests that one of the components of a moral theory of socialist development should be a *prima facie* requirement that socialist planners should avoid exploitative development plans.

It was noted above that there is a close connection between exploitation and coercion: coercion is needed in order to keep an exploited group from spontaneously redistributing the assets of society. This connection suggests that democratic institutions would tend to make exploitation less likely. In application to socialism, this suggests that democratic socialism will not be able to use exploitative means of reform. For if socialist reforms are subject to a democratic process – that is, if affected groups are free to organize politically in defense of their material interests – then exploitation by the state of large groups for the benefit of "socialist progress" will be less likely. Either affected groups (in this case, the peasantry) will effectively organize and block such policies; or else, through the process of political debate, the regime will succeed in persuading the affected groups to accept present sacrifices for more distant socialist goals. In the former case no surplus extraction is successfully performed, while in the latter the surplus is extracted with the consent of affected groups. There is thus an intimate connection between socialist exploitation and the lack of democratic political institutions.[40] The requirement of democratic decision-making processes would exclude Stalin's forced grain transfers from countryside to city, and it would be consistent with the overall structure of Chinese rural development

---

[39] This reply depends on a baseline in which the Gansu peasant has possession of a *per capita* share of Gansu resources. But if the baseline is instead a *per capita* share of China's resources overall, then we are forced to conclude that the Gansu peasantry *is* being exploited; it is being deprived of the benefits of China's collective resources.

[40] Even assuming full democratic rights, it is still *possible* for the majority to exploit a minority economic group. However, full rights of political participation would block many of the most egregious examples of socialist exploitation. This is so because the aim of socialist exploitation is to capture surpluses that can be used by the state for its programs. But the amounts of surpluses that can be squeezed from small groups of poor people (i.e., people close to the average per capita income line) are small enough to make such efforts by the state unlikely. Where a socialist state does have an *a priori* incentive to squeeze is in the case of large productive groups – peasants, miners, fishermen, etc. In these cases the surpluses that could be captured are large enough to be attractive. But these groups are also politically powerful – *if* they have full rights of political participation and organization. So democratic institutions ought to block the most likely cases of socialist exploitation.

schemes.[41] At the same time, it should be noted that this principle would set rather narrow limits on the rate at which socialist reform can proceed; it would exclude, for example, radical initiatives like the Great Leap Forward.

IV. POLITICAL RIGHTS AND POLITICAL RIVALRY

Let us turn now to a second important controversy that arises in the context of socialist reform: the role of political rights within a socialist regime. Much discussion of Marx's position on this issue has centered on rights within Marx's critique of capitalism. But of at least equal significance is the role of rights within post-capitalist institutions. Are there good reasons for a socialist to hold that socialist institutions should embody protections of individual rights – e.g., rights of political association, rights of speech and expression, or rights of religious practice?

Steven Lukes holds that Marxism is theoretically disposed against the notion of individual rights, and that this predisposition leads to important shortcomings in both the ideal theory of socialism and existing socialist institutions.[42] Leaning heavily on Marx's position in "On the Jewish Question," Lukes argues that Marx rejects individual rights on two grounds. First, rights play an ideological role in capitalist society; under the guise of protecting universal human interests, they in fact serve to secure forms of privilege, power, and inequalities in the form of property. Second, and more fundamentally, rights fall within a juridical conception of social life which is suited to bourgeois society but not to full human emancipation. The concept of a right presupposes the idea of conflict among egoistic individuals in circumstances of mutual indifference and scarcity. These circumstances are typical of civil society within a capitalist order, but they are not expected to occur within socialism.[43] Against this deprecation of rights, Lukes holds that certain rights – free communication of thought, freedom of association, freedom from capricious punishment by the state – are important human rights independent from the specific features of capitalist society, and they ought to be institutionally guaranteed in any humane social order. And Lukes maintains that this disregard of individual rights is part and parcel of a normative system which culminated in some of the "moral disasters" of existing socialism.[44]

---

[41] See Dwight Perkins and Shahid Yusuf, *Rural Development in China*, pp. 10–23, for an estimate of the overall balance of trade between urban and rural incomes within the Chinese economy. Their conclusion is that rural revenues provided only a very small portion of the revenues used for industrial development, either directly through taxation or indirectly through artificially low grain prices.

[42] Steven Lukes, *Marxism and Morality*, pp. 65–66.

[43] Likewise, George Brenkert argues, "I shall also argue that Marx rejected the notion of human or natural rights. Those rights claimed to be human rights are, he held, relative to capitalist society." George Brenkert, "Marx and Human Rights," *Journal of the History of Philosophy*, vol. 24 (1986), p. 56.

[44] Steven Lukes, *Marxism and Morality*, p. xii.

16 DANIEL LITTLE

Lukes's position is unduly negative concerning the moral legacy of Marxism; but in order to address the problem in the spirit of the conception of socialist ethics at work here, it is necessary to consider more specific circumstances in which the problem of individual rights might arise. This issue arises most sharply during the process of socialist reform: the extended period in which a socialist government has political power but has not yet effected the destruction of the old social-economic system and the creation of the new. The process of socialist reform will require substantial use of political power, and it will directly offend the interests of groups in society who possessed substantial power, organizational skills, and resources in the old regime. Can a socialist regime permit full and free political expression and organization, while still remaining in a position to effectively pursue the process of socialist reform? And should it do so, given its basic normative commitments? Or are there reasons to expect that the process of socialist reform will be brought into collision with political rights – freedom of expression, freedom of association, and freedom of political activity?

An example derived from Adam Przeworski[45] presents a hard case for political rights and liberties in the context of socialist reform. Suppose a socialist regime has begun a process of nationalization of industry and land reform, and that the economy has suffered a dip in productivity as a result: dislocations in industry and agriculture have led to a significant, though not catastrophic, dip in average family income. Now suppose that a group of former managers and liberal capitalists propose to form a Social-Capitalist party of opposition (the SC party). Their program is *not* restoration of the old order, but rather a political compromise: partial reprivatization of industry and restoration of a degree of profits to managers, alongside of substantial guarantees of workers' rights and income levels. Finally, suppose that their political message is that this system will be more efficient than current socialist management of industry. That is, they offer peasants and workers a "social-capitalist" compromise as an alternative to socialist management. As Przeworski points out, such a program may be genuinely appealing to the material interests of the bulk of the population: it may be that their material interests will be better served, in the short and medium run, by the "social-capitalist compromise" than by the slow process of socialist reform – even if the long-term interests of their class are better served by socialism.[46] How should a socialist government respond to such a challenge? Can a socialist regime tolerate this form of political activity?

Several alternatives present themselves in the face of such a circumstance.

---

[45] Adam Przeworski, "Material Interests, Class Compromise and the Transition to Socialism," pp. 162–88.
[46] *ibid.*, pp. 178–81.

First, most obviously, a socialist government might assess the political appeal of such a program and suppress the SC party if it is judged a potent threat. That is, the government might use its coercive powers to limit the political liberties of the SC group. This is an all-too-familiar recourse from Soviet history.[47] There is a non-repressive alternative, however. Socialist leaders might have a genuine commitment to democratic participation, and might have the political and organizational skills needed to preserve political support in face of the SC challenge. As Przeworski shows, in order to win this sort of political contest, mere appeal to material interests will not suffice; the socialist government will have to make its case for the non-economic values which socialist reform serves, and which the SC program would frustrate, as well as the long-term material interests which socialist reform serves. And through a process of political education and organization, it will have to effectively transmit its vision of the future to the masses of peasants and workers who constitute its political base.[48] On this alternative it is possible for the socialist government to respect political liberties of the opposition, while at the same time preserving the political power needed to carry out the process of reform.

Are there reasons internal to the moral culture of Marxism to hold that the latter is a likely alternative? Lukes holds that there are not, but his case is unpersuasive. There are at least three. First, as was argued above, there is a strong strand of popular democratic values within Marxism, according to which socialist politics should work through the informed participation of its constituency.[49] Consider, for example, Marx's criticisms of Blanqui and his analysis of the failure of the Paris Commune. In *The Civil War in France*, Marx writes with approval both of the popular character of the establishment of the Commune and the democratic institutions which the Communards intended to establish. "While the merely repressive organs of the old governmental power were to be amputated, its legitimate functions were to

[47] Baruch Knei-Paz offers extensive description of this tendency within Stalin's regime in *The Social and Political Thought of Leon Trotsky*, pp. 367–441. Deutscher's *The Prophet Unarmed* is also informative on this point.

[48] An important lesson of the early stages of the Chinese Revolution is the fact that the CCP *was* able to draw the mass of the peasantry along in pursuit of its program of socialist reform, through a combination of material incentives and a vision of a socialist future. Yung-fa Chen holds that the vision of the socialist future was a critical element in the Party's ability to broaden the political horizons of the peasantry. See Yung-fa Chen, *Making Revolution* (Berkeley: University of California, 1986), pp. 503–4. From a different perspective, A.K. Sen emphasizes the importance of non-material incentives in political behavior in a variety of works, including particularly "Rational Fools," eds. Frank Hahn and Martin Hollis, *Philosophy and Economic Theory* (London: Oxford University Press, 1979), pp. 86–109, and *On Ethics and Economics* (London: Basil Blackwell, 1987).

[49] For further arguments to this conclusion, see Andrew Levine, *Arguing for Socialism* (Boston: Routledge & Kegan Paul, 1984), pp. 204–10.

be wrested from an authority usurping preeminence over society itself, and restored to the responsible agents of society. . . . Universal suffrage was to serve the people, constituted in communes."[50] These commitments provide a normative basis for a socialist government's preferring to work through a democratic political process rather than through an authoritarian repression of competing political groups. Free democratic participation is itself a socialist value, not merely a tactical instrument.

Second, there are pragmatic reasons for favoring the second alternative. To the extent that socialist reform depends upon repression rather than mass support, history suggests that the socialist economy will suffer tremendous problems of inefficiency. Here socialist leaders will contemplate the example of Poland; it is possible to drive workers into shipyards at the point of a gun, but it is not possible to coerce them into working efficiently and industriously.

Finally, there is a sufficiently close connection between the desired end state – socialist society – and the process of transition to make it plausible that antidemocratic means of transition will make the end state less accessible. This connection is established through the process of political education gained in the process of reform. It is implausible to expect that free, united men and women will emerge out of an authoritarian political process in which independence of thought and action are repressed. To the extent, then, that socialist politicians are truly concerned to arrive at the basis for communist society, they will be concerned to extend rather than diminish mass political democratic activity. This, in turn, suggests that socialist regimes ought to give meaningful weight to securing political liberties, even to organizations whose goals are inconsistent with the program of socialist reform.

These arguments support a strong commitment to the preservation of the political rights of all citizens within democratic socialism. How far should this commitment extend? What if the outcome of the political contest described above is a victory for the Social-Capitalist party, and the prospect of the partial dismantling of the socialist program? Should the socialist regime simply go down to defeat in these circumstances? If we may take for granted the continuance of democratic institutions under the SC regime, then the commitment to democracy *does* require that the socialist regime relinquish power. Its electoral failure demonstrates that it has not succeeded in persuading the masses that their interests are represented by the socialist program; so it must return to its efforts to garner majority support for its program. Genuine socialism can be attained through democratic means, or not at all.

[50] David Fernbach, ed., *The First International and After*, p. 210.

V. The Use of Force

Let us turn finally to what is perhaps the most difficult problem of political morality for socialism: the role of force in pursuit of a socialist political program. Are there limits internal to Marxian socialism on the use of force in the pursuit of power (revolution), and in the implementation of socialism (socialist reform)? I maintain that there are such limits, and that they derive from the requirements of establishing and preserving *democratic* socialism.

Consider first the problem of the use of force during the quest for state power by a socialist party. This case divides historically into two types: cases in which effective political institutions of representative democracy exist, in which socialist parties can freely compete with other parties; and cases in which an authoritarian, antidemocratic state exists. In the first context, socialist parties should pursue their quest for power through legal electoral means. This is true because of the central commitment to *democratic* socialism. Socialists believe that their program serves the interests of the great majority of modern society; accordingly, it should be possible, within political arrangements in which a socialist party has effective rights of political activity and participation, for a socialist party to win power and control of government. And, because socialism is committed to the value of self-determination of the masses, it ought to choose this means – even if this route appears slow and uncertain. Significantly, these are the circumstances to be found within the political environment of Western Europe, the United States, and Japan today.

It is possible, of course, that parliamentary institutions may break down at the point at which a socialist party appears likely to gain effective power. Threatened classes – the landlord class, for example – may themselves adopt an extralegal strategy to prevent the parliamentary successes of the socialist party from being implemented. Segments of these classes may turn to the military strongman; they may form private militias; they may engage in tactics of violent intimidation of their enemies; and so forth. In these circumstances it is apparent that a socialist movement may exercise the right of self-defense, and form its own police or military forces. In this event, however, the use of force must be carefully controlled and used as an instrument of policy. The goal remains to achieve power through electoral means; force should be used only to help stabilize electoral mechanisms and deter potential enemies from making extralegal uses of power. Thus force should be used only against the paramilitary forces of groups who are attempting to step outside of the legal process (or to subvert the legal process from within – for example, through a declaration of martial law, a suspension of political rights, etc.).

Consider finally those circumstances where democratic institutions do not exist, and where the masses do not have an effective means for affecting government policy in support of their own interests. These circumstances are typically found in cases in which government, in the service of existing elite classes, uses the threat and exercise of violence to enforce its will and silence its enemies. If it is to act at all in these circumstances, a socialist party has no choice but to mobilize support from its followers, and to pursue a forcible overthrow of the dictatorship and establishment of a democratic socialist regime. This case corresponds closely to the experience of socialist revolutions in China, Cuba, and Nicaragua; in each case, an antidemocratic regime which made heavy use of violence and threats to maintain itself was overthrown by a popularly supported socialist movement.

This analysis leads to a preliminary conclusion: socialist parties may not use force, or threat of force, in political systems in which they have effective rights of political activity. They may use force in self-defense, and defense of democratic political institutions, if some groups within a democracy attempt to enforce their will outside of parliamentary processes through the appeal to force. And they may use force in pursuit of their program within any dictatorial political system, or any system in which the masses lack legal means for gaining control of government.

Turn now to the use of force during the process of socialist reform. Under what circumstances is it legitimate for a socialist government to use force to implement its reforms of economic and political institutions? The most objectionable uses of force by socialist governments in this century have occurred in this context – e.g., Stalin's war on the kulaks and Mao's use of the Red Guards during the Cultural Revolution. Here again the requirements of democratic socialism offer the basis for a solution. A socialist government should only use force in order to implement policies that have been adopted through effective democratic institutions of decision-making; for only in these circumstances is it legitimate to hold that the policy represents the will of the masses. On this account, the role of force within socialism is exactly that prescribed by ideal theories of the liberal state: to enforce the system of law adopted through appropriate democratic institutions of decison-making. What this principle prohibits, then, is *dictatorial* uses of force: coercive means that are adopted by the state in order to implement unilateral decrees against a resistant population.

Let us now consider some historically important examples of socialist use of force in light of this discussion: the Chinese Communist Party's use of force against the Guomindang; Stalin's use of force in support of rural collectivization; Mao's use of force during the Cultural Revolution; and the Red Brigade's use of violence to destabilize the Italian democracy (thereby laying the door open for socialist seizure of power).

The Chinese Communist Party's exercise of war against the Guomindang comes out as fully legitimate on the criteria described above. The Nationalist

Government was a military dictatorship which ruthlessly sought out and killed its enemies.[51] There were no effective non-violent means through which socialists could organize and pursue power; consequently, on the grounds described above, it was legitimate for the CCP to use violent means to attempt to overthrow the Guomindang and establish a socialist regime.

Consider next Stalin's use of force against the peasants of the Ukraine in support of rural collectivization. Force was needed in this context exactly because Ukrainian peasants overwhelmingly opposed the policy. If they had possessed effective political rights within the Soviet system, this policy would never have been adopted. It is therefore intrinsic to the policy that it could not be enacted through democratic means; and consequently the use of force by Stalin was wholly illegitimate. It was symptomatic of Stalin's rejection of the requirements of *democratic* socialism; and it should serve as a grim reminder to socialists everywhere of the costs of disregarding democracy.

Mao's Cultural Revolution presents a similar case. Mao was concerned about the bureaucratization of Chinese socialism, and he appealed to an extra-legal institution (the Red Guards) in order to attempt to reverse this perceived tendency. But the violence unleashed by this effort fails the criteria above in several ways: it was not supported by democratic processes, and it was not carefully and judiciously regulated. The Cultural Revolution, then, represents a second example of illegitimate uses of violence and intimidation by a socialist regime.

Consider, finally, the example of the Red Brigades in Italy. Italy possesses effective electoral institutions, within which there are numerous parties of the left and a powerful Communist Party. It cannot be maintained, therefore, that Italy is a dictatorship. The leadership of the Red Brigades despair of a socialist victory through electoral means, however, and choose instead to attempt to undermine the institutions of parliamentary democracy so as to bring about the circumstances in which a violent overthrow of the Italian state is conceivable. By the standards described above, this recourse is illegitimate. If socialism offers an agenda that is genuinely in the interests of the Italian masses, it should be possible for a party of socialists to achieve political successes within existing parliamentary institutions. The terrorist policies of the Red Brigades are in fact subject to the same sorts of criticisms that Marx levelled against Louis Blanqui in the 1840s and 1850s: socialism cannot be achieved through the use of violence by a minority party.

[51] See, for example, John Fairbank's description of some of the means used against Chinese dissidents in the 1930s by the Nationalist Government; on a grander scale, recall Chiang Kai-shek's extermination of the communist workers of Shanghai. See John Fairbank, *Chinabound: A Fifty-Year Memoir* (New York: Harper, 1982), pp. 78–82, and John Fairbank, *The Great Chinese Revolution 1800–1985* (New York: Harper, 1986), pp. 214–25.

This discussion suggests that the problem of the use of force may be resolved by considering the political rights of the majority. If the majority can pursue its goals and interests effectively through existing political institutions, then it has neither need nor right for force. If political arrangements prevent the majority from asserting itself, then it has the right to use force, judiciously and rationally, to achieve its purposes. And within a socialist regime, the same requirement applies: policies must be adopted through democratic means, and force may only be used to implement policies so adopted.

VI. Is Democratic Socialism Feasible?

The three problems considered here, and the solutions presented to them, constitute the core of a political morality for a socialist party in its pursuit of power and the process of socialist reform: socialism should embody and respect the institutional arrangements of democratic decision-making, it should respect individual political rights and activities, it should adopt only those policies which meet with the support of the masses, and it should use force only in implementation of such policies. If socialist politicians and parties had always respected these requirements, the great indignities of socialist regimes during the twentieth century would not have occurred – Stalinism, the Cultural Revolution, or Pol Pot's Cambodia. But before closing, we need to consider – if only briefly – whether these constraints are so narrow as to make the achievement of socialism impossible. For it might be held that the route to socialism *requires* force and class dictatorship.

It should first be noted that the account described above does *not* prevent socialists from using force within dictatorial regimes in which no legal means for achieving power exist – e.g., Nationalist China, Batista's Cuba, or Hitler's Germany. But it does prohibit the use of force in circumstances in which socialists possess effective political rights of activity and participation, and these circumstances exist in liberal capitalist democracies. So let us pose these parallel questions: Is it possible, within idealized institutions of a capitalist democracy, for a socialist party to win control of government through legal electoral means?[52] And is it possible for a socialist government, once in power, to steer a process of socialist reform, including reform of basic social and economic institutions, within a democratic system of decision-making?

Adam Przeworski has devoted much attention to the former problem, and, on his treatment, the answer is underdetermined. One problem is that the traditional constituency of socialist parties – the industrial working class – is

---

[52] I am abstracting from the possibility that the elite classes would themselves abandon parliamentary institutions when a socialist party appears on the brink of attaining power.

not an absolute majority of capitalist democracies. Therefore a socialist party, if it is to arrive at an electoral majority, will have to put forward a program that serves the interests of other groups besides the proletariat. The possibility exists, however, that the interests of other groups – information workers or service workers, for example – will be sufficiently diverse that a straightforward program of abolition of private property in the means of production will not serve all of them. Consequently, in order to win adherents from these other class strata, the socialist party may have to modify its program substantially.

A second problem that arises has to do with the structures of motivation that we attribute to hypothetical voters. If we assume, for example, that voters support a program strictly according to the effect the program would have on their short- or medium-term material interests, then we will arrive at one prediction about the electoral prospects of socialism. If we assume, however, that voters can be motivated by more comprehensive interests – the long-term interests of their class or region, for example, or their political commitments – then we may arrive at a different prediction. These considerations suggest that it is *possible* for a socialist party to win an electoral struggle within a capitalist democracy and to begin to implement a program of socialist reform, but that such a victory is by no means assured.

This conclusion derives from a consideration of idealized electoral institutions within a capitalist democracy. It is sometimes claimed – e.g., by Lenin in *State and Revolution* – that electoral institutions are only stable within capitalist democracy so long as they serve the interests of the economic elites; if the electoral tide begins to turn against the bourgeoisie, electoral institutions will be replaced by more coercive, antidemocratic institutions of government. This prediction does not cast doubt on the moral constraints described above, because when democratic institutions are subverted, the principles above permit a socialist movement to continue its political struggle with force. It would appear, however, that democratic institutions of politics are more robust than this form of skepticism would allow. As a wide range of Marxian political sociologists have concluded, the democratic state is *not* merely the passive tool of the capitalist class within modern western democracies.[53] Instead, the state is affected by a variety of contending powers, including the electoral strength of various non-capitalist groups. And there are quasi-effective constraints limiting the freedom of privileged groups to turn to extralegal means when their interests are not well-served by state policies: widespread popular support for legality and

---

[53] Ralph Miliband, *The State in Capitalist Society* (New York: Basic, 1969); Ralph Miliband, *Capitalist Democracy in Britain*; Nicos Poulantzas, *Political Power and Social Classes* (London: New Left Books, 1975); Adam Przeworski, *Capitalism and Social Democracy*.

existing parliamentary institutions, the probability of social conflict in the event of extralegality, and the possibility that the repressive institutions of the state itself may be brought to bear on the agents of extralegal activity. So the institutions of the democratic state are to some degree autonomous from the interests and powers of the capitalist class. This conclusion provides further support for the view that there is a feasible electoral route to socialism.

These arguments would suggest a basis for conditional optimism for the prospects for socialism within a capitalist democracy: *if* a socialist party can gain an electoral majority, and *if* there are sufficient deterrents in place to block extralegal moves on the part of the capitalist class, *then* a socialist regime will be able to take power and begin to implement a process of socialist reform. And once in place, it should be possible for a democratic socialist regime to construct its program of reform in such a way as to preserve its base of political support among the masses of society. There is no "historical inevitability" for the success of socialism. But political mechanisms exist through which a socialist movement, committed to democratic institutions, can establish itself in government and undertake a process of socialist reform. And if socialism proves not to be attainable through such democratic processes, then this is a powerful argument against the socialist vision of the future.

Philosophy, Colgate University

THE ECONOMIC BASIS OF DELIBERATIVE DEMOCRACY*

By Joshua Cohen

Introduction

There are two principal philosophical conceptions of socialism, corresponding to two interpretations of the notion of a rational society.[1] The first conception corresponds to an instrumental view of social rationality. Captured by the image of socialism as "one big workshop," the instrumental view holds that social ownership of the means of production is rational because it promotes the optimal development of the productive forces. Social ownership is optimal because it eliminates the costs of coordination imposed by the conduct of economic activities in formally independent enterprises, and, more generally, overcomes fetters on development that result from the control of resources by individuals whose particular interests (in profit) imperfectly correspond to a general interest in productive advance.

While controversy continues about the meaning of the thesis that social ownership would remove the fetters imposed by capitalism on productive forces, it is difficult to find a plausible defense of this thesis in contemporary literature. In fact, contemporary arguments for socialism rarely turn on the thesis that social ownership would unfetter productive forces. But whatever the current status of this first conception, I mention it only for the sake of contrast, and will say nothing more about it here.

* This paper develops some ideas that Joel Rogers and I presented in *On Democracy: Toward a Transformation of American Society* (Harmondsworth: Penguin, 1983). esp. ch. 6. I am very much indebted to Joel, both for the joint work that issued in *On Democracy* and for his insightful advice on this paper. I would also like to thank the editors of *Social Philosophy and Policy* for very helpful criticisms of the first draft.

[1] These two philosophical conceptions correspond to two variants of Marxism, the first of which has its most powerful systematization in G.A. Cohen's *Karl Marx's Theory of History: A Defense* (Princeton: Princeton University Press, 1978), the second of which has been elaborated by Jürgen Habermas. For a discussion of the two variants, see Habermas, *Knowledge and Human Interests*, trans. Jeremy Shapiro (Boston: Beacon Press, 1971), chs. 2, 3, 5. For the purposes of this paper, I am putting to the side philosophical conceptions of socialism which appeal to more substantive conceptions of the good life. For a recent account, see Jon Elster, "Self-Realization in Work and Politics: The Marxist Conception of the Good Life," eds. Ellen Paul, Fred D. Miller, Jr., Jeffrey Paul, and John Ahrens, *Marxism and Liberalism* (Oxford: Basil Blackwell, 1986), pp. 97–126.

26 JOSHUA COHEN

The second conception is based on a deliberative view of social rationality. On this view, a commitment to socialism follows naturally from a commitment to democracy, where a democracy is understood to be an association that realizes the ideal of free deliberation among equal citizens.[2] This "extension of democracy" conception provides the focus for this paper, which is composed of three sections. In section I, I sketch four lines of argument that draw broadly socialist conclusions from democratic principles, and that comprise different variants of the extension of democracy conception. In section II, I outline an abstract conception of democratic order that is organized around the notion of deliberative reason. In section III, I indicate how this conception of a deliberative democracy provides a way to unify and deepen the four separate strands of argument from section I, thus enhancing their cumulative force as an argument for a feasible form of socialism.[3]

One final point about the strategy of the paper: my aim is to provide a unifying structure for a family of considerations that lead from a commitment to democratic association to a commitment to a form of socialism. I want, in particular, to locate a set of arguments for socialism within the general framework of political argument provided by the ideal of a deliberative democracy. In pursuing this systematization, I will help myself to a wide range of controversial considerations which require a defense that I do not provide here. For example, I will only respond to a small handful of the many reasonable objections to the four strands of argument discussed in section I. As a consequence, the argument is bound to strike many as proceeding within overly narrow intellectual confines, and as simply assuming what needs to be shown. I do not think that the confines are excessively narrow. Whatever their dimensions, however, the aim is to achieve some clarification by remaining inside them.

[2] For different variants of the extension of democracy conception, corresponding in part to different conceptions of democracy, see V.I. Lenin, The State and Revolution in Lenin, Selected Works in Three Volumes (Moscow: Progress Publishers, 1970), vol. 2, esp. p. 352; Karl Kautsky, The Dictatorship of the Proletariat (Ann Arbor: University of Michigan, 1971); Rosa Luxemburg, Reform or Revolution (New York: Pathfinder, 1970); Michael Walzer, Radical Principles: Reflections of an Unreconstructed Democrat (New York: Basic Books, 1980), chs. 15, 17, and Spheres of Justice (Basic Books: New York, 1983), pp. 291–303; Joshua Cohen and Joel Rogers, On Democracy (New York: Penguin, 1983); Robert A. Dahl, A Preface to Economic Democracy (Berkeley: University of California Press, 1985); Samuel Bowles and Herbert Gintis, Democracy and Capitalism: Property, Community, and the Contradictions of Modern Social Thought (New York: Basic Books, 1986); Roberto Unger, Politics (Cambridge: Cambridge University Press, 1987), vol. 2 (False Necessity), pp. 480–508; Noberto Bobbio, The Future of Democracy: A Defense of the Rules of the Game, trans. Roger Griffin (Minneapolis: University of Minnesota Press, 1987), chs. 1, 4.
[3] Following Alec Nove, I assume that a conception of feasible socialism should not depend on the premise of abundance, should avoid making wild assumptions about human beings or social possibilities, must assume the existence of a state, and must institutionally address tendencies to the abuse of power. See his The Economics of Feasible Socialism (London: George Allan and Unwin, 1983), p. 197.

I. Four Arguments from Democracy

In the discussion that follows, I sketch four lines of argument that fall under the "extension of democracy" conception. Each of the four couples a criticism of capitalism with considerations in support of some form of social ownership of capital. I assume that each is reasonably familiar and so I will present them briefly, giving only as much detail as I will need later on. I save a discussion of objections until section III, though even there I will only address a few of the difficulties that need to be addressed.

The Parallel Case Argument

Several arguments for worker self-management maintain that the case for self-management runs parallel to the case for democratic governance of the state, with both drawing support from the same general principles.[4] These arguments begin by assuming that the state ought to be governed democratically. Next, they argue that the best justification for democratic governance is that the state has some specified characteristic. They then argue that economic enterprises have the specified characteristic as well. They conclude that there ought to be democratic governance of enterprises. They also conclude that since the private ownership of capital interferes with such governance, it ought to be abolished, or at least restricted to very special conditions (e.g., to very small firms).

The most plausible parallel case argument proceeds as follows: the best justification for the requirement of democratic governance of the state is that a political society is a cooperative activity, governed by public rules, that is expected to operate for the mutual advantage of the members. Anyone who contributes to such an activity, who has the capacity to assess its rules, and who is subject to them has a right to participate in their determination. But economic organizations are cooperative activities governed by rules, and they are expected to operate for the advantage of each member. Workers in such enterprises contribute to the cooperative activity, have the capacity to assess the rules that regulate it, and are subject to them. So they have a right to determine the regulative rules in their workplaces. Since the private ownership of capital conflicts with that right, it ought to be abolished, or at least carefully circumscribed.[5]

---

[4] The clearest version is in Robert Dahl, *A Preface to Economic Democracy* (Berkeley: University of California Press, 1985), ch. 4. See also Bowles and Gintis, *Democracy and Capitalism*, ch. 3; Walzer, *Radical Principles*, chs. 15, 17, and *Spheres of Justice*, pp. 291–303.

[5] Any particular system of self-management would need to settle such important issues as which workers have the relevant rights (whether a "residency requirement" is permissible), precisely how those rights should be protected, what methods of debt financing are consistent with self-management, and how to render self-management consistent with such concededly permissible forms of "outside" regulation as rules regulating product safety and the release of pollutants into the environment. But the fact that these are open questions which would almost certainly be answered in different ways in different cases is not a problem for the parallel cases argument. Similar questions always arise for local jurisdictions within a state.

The Structural Constraints Argument

According to the structural constraints argument, the private control of investment importantly limits the democratic character of the state by subordinating the decisions and actions of the democratic state to the investment decisions of capitalists.[6] Political decisions are structurally constrained because the fate of parties and governments depends on the health of the economy, the health of the economy on investment decisions by capitalists, and investment decisions by capitalists on their expectations of profits. While groups other than capitalists also control strategic resources, and can use that control to constrain decision-making, the structural constraints argument holds that the power of capitalists and the fact that everyone's welfare depends on their decisions singles them out for special attention.

Suppose, for example, that citizens in a capitalist democracy want simultaneously to increase the rate of growth and to redistribute income.[7] Suppose further that doing so requires both stimulating investment and increasing the progressivity of the tax system. The private control of investment is an obstacle to this combination of policies. Rational capitalists will not invest more when they expect that more of their gains will be taxed away. Since declining investment would impose long-term material losses on citizens, rational citizens, anticipating the choices of capitalists, will not introduce the scheme. So, even if political parties are perfect representatives of citizens, no party in power will consistently advance the desired policies. Since the private control of investment thus imposes important constraints on the collective choices of citizens, public control of investment is required as a remedy.

The Psychological Support Argument

The psychological support argument focuses on the forms of association "outside" the state, particularly in the economy, that strengthen the forms of thought, feeling, and self-understanding that give substance to democratic citizenship.[8] Two psychological conditions are of special importance in a

---

[6] On structural constraints, see Adam Przeworski, *Capitalism and Social Democracy* (Cambridge Cambridge University Press, 1985), ch. 4; Adam Przeworski and Michael Wallerstein, "Structural Dependence of the State on Capital," *American Political Science Review*, forthcoming; Charles Lindblom, *Politics and Markets: The World's Political-Economic Systems* (New York: Basic Books 1977), ch. 13; Cohen and Rogers, *On Democracy*, ch. 3.

[7] Here I summarize the discussion in Przeworski and Wallerstein, "Structural Dependence."

[8] On the psychological support thesis, see Carole Pateman, *Participation and Democratic Theory* (Cambridge: Cambridge University Press, 1970); Dahl, *Preface to Economic Democracy*; Ronald M. Mason, *Participatory and Workplace Democracy* (Carbondale: Southern Illinois University Press 1982); J. Maxwell Elder, "Political Efficacy at Work: The Connection Between More Autonomous Forms of Workplace Organization and a More Participatory Politics," *American Political Science Review*, 75 (1981), 43–58. It is suggested as well in John Stuart Mill, *Principles of Political Economy* Book 4, ch. 7, secs. 4, 6. For a skeptical discussion, see Edward Greenberg, *Workplace Democracy: The Political Effects of Participation* (Ithaca: Cornell University Press, 1986), chs. 5, 6, 8. Greenberg skepticism is, however, consistent with my use of the psychological support argument (see h remarks on pp. 167–68).

well-functioning democracy. The first is what Mill called an "active character" – the sense that social arrangements are malleable and subject to improvement, and that one's own efforts can contribute to their improvement.[9] The second is a sense of the common good – the capacity to judge in terms of common good, and an effective desire to act on such judgments. The psychological support argument holds that the extension of self-government into the traditionally undemocratic sphere of work contributes to both the formation of an active character and to the development of a sense of the common good, and thus contributes to a more fully democratic state. Since capitalist property relations vest final authority in the owners of capital, they limit the extent of intra-firm democracy, thereby fostering passivity and a narrower basis of political judgment. For these reasons, they are not well-suited to a democratic society.

The Resource Constraint Argument

Finally, the resource constraint argument is that the unequal distribution of wealth and income characteristic of capitalism limits the democratic character of politics by undermining the equal access of citizens to the political arena and their equal capacity to influence outcomes in that arena (quite apart from the structural constraints imposed by the private control of investment).[10] Citizens in a democracy are formally equal, and democratic procedures officially vest power in numbers. But because economic resources provide the material basis for organized political action, groups that are materially disadvantaged face important organizational and political disabilities. A well-functioning democracy, based on the principle that political opportunity should not be a function of economic position, would therefore be aided by a more equal distribution of material resources than is characteristic of capitalism. And greater distributional equality would plausibly be fostered by a scheme in which capital is socially owned.

Each of these four lines of argument identifies a source of tension between capitalism and democracy. Each suggests that some form of social ownership would be more suited to democratic ideals. But the arguments are, at least on the surface, quite disparate. Drawing on distinct conceptions of democracy, they point to different aspects of capitalism in their diagnosis of its undemocratic character, and lead to different conclusions about suitable alternatives. The structural constraints argument, for example, focuses on the control of investment, while the parallel case argument focuses on the undemocratic character of the organization of work. Embracing the latter is consistent with affirming the fully democratic character of politics in capitalist democracies, while endorsing the former is not. Still, there is a

---

[9] John Stuart Mill, *Considerations on Representative Government* (London: J.M. Dent, 1972), pp. 193, 211–18; Pateman, chs. 2, 3.

[10] On the resource constraint argument, see Anthony Downs, *An Economic Theory of Democracy* (New York: Harper and Row, 1957), part 3; Cohen and Rogers, *On Democracy*, ch. 3.

certain affinity among them, and they have considerable cumulative force. What is needed is a more abstract and comprehensive point of view from which they all can be brought into play. The aim of section II is to outline a conception of democratic order – of deliberative democracy – which provides that standpoint.

II. DELIBERATIVE DEMOCRACY[11]

The notion of a deliberative democracy is rooted in the intuitive ideal of a form of social order in which the justification of the terms of association proceeds through public argument among equal citizens.[12] A deliberative democracy is a social order whose basic institutions embody that ideal. The members of a deliberative democracy share a commitment to the resolution of problems of collective choice through public reasoning, and regard their basic institutions as legitimate insofar as they establish a framework for free public deliberation.

In the remarks that follow I aim to elaborate this intuitive ideal. I begin by providing a fuller and more explicit statement of the ideal itself, presenting what I will call the "formal conception" of a deliberative democracy. Proceeding from this formal conception, I develop a more substantive account of deliberative democracy by sketching an ideal deliberative procedure. The procedure captures the notion of justification through free deliberation among equals ingredient in the democratic ideal, and serves in turn as a model for deliberative institutions.

[11] This section of the paper is based on my "Deliberation and Democratic Legitimacy," in eds. Alan Hamlin and Phillip Petit, *The Good Society* (London: Basil Blackwell, forthcoming). For related views, see Jon Elster, "The Market and the Forum: Three Varieties of Political Theory," in eds. Jon Elster and Aanund Hylland, *Foundations of Social Choice Theory* (Cambridge: Cambridge University Press, 1986), pp. 103–32; Bernard Manin, "On Legitimacy and Political Deliberation," *Political Theory*, vol. 15 (August 1987), pp. 338–68; Jürgen Habermas, *The Legitimation Crisis of Late Capitalism*, trans. T. McCarthy (Boston: Beacon Press, 1975), and *The Theory of Communicative Action*, trans. T. McCarthy, vol. 1 (Boston: Beacon Press, 1984). Apart from its representation in "high political theory," the notion of deliberative democracy plays a role in the "responsible party" tradition in American political science. I am indebted to Lee Perlman for his lucid explanations of the main elements of that tradition. See his "Parties, Democracy, and Consent," unpublished. The notion also figures in recent discussions of American public law. See, among others, Cass Sunstein, "Naked Preferences and the Constitution," *Columbia Law Review*, vol. 84 (November 1984), pp. 1689–1732, "Interest Groups in American Public Law," *Stanford Law Review*, vol. 38 (November 1985), pp. 29–87, "Legal Interference with Private Preferences," *The University of Chicago Law Review* vol. 53 (Fall 1986), pp. 1129–84; Frank Michelman, "The Supreme Court, 1985 Term – Foreword: Traces of Self-Government," *Harvard Law Review*, vol. 100 (November 1986), pp. 4–77; Bruce Ackerman, "The Storrs Lectures: Discovering the Constitution," *Yale Law Journal*, vol. 93 (May 1984), pp. 1013–72, and "Discovering the Constitution," unpublished.

[12] For a contrast between this ideal and the intuitive ideal of fairness that Rawls draws on in *A Theory of Justice*, see my "Deliberation and Democratic Legitimacy."

The Formal Conception

The formal conception of a deliberative democracy has four main features:

— D1: A deliberative democracy is an ongoing and independent association whose members share (and it is common knowledge that they share) the view that the appropriate terms of association are those that either provide a framework for or are the results of their own deliberation. They share a commitment to coordinating their activities within institutions that make deliberation possible and according to norms that they arrive at through their deliberation. For them, free deliberation among equals is the basis of legitimacy.

— D2: A deliberative democracy is a pluralistic association. The members have diverse preferences, convictions, and ideals concerning the conduct of their own lives. While sharing a commitment to the deliberative resolution of problems of collective choice (D1), they also have aims that diverge, and do not think that some particular set of preferences, convictions, or ideals is mandatory.

— D3: Because the members of a democratic association regard deliberative procedures as the source of *legitimacy*, it is important to them that the rules of association not merely *be* the results of their deliberation, but that it be *manifest* to them that this is so. They prefer institutions in which the connections between deliberation and outcomes are more evident to ones in which they are less so.[13]

— D4: The members recognize one another as having deliberative capacities, i.e., the capacities required for entering into a public exchange of reasons and for acting on the result of such public reasoning.

In the discussion that follows, I try to give substance to this formal conception by characterizing the ethical and institutional consequences of a shared commitment to manifestly deliberative forms of collective choice. To connect the formal ideal to these consequences, I consider an ideal deliberative procedure. This procedure provides an explicit statement of the

[13] The force of the notion of manifestness is indicated in, for example, discussions of campaign finance. In upholding limits on campaign contributions under the Federal Election Campaign Act, the U.S. Supreme Court approved of what they took to be "the Act's primary purpose – to limit the actuality and *appearance* [my emphasis] of corruption resulting from large individual campaign contributions." Buckley v. Valeo, 424 U.S. 1 (1976). For philosophical discussions of the importance of manifestness or publicity, see Immanuel Kant, "To Perpetual Peace: A Philosophical Sketch," in *Perpetual Peace and Other Essays*, trans. Ted Humphrey (Indianapolis: Hackett, 1983), pp. 135–39; Rawls, *A Theory of Justice* (Cambridge: Harvard University Press, 1971), p. 133 and section 29; Bernard Williams, *Ethics and the Limits of Philosophy* (Cambridge: Harvard University Press, 1985), pp. 101–2, 200; Bobbio, *The Future of Democracy*, ch. 4.

features of deliberative decision-making – of free deliberation among equals – that are suited to the formal conception, and thereby indicates the properties that the framework of deliberative institutions should, so far as possible, embody. It thus provides a model for institutions, and in the first instance for those institutions in which collective choices are made and social outcomes publicly justified.[14]

The Ideal Procedure

There are four main aspects of deliberation: setting the agenda, proposing alternative solutions to the problems on the agenda, supporting those solutions with reasons, and concluding by settling on some alternative. The democratic conception can be represented in terms of the requirements that it sets on such procedures. In particular, outcomes are democratically legitimate if and only if they would be the object of an agreement arrived at through a free and reasoned consideration of alternatives by equals.[15]

— I1: Ideal deliberation is *free* in part because the participants regard themselves as bound only by the results of their deliberation and by the preconditions for that deliberation. Their consideration of proposals is not constrained by the authority of prior norms or requirements. Further, it is free because the participants suppose that they can act from the results, that they can take the fact that a decision is arrived at through their deliberation as a sufficient motivation for complying with it. Thus the democratic conception is not only a standard of justification, but is a source of motivation as well.

— I2: Ideal deliberation is *reasoned* in that the parties to it are required to state their reasons for advancing proposals, supporting them, or criticizing them. They give reasons with the expectation that those reasons (and not, for example, their power) will settle the fate of their proposal.[16] Reasons are offered with the aim of bringing others to accept the proposal, subject to the understanding that they have disparate ends (D2) and are committed to settling the conditions of their association through free deliberation among equals (D1). Proposals may be rejected because they are not defended with

[14] The procedure is not an initial choice situation in which principles or institutions are themselves selected. On the distinction between the role of the procedure and the role of a choice situation, see "Deliberation and Democratic Legitimacy." This distinction will be important in the later discussion of motivation formation (see below, pp. 34–35).

[15] I do not wish to endorse the view that all moral norms have a deliberative justification. The conception of deliberative democracy is, in Rawls's term, a "political conception," and not a comprehensive moral theory. On the distinction between political conceptions and comprehensive moral theories, see John Rawls, "The Idea of an Overlapping Consensus," *Oxford Journal of Legal Studies*, vol. 7 (1987), pp. 1–25.

[16] As Habermas puts it, "no force except that of the better argument is exercised." *Legitimation Crisis*, p. 108.

acceptable reasons, even though they could be defended with such reasons. On the deliberative conception, it is important that collective choices be *made in a deliberative way*, and not simply that those choices conform to the preferences, convictions, and ideals of citizens.[17]

— I3: In ideal deliberation, parties are both formally and substantively *equal.* They are formally equal in that the rules defining the procedure do not single out individuals for advantage or disadvantage. Everyone with deliberative capacities has equal standing at each stage of the deliberative process. Each can put issues on the agenda, propose solutions, and offer reasons in support of or in criticism of proposals, and each has an equal voice in the decision. The participants are substantively equal in that the existing distribution of power and resources does not shape their chances to contribute at any stage of the deliberative process, nor does that distribution play an authoritative role in their deliberation. The participants in the deliberative procedure do not regard themselves as bound by the existing system of rights, except insofar as that system establishes the framework of free deliberation among equals.[18] Instead, they regard that system as a potential object of their deliberative judgment.

— I4: Finally, ideal deliberation aims to arrive at a rationally motivated consensus – to find reasons that are persuasive to all who are committed to acting on the results of free deliberation among equals. Even under ideal conditions, there is no promise that there are such reasons. If there are not, then deliberation concludes with voting, subject to some form of majority rule. The fact that it may so conclude does not, however, eliminate the distinction between deliberative forms of collective choice and forms that aggregate non-deliberative preferences. The institutional consequences are likely to be different in the two cases, and the results of voting among those who are committed to finding reasons that are persuasive to all is likely to differ from the result of an aggregation that proceeds in the absence of this commitment.[19]

Drawing on this characterization of ideal deliberation, can we say anything more substantial about a deliberative democracy? What are the implications of a commitment to deliberative decisions for the framework of social order? In the remarks that follow, I provide an initial answer to these questions by indicating the ways that this commitment carries with it a commitment to a

[17] For a discussion of this distinction in the context of American constitutional and administrative law, see Sunstein, "Interest Groups," secs. 4–6.
[18] The importance of this qualification becomes clear later. See pp. 37–38, 40.
[19] On the need to drop the assumption of unanimity from deliberative views, see Manin, "Legitimacy and Deliberation," pp. 359–61.

framework of order that advances the common good and respects individual autonomy.

Common Good and Autonomy

Consider first the notion of the common good. The requirements of reasonableness (I2) and consensus (I4) link the notion of deliberative democracy to the common good. Since the condition of pluralism obtains (D2), and the aim of deliberation is to secure general agreement among all who are committed to free deliberation, the focus of deliberation is on ways of advancing the diverse aims of the parties to it. While no one is indifferent to his or her own good, everyone also seeks to arrive at decisions that are acceptable to all who share the commitment to deliberation (D1). As we shall see just below, taking that commitment seriously will likely require a willingness to revise one's understanding of one's own preferences and convictions. Thus the characterization of an ideal deliberative procedure links the formal notion of deliberative democracy with the more substantive ideal of a democratic association in which public debate is focused on the common good of the members.

Of course, talk about the common good is one thing; sincere efforts to advance it are another. While public deliberation may be organized around appeals to the common good, those appeals may reflect cynical (or sincere) efforts to disguise personal or class advantage as the common advantage. Considering the motivational effects of deliberation may provide a response to this difficulty.[20] A consequence of the reasonableness of the deliberative procedure (I2) is that the mere fact of having a preference or conviction does not, by itself, provide a reason in support of a proposal. While I may take my preferences as a sufficient reason for advancing a proposal, deliberation under conditions of pluralism requires that I find reasons that make the proposal acceptable to others who cannot be expected to regard my preferences as sufficient reasons for agreeing. The motivational thesis is that the need to find and to present such reasons will contribute to shaping the preferences and convictions that are brought to the deliberative procedure in ways that will make it more workable.

First, the practice of presenting reasons will contribute to the formation of a commitment to the deliberative resolution of problems of collective choice (D1). Given that commitment, the likelihood of a sincere representation of preferences and convictions should increase, and the likelihood of their strategic misrepresentation should decrease. Second, it will shape the content of those preferences and convictions as well. Assuming a commitment to deliberative justification, the discovery that I can offer no persuasive reasons

---

[20] See Elster, "The Market and the Forum," pp. 112–13; Habermas, *Legitimation Crisis*, p. 108, and *Communication and the Evolution of Society*, trans. T. McCarthy (Boston: Beacon Press, 1979), ch. 2.

on behalf of a proposal of mine may transform the preferences that motivate the proposal. Aims that I recognize to be inconsistent with the requirements of deliberative agreement may tend to lose their force, at least – and this qualification needs to be underscored – when I expect others to proceed in reasonable ways, and expect that the outcome of deliberation will regulate subsequent action.

Consider, for example, the desire to be wealthier, come what may. I cannot appeal to this desire itself in defending policies. The motivational claim is that the need to find an independent justification that does not appeal to this desire will tend to shape it into, e.g., a desire to have a level of wealth that is consistent with a level that others find acceptable. I am, of course, assuming that the deliberation is known to be regulative, and that the wealth cannot be protected through wholly non-deliberative means.[21]

Deliberation, then, focuses debate on the common good. And the relevant conceptions of the common good are not composed simply of interests and preferences that are antecedent to deliberation. Instead, they are shaped by deliberation itself, and are interests that, on public reflection, we find it legitimate to appeal to in making claims on social resources.

The ideal deliberative scheme also indicates the place of autonomy in a deliberative democracy. In particular, it is responsive to two threats to autonomy. As a general matter, actions fail to be autonomous if the preferences on which an agent acts are, roughly, given by the circumstances, and not determined by the agent. There are two paradigm cases of "external" determination. The first is what Elster has called "adaptive preferences."[22] These are preferences that shift with changes in the circumstances of the agent without any deliberate contribution by the agent to that shift. This is true, for example, of the political preferences of instinctive centrists who move to the median of the political distribution, wherever it happens to be. The second I will call "accommodationist preferences." While accommodationist preferences are deliberately formed, they represent psychological adjustments to conditions of subordination in which individuals are not recognized as having the capacity for self-government. Take the case of Stoic slaves. With a view to minimizing frustration, they deliberately shape their desires to match their powers. Recognizing that slavery is their only possibility, they cultivate desires to be slaves, and then act on those desires. While their motives are deliberately formed, the Stoic slaves do not act autonomously when they seek to be good slaves. The absence of alternatives and consequent denial of scope for the deliberative capacities that define the

---

[21] This qualification has implications for the role of deliberation in moving from non-ideal to ideal conditions. See below, p. 37.

[22] See "Sour Grapes," eds. Amartya Sen and Bernard Williams, *Utilitarianism and Beyond* (Cambridge: Cambridge University Press, 1982), pp. 219–38.

condition of the slaves support the conclusion that their desires result from
their circumstances, even though those circumstances shape the desires of
Stoic slaves through their deliberation.[23]

There are, then, at least two dimensions of autonomy. The phenomenon of
adaptive preferences underlines the importance of conditions that permit
and encourage the deliberative formation of preferences; the phenomenon of
accommodationist preferences indicates the need for favorable conditions for
the exercise of the deliberative capacities. Both aspects are present in forms of
collective decision-making that conform to the ideal deliberative procedure.
Relations of power and subordination are neutralized (I1, I3, I4), and each
citizen is recognized as having deliberative capacities (D4), thus addressing
the problem of accommodationist preferences. And the requirement of
reasonableness (I2) also discourages adaptive preferences. While preferences
are formed by the deliberative procedure, this type of preference formation is
consistent with autonomy. For preferences that are shaped by deliberation
are not simply given by external circumstances. Instead, they are the result of
the public use of reason.

Beginning, then, from the formal idea of a deliberative democracy, we
arrive at the more substantive ideal of an association that is regulated by
deliberation, aimed at the common good, and respectful of the autonomy of
the members. And so, in seeking to embody the ideal deliberative procedure
in institutions, we seek, *inter alia*, to design institutions that focus political
debate on the common good, and that provide favorable conditions for the
exercise of deliberative powers.

Three Criticisms

Before concluding the presentation of the deliberative conception and
returning to the issue of socialism, I want to elaborate on the motivations for
the conception by responding to three criticisms of it.

First, the conception of deliberative democracy might be thought to
embrace an implausible view about social change. Emphasizing the
importance of rational deliberation might suggest the view that deliberation
under non-ideal circumstances is always the best way to advance the
deliberative ideal, "that one will in fact approach the good society by acting as
if one has already arrived there."[24] The view that I have suggested here has
no such implication. In fact, considerations internal to the account of
deliberative democracy provide some ground for skepticism about the role of
rational public argument – rather than "something like irony, eloquence, or

---

[23] I should emphasize that the historical evidence shows that Stoic slavery is largely a philosopher's
construction. For a discussion of the evidence, see my "The Moral Arc of the Universe – The Case of
Slavery" (unpublished).

[24] See Elster, "Market and Forum," p. 119; he suggests that Habermas's view suffers from this
defect.

propaganda"[25] – in moving from non-ideal to more ideal conditions. One of the features of non-ideal circumstances is that one cannot count on others to be moved by public deliberation. But the motivational mechanism described earlier that leads to a sincere concern for the common good depends on the belief that others are so moved. So while it is not inconsistent with the deliberative view that deliberation works its effects under non-ideal conditions, the basic commitments of the theory do not mandate the conclusion that the elimination of "political and economic domination ... can be brought about by rational argumentation."[26]

Second, I have been treating the ideal of democracy as the basic organizing ideal for a political conception. But it is commonly assumed that the ideal of democracy (by contrast, for example, with the ideal of fairness) is not suited to this role because it fails, for example, to provide a secure foundation for fundamental liberties (for example, the liberties of thought and expression).[27] It fails because it entrusts their protection to the shifting opinions of majorities about the value of thought and expression. To be plausible, then, the conception of democracy must be supplemented with additional principles requiring fundamental liberties. The resulting hybrid view will strike a compromise between political equality and individual liberty. This second objection is of particular relevance to the problem of socialism, because the additional principles required to accommodate the liberties might themselves provide a basis for an argument against social ownership. Thus, if a defense of the liberties of thought and expression carried with it a requirement of "economic liberty," understood as the liberty to own the means of production, then the extension of democracy argument would lose its force.[28]

Both the objection and the claim that there is a need for compromise rest on a misconstrual of the democratic ideal. The objection supposes that thought and expression are simply objects of public evaluation – goods that are evaluated through deliberation, and that might be judged to have a

---

[25] ibid., p. 120.

[26] ibid., p. 119.

[27] For discussion of the connections between democracy and free expression, see Rosa Luxemburg, *The Russian Revolution* (Ann Arbor: University of Michigan Press, 1961), pp. 66–72; Alexander Meiklejohn, *Free Speech and Its Relation to Self-Government* (New York: Harper and Row, 1948); John Hart Ely, *Democracy and Distrust* (Cambridge: Harvard University Press, 1980), pp. 93–94, 105–16. I believe that the democratic conception can also provide a satisfactory account of the liberty of conscience and the liberties associated with privacy and personhood. As a general matter, one needs to show that other fundamental liberties must be protected if citizens are to be able to engage in and have equal standing in public deliberation without fear that such engagement puts them at risk for their convictions or personal choices. This is a matter for detailed treatment elsewhere.

[28] For rejection of the view that it does, see Rawls, *Theory of Justice*, pp. 270–74, 280–82; Ronald Dworkin, *Taking Rights Seriously* (Cambridge: Harvard University Press, 1978), chs. 11, 12.

negligible value. But this is an incorrect account of their role in the deliberative conception. The preferences and convictions that are relevant to the collective evaluation of alternatives are those that arise from or are confirmed through deliberation. And the reasoned evaluation of alternatives that comprises deliberation can only proceed within a framework that secures free expression. It is implausible to think that such evaluation might proceed in an environment in which the liberties of thought and expression are not institutionally secured and given broad scope. It violates the core of the ideal of free deliberation among equals to fix preferences and convictions by restricting advocacy, or by barring people from access to advocacy, or by preventing the expression that is essential to having convictions at all.

So the objection fails because the liberties comprise part of an institutional framework that makes free deliberation among equals possible; they are not simply among the goods to be evaluated through public deliberation, but part of a framework for making the relevant evaluations. The protection of basic liberties, then, follows naturally from the most plausible interpretation of the ideal of democracy itself. Furthermore, that interpretation does not support the view that the defense of the liberties of thought and expression carries with it the liberty to own the means of production. While it is plausible that the right to personal property is a requisite for individual autonomy and the independence required to participate in public deliberation, there is no similarly plausible case that links the right to own the means of production with such participation. So while a wide range of extraordinarily complicated problems about the content of different liberties, their relative significance, and the proper reach of majoritarian procedures needs to be addressed to fill out the democratic conception, I do not think that addressing them forces a compromise between the democratic conception and a wholly independent set of political principles.

The third objection is that the ideal of deliberative democracy is objectionably sectarian because it depends on a particular view of the good life, the ideal of active citizenship. In discussing this objection, I will put to the side current controversy over the thesis that "sectarianism" is avoidable and objectionable, and assume that it is both.[29]

Views of the good figure in political conceptions in at least two ways. First, the *justification* of some conceptions appeals to notions of the good. Aristotelian views, for example, endorse the claim that the exercise of the deliberative capacities is a fundamental component of a good human life, and

[29] Contrasting views on the problem of "sectarianism" are argued in Rawls, "The Idea of an Overlapping Consensus"; Ronald Dworkin, *A Matter of Principle* (Cambridge: Harvard University Press, 1985), Part 3; Alasdair MacIntyre, *After Virtue* (Notre Dame: University of Notre Dame Press, 1981); and Michael Sandel, *Liberalism and the Limits of Justice* (Cambridge: Cambridge University Press, 1982).

conclude that a political association ought to be organized to encourage the realization of those capacities through participation in public affairs. Second, the *stability* of a society may require widespread allegiance to a specific conception of the good, even though the justification of its basic institutions is free of any appeal to that conception. For example, an order whose justification makes no reference to the ideal of public service may depend for its stability on a general consensus that a life of virtuous public service is a good life. Thus Rousseau's justification of a state regulated by a general will does not rest on the view that political participation is a supreme good in human life. But he thought that the stability of an order regulated by a general will required citizens to value participation above their private affairs.[30]

The charge of sectarianism is most commonly and forcefully directed against views that rely on conceptions of the good at the level of justification. But if this is the source of the problem of sectarianism, then the democratic conception is not objectionably sectarian. It is organized around a view of public justification – that justification proceeds through free deliberation among equal citizens. It does not depend on the view that the best life is a life devoted to participation in public affairs. It is plausible that the stability of a deliberative democracy would depend on encouraging the ideal of active citizenship. But this dependence does not suffice to show that it is objectionably sectarian.

III. Democracy and Socialism

I now turn to the connections between deliberative democracy and socialism. I will begin by enumerating a few of the features of a feasible form of socialism. Then, concentrating on certain components of the description (the others serve as important background assumptions in the discussion), and drawing on the four lines of argument sketched in section I, I will indicate how these components would contribute to establishing a framework of free public deliberation among equals.[31] The aim is not to show that these features would be arrived at through such deliberation, but rather that they help to comprise a system of institutional conditions in which free deliberation among equals can proceed in the first place.

1. A socialist scheme suited to the deliberative conception requires a framework of legally codified rights to personal security, and to the liberties of thought, expression, association, and political participation. I indicated the

[30] Thus the account of participation in the *Social Contract* is presented as part of a discussion about "How Sovereign Authority Is Maintained" (Book III, chs. 12–14). It does not figure in the contractual argument that justifies the sovereignty of the general will (Book I, ch. 6). See Jean-Jacques Rousseau, *On The Social Contract*, ed. Roger D. Masters, trans. Judith R. Masters (New York: St. Martin's, 1978).

[31] In the discussion that follows I draw on Cohen and Rogers, *On Democracy*, ch. 6.

reasons for the liberties of thought and expression earlier; the same general rationale carries over to the other liberties. The legal codification of the liberties – their representation as rights – serves both for their protection and as a way of expressing a public commitment to maintaining a deliberative framework that depends on their security.[32]

2. A socialist realization of the ideal of deliberative democracy depends on the existence of competing political parties (including, I assume, non-socialist parties) that advance programs addressed to the common good. The existence of political parties, of course, does not ensure that the parties will play this role. They may instead serve to exaggerate conflict, encourage the "spirit of faction," or simply advance the careers of functionaries. But you can't beat something with nothing. And no plausible organizational alternative exists to parties as a way to organize large-scale political debate in ways that focus that debate on projects that advance the common good. Furthermore, to support the manifest equality of citizens required by the deliberative view (I3), access to and influence in deliberative arenas should be independent of material position. And this would be encouraged if the costs of party competition were publicly assumed.

3. A third condition is the public control of investment, realized through a scheme in which publicly owned means of production are operated by worker-managed firms (see condition 4 below). Countless details of a system of public control that are crucial in practice are pointless to specify here. The main idea is that in such a scheme, the share of national income to be devoted to investment and the desired pattern of that investment is fixed by public debate and decision. Those decisions are implemented by fixing the terms on which capital is rented to firms, but not by providing detailed directives about the conduct of those firms. Any institutions responsible for the conduct of these policies are of course subject to legislative oversight. In the multi-party environment characteristic of a deliberative democracy, parties would be expected to formulate programs about the direction and scope of investment. And the existence of programs of this sort would, in turn, encourage public deliberation about the terms of material development.

4. Socialist firms are to be worker-managed. In such firms, all and only the workers in the firm have voting rights concerning the operations of the firm – including what to produce, how much to produce, what the distribution of earnings among members should be, and whether to expand the scale of operations. In referring to these firms as "worker-managed," I am not

---

[32] Thus I find objections to "rights consciousness" implausible. Representing individuals as having rights provides public expression for the notion of the dignity of citizens, and thus provides a basis for social unity. The classical objection is stated in Karl Marx, "On the Jewish Question," ed. Robert Tucker, *Marx-Engels Reader*, 2nd edition (New York: Norton, 1978), pp. 26–52; and most clearly in Evgeny Pashukanis, *The General Theory of Law and Marxism*, in *Soviet Legal Philosophy*, trans. H.H. Babb (Cambridge: Harvard University Press, 1951).

assuming that there must be a regular sharing of the tasks of management by workers (any more than a democratically organized state requires a regular rotation of citizens through administrative positions). The conception does, however, require that workers in a firm have the right to fix the terms on which they are managed. But different firms could be expected to arrive at different views about the delegation of authority to managers, the extent of cooperation in work itself, and the distribution of enterprise earnings.[33] As a result, a wide variety of forms of association – small and large, centralized and decentralized, cooperative and atomistic – could be expected to appear and to flourish, corresponding to the plurality of associational ideals in a deliberative democracy.[34]

5. Finally, it seems clear enough that any version of socialism that is plausibly an expression of the deliberative ideal will make important use of markets and other non-command forms of transaction and collaboration among firms.[35] The reason for this is that we lack a plausible account of fully non-market coordination that does not threaten to undermine basic liberties by placing such coordination in the hands of a 'papacy of production' that will serve as a "despotic ruler of production and trustee of distribution."[36] In the absence of an institutionally rich and empirically defensible account of how to combine fully non-market forms of coordination with a democratic regime, across-the-board opposition to market forms seems unreasonable.

The Socialist Components

Having sketched certain features of a reasonable form of socialism, I now want to indicate how the deliberative conception in conjunction with the four lines of argument from section I provides a framework of argument for them. I focus on conditions 3 and 4, the public control of investment and worker self-management.

1. Consider first the public control of investment. The rationale for this in the deliberative conception is provided, in the first place, by the structural constraints argument. By effectively removing a central feature of social cooperation from democratic review, the private control of investment limits the scope of public deliberation. The aim of the public control of investment

---

[33] Here I follow Louis Putterman, "On Some Recent Explanations of Why Capital Hires Labor," *Economic Inquiry*, vol. 22 (1984), pp. 171–72.

[34] On the importance of this point, see my "Contractualism and Property Systems: Response to John Gray," *Nomos*, forthcoming.

[35] By "other non-command forms" I mean to include long-term contracts, joint ventures, and quasi-integration. For discussion of different forms, see Alexis Jacquemin, *The New Industrial Organization: Market Forces and Strategic Behavior*, trans. Fatemeh Mehta (Cambridge: MIT Press, 1987), ch. 5. For an interesting account of current shifts in forms of collaboration, see Charles Sabel, "The Reemergence of Regional Production: Changes in the Scale of Production," forthcoming in SSRC Western European Committee volume, *Experimenting With Scale*.

[36] The phrases come from Karl Marx, *Grundrisse*, trans. Martin Nicolaus (New York: Random House, 1973), p. 156, and are directed against the followers of Saint-Simon.

is to lift this limit on deliberation, and to contribute to its regulative role, by making the conditions of economic life part of the subject matter of political debate. The requirement of manifestness (D3) provides additional support for this conclusion. On the deliberative view, it is important that the terms of association be regulated by deliberation aimed at the common good, and that that regulation be manifest. The initiation of a scheme of public control of investment is meant to make the connection between public debate about the economy and the development of the economy more evident than it is under a system of private control subject to administrative regulation.

Support for public control is provided as well by the psychological claims of the deliberative view, in particular the role of public reasoning in the formation of motivations. The removal of important areas of social order from public debate weakens the regulative role of deliberation in setting the terms of association, and this in turn can be expected to weaken the influence of deliberation on the formation of motivations. It thus encourages the pursuit of pre-deliberative interests in public arenas, and undermines the formation of a sense of the common good.

Several considerations drawn from the notion of deliberative democracy thus support the public control of investment. But there are at least three important objections to it. The first objection is that "public" control of investment in fact amounts to the control of investment by a bureaucracy that represents itself as an agent for the public. Two considerations provoke this skepticism. First, the notion of "public" control assumes that there are coherent collective judgments for bureaus to implement. But far from being coherent, collective judgments are globally unstable.[37] Second, even if collective judgments were coherent, bureaus could not be expected to implement them. Instead, they would advance their own budget-maximizing programs. Under the guise of public control, we would have the rule of the "papacy of production."

Both of these problems are of considerable importance, and full answers are beyond the scope of this paper. Stated in these general terms, however, neither provides a compelling objection.

Let's begin with the problem about the "public" that is supposed to be controlling investment. On the deliberative view, public judgments are judgments that arise through deliberation, within institutions that establish the framework for deliberation. They are not based on an institution-free aggregation of predeliberative preferences. But theorems concerning the

---

[37] For discussion of instability theorems and their relevance for democratic theory, see William Riker, *Liberalism Against Populism: A Confrontation Between the Theory of Democracy and the Theory of Social Choice* (San Francisco: W.H. Freeman, 1982), chs. 5–7; Jules Coleman and John Ferejohn, "Democracy and Social Choice," *Ethics*, 97 (October 1986), pp. 6–25; Joshua Cohen, "An Epistemic Conception of Democracy," *Ethics*, 97 (October 1986), pp. 26–38.

global instability of majority rule arise precisely in this latter context. Since there is no general instability theorem for the case that is relevant here, the first consideration provides premature condemnation of the notion of public control. Second, skepticism about the claims of bureaus to be acting as perfect agents for the public (or even for the legislature) is well-founded. On the other hand, there is no general argument that is robust across different institutional settings (much less different motivational assumptions) for the conclusion that bureaus must dominate policy and produce an inefficient oversupply of the goods whose provision they supervise.[38] Ensuring that they do not dominate policy provides a difficult problem in institutional design. But, once again, the existence of the problem should not serve as grounds for premature condemnation.

The second main objection is that the conjunction of the deliberative conception and the structural constraints argument does not establish even a *prima facie* case for direct public control of investment. For consider the deliberative argument for the liberties of thought and expression. According to that argument, the scope of public deliberation must be constrained by various constitutional devices in order to ensure the preservation of the deliberative framework itself. So the fact that the private control of investment also imposes constraints on deliberation – assuming that it is a fact – does not by itself provide any reason for opposing it.

This argument is mistaken, and rests on a misstatement of the case for those liberties. As I indicated earlier, the liberties do not impose *constraints* on public deliberation; they help to establish the framework of conditions under which it can proceed at all. So the *prima facie* case stands, unless it could be shown that the liberty to own the means of production is similarly a precondition of deliberation. But as I indicated earlier (p. 38), this seems unwarranted.

The third objection is that public deliberation about the economy can proceed perfectly well, and, in fact, proceeds best without public ownership and control of investment.[39] The policy instruments available to a democratic state permit, as Keynes put it, a "somewhat comprehensive

---

[38] On the model of bureau-dominance, see William Niskanen, *Bureaucracy and Representative Government* (Chicago: Aldine, 1971). For criticism focusing on the special assumptions that fuel Niskanen's view, see Gary Miller and Terry Moe, "Bureaucrats, Legislators, and the Size of Government," *American Political Science Review*, vol. 77 (1983), pp. 297–323; Terry Moe, "The New Economics of Organization," *American Journal of Political Science*, vol. 28 (1984), pp. 765–72; John A.C. Conybeare, "Bureaucracy, Monopoly, and Competition: A Critical Analysis of the Budget-Maximizing Model of Bureaucracy," *American Journal of Political Science*, vol. 28 (August 1984), pp. 479–502.

[39] An especially clear statement of this view can be found in John Maynard Keynes, *General Theory of Employment, Interest, and Money* (New York: Harcourt, Brace, and World, 1964), ch. 24 ("Concluding Remarks on the Social Philosophy to Which This Theory Might Lead"). The remarks in the rest of the paragraph summarize Keynes's discussion.

socialisation of investment,"[40] while retaining a framework of private ownership of capital and decentralized economic coordination. Further, reasons of individual liberty dictate that we choose these alternative instruments for the socialization of investment. Politicizing and centralizing the decisions about the pace and direction of investment would lead to a centralization of political power, and this in turn would threaten the liberties required for the deliberative order. Since an alternative scheme for the socialization of investment is available, the argument from democracy provides no reason for preferring socialism to capitalism.

This objection can be interpreted in two ways. On the first, the thesis is simply that the structural constraints argument is wrong. A system of private investment decisions is consistent with public control because a democratic state can establish a system of incentives which will lead individual decision-makers to conform to the "general will," whatever the content of that will. Consistent with the narrow confines that limit this paper, I will simply assume (what I take to be true) that the structural constraints argument is right, and so put the first interpretation to the side.

The second interpretation concedes that the private control of investment imposes structural constraints on public deliberation, and allows that those constraints establish a *prima facie* case for public control. But it concludes that the *prima facie* case is overridden by other considerations. Structural constraints are, in fact, legitimate and reasonable because their absence would produce even more severe constraints on public deliberation. Just as it is commonly thought to be legitimate and reasonable to limit particular liberties in order to strengthen an overall system of liberties, it is also legitimate and perhaps reasonable to constrain political deliberation along certain dimensions in order to strengthen the system of public deliberation. Leaving investment decisions in private hands is, on this view, analogous to familiar forms of constitutional self-restraint; citizens themselves might deliberately choose to restrain the exercise of their authority out of a concern that lack of restraint would undermine the framework of public deliberation.

To underscore the force of the point, recall that according to the structural constraints argument itself, it is rational for citizens in a capitalist democracy to consent to the appropriation of profits by capitalists, since their own long-term material well-being depends on investment by capitalists and investment depends on profits. But if it is rational for workers to consent to profit-taking *given* private control of investment, then why couldn't it be rational for everyone to consent to private control of investment in the first place, in view of threats to deliberative order that might issue from the

[40] *ibid.*, p. 378.

politicization and centralization of the economy promised by public control of investment?[41]

I can see no *a priori* problem with this argument. It is certainly true that some issues that could legitimately be placed on the political agenda are best removed from it.[42] Nevertheless, there are at least three reasons for remaining unpersuaded in the case at issue. First, it is difficult to see the rationale for drawing the lines around the control of investment. Decisions about war and peace, for example, are literally matters of life and death, and commonly the focus of contentious and passionate political conflict. But the contention that surrounds them does not support the conclusion that decisions about war and peace, or about matters that bear directly on them, ought to be left in private hands in order to avoid upsetting the public order. As a general matter, it seems unreasonable in a democratic society to remove issues that bear on common interests from the political agenda, since doing so threatens to deprive democratic politics of its substance and interest. At the same time, leaving issues on the official agenda, but subjecting them to the real control of non-deliberative mechanisms, can foster cynicism and apathy.

Perhaps the reason for drawing the line around the control of investment is drawn from the experience of single-party states with command economies. This experience encourages the view that the public control of investment threatens the civil and political liberties that comprise part of the deliberative framework. But (and this leads to my second response) certain elements in the scheme I discussed earlier aim to avoid the forms of concentration of power that motivate this objection. The socialist scheme that conforms to the deliberative ideal requires a multi-party system, and rejects command planning and the central direction of labor as inconsistent with the framework of liberties that helps to define a deliberative democratic order. Furthermore, the arrangement that I sketched earlier combines public control of investment with a regime of self-managed firms. It is reasonable to expect that self-management would enhance the political capacity of workers, thus enabling them to better resist the pressures of consolidated authority.

Third, within a scheme of public control of investment, various additional institutional devices can be introduced to address concerns about the concentration of power that would issue from such control. Take, for example, a proposal recently advanced by Roberto Unger. He suggests a three-tiered economic order: the first tier would be a social investment fund

[41] For a discussion of broadly parallel political arguments for capitalism in its early development, see Albert O. Hirschman, *The Passions and the Interests: Political Arguments for Capitalism Before its Triumph* (Princeton: Princeton University Press, 1977), esp. Part 2.

[42] See Stephen Holmes, "Gag Rules, Or the Politics of Omission," unpublished, for an interesting account of reasons for putting issues off the agenda, and the many devices that serve that end.

that is controlled by democratically elected executive and representative bodies, that fixes the institutional and economic framework within which the rest of the order operates, and that lends capital to funds at the second tier. That tier, in turn, would be a system of subordinate investment funds controlled by semi-independent bodies that borrow from the central fund and lend to enterprises within the limits set by the central fund. The third tier would be composed of firms that borrow capital from the subordinate investment funds and that transact with one another within the rules fixed by the funds. A central aim of the system is to avoid direct links between the central fund and firms themselves. In the absence of such links, the central fund could not issue detailed directives to firms, thus institutionally limiting its capacity for political and economic domination.[43] So while the institutional dispersion of power is important, a wide range of devices might contribute to it consistent with a system of public control of investment that provides the framework for free public deliberation about the conditions of material prosperity.

2. Let us now turn to the issue of worker self-management. The conception of deliberative democracy provides a way of unifying several considerations in support of it. The deliberative conception carries with it a commitment to autonomy, and thus a commitment to ensuring favorable conditions for the exercise of the deliberative capacities. Workplace democracy provides these conditions because democratic ordering within firms provides scope for the exercise of those capacities. The parallel case argument strengthens this conclusion. Since enterprises comprise forms of cooperation for common benefit, and workers have the capacity to assess the rules that regulate workplace cooperation, they have a right to determine those rules through their own deliberation. The deliberative ideal of justification carries over from the state to firms.

The argument from psychological support strengthens the case for workplace democracy. The workplace provides a context in which deliberative capacities can be developed and exercised, thus facilitating their exercise in the political arena. Exercise of these capacities in an arena that bears directly on everyday life plausibly contributes to an active character. By regularly encouraging members to widen the range of interests that they consider, this kind of exercise can be expected to aid the development of a sense of the common good. Since the conception of deliberative democracy depends on that sense, worker self-management contributes to deliberative democracy.

Finally, the resource constraint argument provides additional support for this arrangement. The deliberative conception requires (I3) that citizens have equal standing in deliberative arenas, and that material inequalities

[43] Unger, *Politics*, vol. 2, pp. 491–500, 505–6.

should not fix their access to or influence in deliberative arenas. But as the resource constraint argument emphasizes, material inequalities threaten to undermine that equality. A regime of workplace democracy, in which remuneration is determined by worker decisions, could reasonably be expected to generate less inequality in the normal course of its operations than the inequality that is characteristic of capitalism.[44] And, by so doing, it would support the equality required by the deliberative view.

The deliberative view thus brings together several considerations that support self-management. I want now to address three problems about self-management that come into prominence when it is presented in this framework. The first assumes the plausibility of the psychological support argument – that is, that firm democracy would broaden interests and enhance the sense of efficacy – but questions whether the consequences would, in fact, be consistent with the aims of a deliberative democracy. The problem is that the scheme of self-managed firms might produce narrow group or corporate identities rooted in particular enterprises, rather than encouraging a sense of the common good that extends beyond those firms. While broadening the scope of interests to encompass others in the same enterprise, and enhancing the sense of political efficacy, a system of self-managed enterprises might encourage a system of political bargaining in which well-positioned firms and industries act to solidify their privileged position.

This objection has greater force against classical schemes of council democracy than it does against the view advanced here. Since political representation in the deliberative view is not organized around a scheme of worker councils, it is not to be expected that an 'identity' formed at work would provide the sole or primary basis for the formation and articulation of political interests. Debate within and between political parties, for example, could serve to articulate more comprehensive programs of economic and political action, and thus to widen the motivations of citizens beyond those that they develop as workers.

A second objection is that the virtuous psychological effects of self-management require smaller-scale enterprises. But restrictions on size would prevent firms from taking advantage of scale economies. The objection is not that self-management is impossible for firms above a certain size, but that in the absence of limits on scale, it would not have the psychological effects discussed earlier. Since limits on size may undermine scale economies, a

[44] For some evidence, see Frank Stephen, ed., *The Performance of Labor-Managed Firms* (New York: St. Martins, 1982), esp. chapters by Oakeshott, Estrin; Christopher Eaton Gunn, *Worker's Self-Management in the United States* (Ithaca: Cornell University Press, 1984), pp. 87, 119, 167, 180; Dahl, *Preface to Economic Democracy*, pp. 105–7.

system of self-management might well impose considerable material sacrifices.

In responding to objections along these lines, it is sometimes argued that self-managed firms have considerable efficiency advantages, and that these advantages might compensate for restrictions on scale. I will put these alleged advantages to the side in part because the evidence for them is very spotty, and in part because problems of sample bias in studies of self-managed firms are nearly overwhelming.[45] But even abstracting from the alleged advantages, it is still not clear how serious the size difficulties are. Consider the actual size distribution of firms. For example, taking Japan, Sweden, Austria, Belgium, France, and Italy together, the average firm in manufacturing employs 80 workers. And nearly 70 percent of manufacturing workers work in firms with fewer than 500 workers.[46] While precise judgment is impossible, it seems reasonable to conclude that most manufacturing workers now work in firms that are not large enough to undermine the force of the psychological support argument.

In addition, organizational experimentation might enable larger-scale enterprises to achieve the psychological effects of democracy without sacrificing the benefits of scale. For example, in multi-divisional firms, self-management can proceed in the first instance at the level of the division.[47] So while any actual system would need to work out complex organizational problems, and working out those problems would require a highly detailed understanding of organizational and technological issues that I lack, the size issue does not itself appear to present insuperable difficulties.[48]

The final difficulty is that a system in which all firms are self-managed might be thought to impose objectionable constraints on the liberty of those citizens who wish simply to work for a wage.[49] This objection strikes me as having little force, since I do not see what fundamental interest is protected by the liberty to sell labor for a wage. Constraints against wage-labor, or its confinement to special circumstances, seem in principle no more

[45] See Bowles and Gintis, *Democracy and Capitalism*, pp. 75–79, for a discussion of the alleged advantages.

[46] See Janos Kornai, "The Hungarian Reform Process: Visions, Hopes, and Reality," *Journal of Economic Literature*, vol. 24 (December 1986), p. 1699 (Table 3). Kornai emphasizes that firm size in Hungary is considerably larger. But since Hungarian socialism is not the socialism advocated here, I do not draw what may seem to be the obvious conclusion.

[47] For a discussion of the ways that divisionalization aids transactional efficiency and self-management, see Stephen R. Sacks, *Self-Management and Efficiency: Large Corporations in Yugoslavia* (London: George Allen and Unwin, 1983).

[48] For a recent analysis of trends in the scale and organization of production that reinforces both points in the paragraph, see Charles Sabel, "The Reemergence of Regional Production."

[49] See John Gray, "Contractarian Method, Private Property, and the Market Economy," *Nomos*, forthcoming; and my "Contractualism and Property Systems."

objectionable than constitutional prohibitions of slavery or the requirement in the U.S. Constitution that there be republican forms of government in the states. Those who embrace the social ideal of slavery and the political ideal of monarchy are confined by these prosciptions. Furthermore, it would be a mistake to suppose that the system of worker self-mangement denies the value of choice. It rejects the allocation of labor through command and it permits a wide range of forms of enterprise and associational ideals to flourish. So the "objectionable constraint" objection is not telling.

CONCLUSION

At the beginning of this paper, I said that I would discuss the ways that the deliberative conception of democracy provides the core of a philosophical conception of socialism. But it might be argued that I have not been discussing socialism at all, because I have not adequately captured the central socialist notion – the collective ownership of the means of production. Genuine collective ownership, it might be argued, requires that some organized collectivity have the same bundle of legal powers with respect to the means of production that (idealized) capitalists do. But on the view advanced here, no single institution or collectivity has precisely those powers. The ownership atom is split,[50] with decisions about the use of resources and decisions about the control of investment falling into separate hands. The dispersion of the components of the ownership bundle, together with the attention given to the problems of concentrated power, run counter to a classical understanding of the collective ownership of the means of production.

It is certainly true that normative accounts of socialism commonly focus on the question: *Who* should have the bundle of rights that comprises the ownership of capital? But this question should be criticized, not answered. Arguments in social philosophy should not premise a highly unified conception of property and confine our attention to different ways of shifting the bundle around.[51] A more suitable procedure is to "unbundle" ownership, and then to consider the different ways of distributing the rights that comprise it.[52] Pursuing this strategy, I have suggested that a central normative ideal in the socialist tradition is the ideal of a democratic association, and that the concentration of the powers of ownership in a single

[50] The phrase was suggested to me by Joel Rogers.
[51] See Unger, *Politics*, vol. 2 for extended discussion of this Legal Realist thesis; also Thomas C. Grey, "The Disintegration of Property," eds. J. Roland Pennock and John W. Chapman, *Property: Nomos 22* (New York: New York University Press, 1980), pp. 69–85.
[52] It is consistent with this second procedure to arrive at the normative conclusion that the property bundle ought to be retied. The objection here is only to letting the unified conception serve as a premise in political argument.

institution does not accommodate that ideal. Its realization requires departures from classical understandings of collective ownership, and particular attention to the institutional dispersion of powers. But those departures preserve enough of the ideals and institutions associated with the socialist tradition that there is no reason to reject the term "socialism" in describing the institutions that embody the democratic ideal.

Philosophy and Political Science, Massachusetts Institute of Technology

IN WHAT SENSE MUST SOCIALISM BE COMMUNITARIAN?*

By David Miller

Introduction

This paper stands at the confluence of two streams in contemporary political thought. One stream is composed of those critics of liberal political philosophy who are often described collectively as 'communitarians'.[1] What unites these critics (we shall later want to investigate how deep their collegiality goes) is a belief that contemporary liberalism rests on an impoverished and inadequate view of the human subject. Liberal political thought – as manifested, for instance, in the writings of John Rawls, Robert Nozick, and Ronald Dworkin – claims centrally to do justice to individuality: to specify the conditions under which distinct individuals, each with his own view about how life should be lived, can pursue these visions to the best of their ability. But, the critics claim, liberalism is blind to the social origins of individuality itself. A person comes by his identity through participating in social practices and through his affiliation to collectivities like family and nation. An adequate political philosophy must attend to the conditions under which people can develop the capacity for autonomy that liberals value. This, however, means abandoning familiar preoccupations of liberal thought – especially the centrality it gives to individual rights – and looking instead at how social relationships of the desired kind can be created and preserved. It means, in short, looking at communities – their nature and preconditions.[2]

The other stream comprises various attempts to recast the principles of socialism with the aim, broadly speaking, of bringing it more closely into line

---

* I should like to thank the participants in the conference on "Capitalism and Socialism" organized by the Social Philosophy and Policy Center for helpful discussion of an earlier draft of this paper, and Jerry Cohen, Andrew Williams, and Lesley Jacobs for sending valuable written comments.

[1] See, for instance, Amy Gutmann, "Communitarian Critics of Liberalism," *Philosophy and Public Affairs*, vol. 14 (1985), pp. 308–22.

[2] This sketch of communitarianism is deliberately ambiguous in one aspect. We may read the communitarian critics as basing their argument on a core liberal ideal – personal autonomy – but as proposing a more adequate account than mainstream liberalism of the conditions under which autonomy can be realized. Alternatively, we can read them as departing in a more fundamental way from liberal assumptions, substituting a different conception of the self, a different conception of freedom, and so forth. This ambiguity runs deep in communitarian writing (I return to the point later, particularly in relation to Charles Taylor): does communitarianism come to fulfill liberalism or to destroy it?

with the aspirations of the majority of people (including the majority of workers) in the advanced societies. This means not only discarding outdated policy proposals, such as extensive schemes of nationalization, but at a more fundamental level looking critically at traditional socialist ideals (for instance, the belief that it is intrinsically better for people to enjoy goods and services in common than to enjoy them privately as individuals). We can identify the central ideal of the new socialism as equality of effective choice: people should have the rights, opportunities and resources that enable them to choose effectively how they are to live their lives. Socialism is not the enemy of freedom, but its best friend; whereas libertarians and liberals claim that their proposals provide people with the greatest equal liberty, only socialist policies can make that liberty effective.[3]

How are these two streams of thought related? In one, we find people attacking liberalism in the name of community: in the other, we find socialists trying to divest themselves of traditional commitments, including communitarian commitments, and to outflank liberals in their devotion to individual freedom. Should the communitarian critique give the new socialists any pause for thought? Are the ideas it advances in any way integral to socialism itself? Or should it be regarded as an essentially conservative response to liberal institutions with which a modernizing socialist should have nothing to do? To answer these questions, we need to look more closely and critically at the often obscure views of the 'communitarians'. First, though, I shall offer a schematic interpretation of the socialist tradition which is intended to bring the questions above into sharper focus.

I. TWO STRANDS IN THE SOCIALIST CRITIQUE OF CAPITALISM

It hardly needs saying that 'socialism', like other terms designating ideologies, resists straightforward definition. It is impossible to provide a set of necessary and sufficient conditions for a political outlook to be socialist. Wittgenstein's strictures about family-resemblance terms like 'game' apply with their full force here. We can, however, say uncontroversially that socialism arose as a radical reaction to nineteenth-century capitalism, and it is certainly a necessary condition for an outlook to be socialist that it advocate a major transformation of that order. For the purposes of the present discussion I want to isolate and contrast two strands in the socialist critique of capitalism, which I think on any reckoning would count as fairly central — though this is not to say that every socialist has embraced them both.[4]

---

[3] For statements of this view by two prominent members of the British Labour Party see Bryan Gould, *Socialism and Freedom* (London: Macmillan, 1985); Roy Hattersley, *Choose Freedom: The Future for Democratic Socialism* (London: Michael Joseph, 1987).

[4] Nor do I want to say that the socialist critique is exhausted by the two elements I identify. It has other strands too: for instance one charge often made by socialists is that capitalism is a highly

The first element in the socialist critique focuses on the distributive inadequacies of capitalism. Capitalism, it is alleged, distributes resources, freedom and power in a way that is grossly unfair and/or prevents a large section of the population from receiving decent quantities of these benefits. Socialist institutions would allocate such benefits in a far more egalitarian fashion, in order to conform with socialist criteria of justice (which, in the extreme view, would prescribe perfect equality – in less extreme views, those criteria would find a place for limited inequalities based on desert or merit). The most obvious target of this critique is the distribution of wealth and income in capitalist society. As I interpret it here, however, the critique also extends to issues such as the distribution of labor-time (workers sweat while capitalists stand idle), the distribution of power in economic enterprises (capitalists command while workers obey), and the distribution of power in society more generally (capitalists control the state, benefit from the legal system, etc.). If we construe 'resources' *very* broadly to include benefits such as these, we can summarize the socialist charge as one of maldistribution of resources: the indictment of capitalism is not that it generates the wrong resources, but that it allocates them in a way that is unfair and inhumane.[5]

The second element in the socialist critique, in contrast, focuses on the quality of life in capitalist society, including the quality of the resources it generates. Included here, we find a number of different charges: for instance, capitalism involves production for profit rather than production for use, and therefore fails to provide people with the goods and services that they really need; it stifles creativity and robs work of its aesthetic content; it promotes the consumption of privately-purchased commodities, rather than enjoyment of goods and services in common; it fosters competitive relationships between people rather than relations of cooperation and fraternity; it renders

---

inefficient system, making poor use of the welfare-generating resources available to it. There is a good discussion of efficiency arguments in Allen Buchanan, *Ethics, Efficiency and the Market* (Oxford: Clarendon Press, 1985), ch. 2.

[5] Marxists often claim that their critique of capitalism does not involve a charge of maldistribution. Their meaning, I think, is that they are not centrally concerned with the allocation of income; in particular, they want to dismiss the suggestion that capitalism can be made acceptably fair by income redistribution schemes. What this suggests is *either* that they see a fairly rigid connection between distribution in the narrow sense (income distribution) and the structural inequalities of capitalism (e.g., the power structure of enterprises) *or* that they see distribution in the former sense as a comparatively trivial matter. In my wider sense, however, the Marxist critique, in this aspect, would properly count as a distributive critique.

Marx himself recognized that his critique of capitalism could be expressed in distributive terms. For the evidence, see G.A. Cohen, "Freedom, Justice and Capitalism," *New Left Review*, vol. 126 (March–April 1981), pp. 13–14 n. 7.

people's interactions instrumental and formal, rather than encouraging the spontaneous meeting of human hearts (and so forth). These claims, made singly or in combination, add up to the thesis that capitalism does not and cannot provide the good life for man, and that what must be brought about is not a mere reshuffling of resources, however radical, but a qualitative change in human relationships and motivations.

These two components of the socialist critique are not, of course, mutually exclusive, and can indeed be employed in tandem to good effect. In Marx, for instance, the first element is represented by the idea of exploitation – the claim that, under capitalism, the surplus value created by the labor of workers is systematically expropriated by capitalists – and the second is represented by the idea of alienation – the claim that work under the conditions of capitalism fails to realize man's "species-being" (i.e., his nature as a creative and communally-oriented being). Nevertheless, it is in most cases possible to disentangle the two elements, and doing so may throw some light on the revisionary socialist project mentioned at the beginning of the paper. For that project can be interpreted as one of pursuing the distributive critique to the exclusion of what I have identified as the "quality of life" critique. Socialism, on this view, is entirely a matter of the fair distribution of resources, taking "resources" in the broad sense as above. It is not concerned with what people may do with the resources they are allocated, with what motivates them, or how they are related to one another – except insofar as these matters have repercussions for the allocation of resources itself.

It is not difficult to understand the pressures that push contemporary socialists in this direction. First of all, the distributive critique can be reconciled with major features of modern industrial societies far more readily than the "quality of life" critique. Consider two of these features: the market economy and the legal system. There is *prima facie* no incompatibility between the distributive critique and economic markets as such; that is, it seems a feasible project to reallocate resources in such a way that markets produce outcomes that are acceptable on grounds of distributive justice. How this could be done would depend on the criterion of distributive justice employed, but I am thinking generally of schemes such as equalization of capital holdings, the conversion of enterprises into worker cooperatives leasing capital, progressive income taxes, and so forth. To oppose this, one would have to hold that there was an inexorable connection between markets and capitalism such that, if markets are allowed to flourish, standard capitalist patterns of ownership must inevitably re-emerge; or, on the other hand, if these arrangements are outlawed, markets will be unable to work effectively. (Although this view is sometimes expressed – both by Marxists and by libertarians – the argument for it remains obscure to me.)

By contrast, most versions of the "quality of life" critique – including the

Marxian theory of alienation[6] – entail the condemnation of market relationships as a distortion of genuine human relationships. No matter how radically resources are redistributed, activity in the market must be governed by norms of instrumental rationality, people must behave non-tuistically (that is, each must aim to maximize his holdings, regardless of the welfare of his partners in exchange), and so forth. The "quality of life" critique seems therefore inevitably to point beyond markets towards some other method of coordinating economic behavior. By the same token, however, it lays itself immediately open to a charge of utopianism. If we want a feasible form of socialism, it seems that we have to accept a major role for markets, and to that extent we must abandon the "quality of life" critique.[7]

A similar point can be made with respect to the legal system. A modern legal system can be regarded as a system of uniform general rules enforced by formal procedures, which confer rights on individuals. The distributive critique includes nothing at odds with this idea of legality itself. Socialists characteristically allege that, in capitalist societies, a particular set of rights favorable to capitalist interests is embodied in the law, and moreover that enforcement procedures favor those already well-endowed with resources. A socialist system would rectify these defects by, for instance, recognizing enforceable rights to welfare and allocating resources in such a way that access to the legal system was effectively equalized. In contrast, the "quality of life" critique contains elements hostile to the very idea of legality: rights are dismissed as "the prized possessions of alienated persons,"[8] and the formality of the law is contrasted with arrangements whereby people could deal with one another as complete human beings, each responding to the full particularity of the other. The problem, once again, is to see how an alternative to the legal system can be made to seem feasible in a modern industrial society.[9]

Considerations of realism, then, are one major pressure inducing contemporary socialists to abandon the "quality of life" critique in favor of the distributive critique of capitalism. A second pressure is loss of faith in the assumptions needed to back up the former critique. The "quality of life" critique requires us to judge some modes of human life as better than others,

---

[6] I have examined this theory critically in "Marx, Communism and Markets," *Political Theory*, vol. 15 (1987), pp. 182–204.

[7] Evidence for believing that a feasible form of socialism must allow a major role to markets is usefully presented in Alec Nove, *The Economics of Feasible Socialism* (London: Allen and Unwin, 1983).

[8] Ruth Anna Putman, "Rights of Persons and the Liberal Tradition," ed. Ted Honderich, *Social Ends and Political Means* (London: Routledge and Kegan Paul, 1976), p. 102.

[9] I have argued this point briefly in *Anarchism* (London: Dent, 1984), ch. 12. For a fuller defense of the idea of legality against left-wing criticism, see Tom D. Campbell, *The Left and Rights* (London: Routledge and Kegan Paul, 1983), esp. ch. 3.

regardless of the preferences that people actually display. If we are going to condemn competition, say, or the kinds of goods produced for consumption in market economies, we must be able to deploy some theory of human good which allows us to make the necessary discrimination. But the contemporary intellectual climate is very hostile to any such theory. The high-minded assumptions about the nature of the good life that socialists made a century ago – as indeed did many liberals, most notoriously John Stuart Mill – now strike us as elitist and somewhat pious. We are far more self-critical in the matter of elevating our own preferred mode of life to the status of universal truth. And while most socialist intellectuals privately persist in their taste for improving literature, healthy hikes in the country, and political discussion as forms of recreation, they are far less keen to have those predilections held up as the image of socialism itself. The current preference is, if anything, for 'designer socialism,' that is a view of socialism that warmly allies itself to current fashions in clothes, music and life-style generally. It is clearly impossible to celebrate modes of consumption thrown up by present-day capitalism while at the same time holding on to a view of socialism that embodies a strong "quality of life" critique of that very system.

These are two of the pressures, therefore, that incline contemporary socialists to put forward a slimmed-down version of socialism, defined more or less entirely in distributive terms. Socialism, then, is exclusively a matter of allocating resources (broadly conceived) in the appropriate manner. As examples of this tendency in political philosophy, I would cite the following: Hillel Steiner's proposals for a laissez-faire economy grounded in equal entitlements to natural resources;[10] Ronald Dworkin's conception of equality of resources, including an insurance scheme to compensate for inequalities in personal endowments;[11] John Roemer's argument for equality of productive assets as the best way of capturing the point of the Marxian theory of exploitation;[12] Robert Van der Veen and Philippe Van Parijs's advocacy of a "Capitalist road to Communism" whereby returns to labor and capital are taxed at progressively higher rates to provide each person with an unconditional grant to satisfy their needs.[13] Although these

[10] See Hillel Steiner, "The Natural Right to the Means of Production," *Philosophical Quarterly*, vol. 27 (1977), pp. 41–49; "Slavery, Socialism and Private Property," eds. J. Roland Pennock and John W. Chapman, *Nomos XXII: Property* (New York: New York University Press, 1970); "Liberty and Equality," *Political Studies*, vol. 29 (1981), pp. 555–69.

[11] Ronald Dworkin, "Equality of Resources," *Philosophy and Public Affairs*, vol. 10 (1981), pp. 283–345.

[12] John Roemer, "Equality of Talent," *Economics and Philosophy*, vol. 1 (1985), pp. 151–87; "Should Marxists Be Interested in Exploitation?", Working Paper No. 221, Department of Economics, University of California, Davis.

[13] Robert J. Van der Veen and Philippe Van Parijs, "A Capitalist Road to Communism," *Theory and Society*, vol. 15 (1986), pp. 635–55.

proposals differ in important respects, they share the aim of radically altering the distributive outcome of conventional capitalism, but without requiring any corresponding change in the quality of human relationships that prevail under that system.

I should make it clear that I am broadly in sympathy with this tendency towards a justice-based socialism; in particular, I have been arguing for some time that markets are both an economically essential and an ethically acceptable component in a viable form of socialism.[14] Nevertheless, I do not believe that socialists can discard everything in the "quality of life" critique of capitalism; they especially need to hold on to *some* form of community as an essential part of their vision. *Which* form of community is the major issue addressed in this paper. But first let me present the minimalist case for communitarianism of some kind as an ineliminable part of the socialist project.[15]

In presenting this case, I make two assumptions which I hope are not controversial. The first is that we want our version of socialism to be democratically suported: whatever view is taken about the transition to socialism, socialist institutions should command the willing assent of at least the majority of the population once those institutions are installed. The second is that the rules of the system (the rules governing economic transactions, etc.) should, for the most part, be complied with voluntarily: the level of coercive enforcement should be no higher than, say, that prevailing under present-day capitalism; and preferably it should be a good deal lower. Clearly, if such assumptions are to hold good, the socialist arrangements we

---

[14] See David Miller, "Socialism and the Market," *Political Theory*, vol. 5 (1977), pp. 473–90; "Jerusalem Not Yet Built: A Reply to Lessnoff on Capitalism, Socialism and Democracy," *Political Studies*, vol. 28 (1980), pp. 584–89; "Marx, Communism and Markets"; David Miller and Saul Estrin, "Market Socialism: A Policy For Socialists," ed. I. Forbes, *Market Socialism: Whose Choice?*, Fabian pamphlet No. 516 (reprinted as "A Case for Market Socialism," *Dissent*, Summer 1987, pp. 359–67). These ideas are developed more systematically in a forthcoming book, *Market, State and Community* (Oxford: Clarendon Press, 1989).

[15] I call this the minimalist case because it hinges the argument for community entirely on elements drawn from the distributive critique; it makes no appeal to the inherent value of community. Now an argument of this kind might appear inherently paradoxical, at least insofar as it is addressed to the public at large. For either the addressees already see themselves as belonging to a community, or they do not. If they do, then it is redundant to offer them a justifying argument that appeals to extrinsic distributive considerations; if they do not, then a sense of community cannot be conjured out of thin air because it would be helpful from a distributive point of view were it to exist. Thus the argument that follows might seem to have an unavoidably esoteric character.

We may, however, take the addressees of the argument to be people who both see themselves as members of a community and espouse principles of distributive justice, but who as yet see no necessary relationship between these commitments. Community membership is felt to be inherently valuable, but irrelevant from a distributive point of view. The purpose of my argument is to enhance the value of community by connecting the two commitments. This has a practical point insofar as we are now in a position to make political decisions that will influence the nature of our community in the future – strengthening or weakening people's allegiance in the long run.

have in mind must be legitimated, in the sense that most people must hold a conception of justice that corresponds to the one that these arrangements embody. For instance, insofar as the arrangements we envisage rest on a conception of equality, the people subject to them must be, or become, egalitarians.

Now, on one view of the matter, this question of legitimation poses no real problem. If we think that good, rational arguments can be given for the view of justice that we favor, then we may believe that most people – given sufficient time, perhaps – will come to share this view, and so the appropriate conception of justice can be developed apart from, and prior to, the arrangements of socialism itself. In particular, the view of justice people hold doesn't depend on the kind of relationships they have with those around them, so the order of decision goes as follows: first, a consensus emerges on justice itself; second, this consensus is embodied in institutions which allocate resources to people; third, people use the resources they have been allocated to pursue their personal goals, perhaps including the goal of developing relationships of particular kinds. This, very crudely, is how John Rawls sees the matter,[16] and his idea has been influential among many, including some socialists who interpret the *substance* of justice in a more egalitarian way than he does himself.

I hold this view to be badly in error. Against it, I want to argue that our ideas of distributive justice are powerfully affected by our perception of the relationships generally prevailing in the set of people within which the distribution is going to occur. Perhaps this is best illustrated by starting with an extreme case. Suppose we conceived of a 'society' made up of individuals who had no social relations with one another, each living an entirely independent and self-contained life – a set of Robinson Crusoes, each on his own island. What would justice mean to the inhabitants of such a 'society'? They would endorse something like Nozick's view that justice means non-interference with the rights that each has acquired by his own legitimate efforts (where "legitimate" is in turn spelled out in terms of non interference). Charles Taylor has put this point well:

> ... there is a mode of justice which holds between quite independent human beings, not bound together by any society or collaborative

---

[16] This is not the place to discuss the finer details of Rawls's theory. He expresses some concern about what he calls the "strains of commitment" – the possibility that people might no longer be able to accept the principles of justice they have endorsed in the abstract when faced with their concrete results – but he sees this as a problem about justice and material interests: can people who do badly out of the application of a theory of justice be expected to continue embracing it? (See John Rawls, *Theory of Justice* (Cambridge: Harvard University Press, 1971), esp. section 29.) He does not raise the question whether the practical acceptability of a theory of justice might not depend on the quality of social relationships *in general*.

arrangement. If two nomadic tribes meet in the desert, very old and long-standing intuitions about justice tell us that it is wrong (unjust) for one to steal the flocks of the other. The principle here is very simple: we have a right to what we have.[17]

Conversely, any view that is more redistributive than Nozick's – any view holding that people can make claims on one another that go beyond simple non-interference – must presuppose a background set of social relationships against which claims of this sort would appear legitimate.[18] This, indeed, is the nub of Michael Sandel's criticism of Rawls.[19] Rawls advances a distributive principle – the difference principle – which gives people a claim on what others have produced by exercising their talents and skills, but says nothing about the communitarian relationships which, in practice, would be needed to underpin this principle. What applies to Rawls applies *a fortiori* to principles of distributive justice that are more strictly egalitarian. These principles may deprive some asset-holders of large quantities of the holdings they would have enjoyed under the "Nozick Constitution" which we are using as a benchmark. We can only expect them to consent to institutions that enforce the preferred distribution if they regard themselves as bound to the beneficiaries by strong ties of community: the stronger the ties, the more egalitarian the distribution can be.[20]

It is not an adequate answer to this line of thought to say that a distributive practice can, of itself, create the necessary ties. No doubt there is a process of reinforcement such that implementing a practice of distributive justice appropriate to a particular community will tend to buttress the sense of community that already exists. But if, starting from the Crusoe 'society,' an external agency were to impose an egalitarian redistribution of assets but do

---

[17] Charles Taylor, "The Nature and Scope of Distributive Justice," *Philosophy and the Human Sciences: Philosophical Papers II* (Cambridge: Cambridge University Press, 1985), p. 289.

[18] Let me stress that I am concerned here about the conditions under which a socialist system of distribution could be legitimate, in the sense of being congruent with widely-held and spontaneously-formed notions of justice. I am not directly concerned with the transition to socialism, i.e., with the circumstances under which those who are the chief beneficiaries of capitalism would be willing to renounce the privileges they already enjoy. Although democratic socialists will want both the transition and the ensuing arrangements to have broad popular support, it would be unrealistic to set the standard of consent as high for the former as for the latter.

[19] See Michael Sandel, *Liberalism and the Limits of Justice* (Cambridge: Cambridge University Press, 1982), ch. 2.

[20] Obviously, this is not a claim about logic but a claim about social psychology. Although social psychologists cannot create genuine communities in the laboratory, their simulations provide some support for the claim. In particular, people give less weight to merit and more weight to equality in distribution when they expect to interact with their partners over a period of time. See E. Gary Shapiro, "Effect of Expectations of Future Interaction on Reward Allocation in Dyads: Equity and Equality," *Journal of Personality and Social Psychology*, vol. 31 (1975), pp. 873–80; Melvin J. Lerner, The Justice Motive: 'Equity' and 'Parity' among Children," *Journal of Personality and Social Psychology*, vol. 29 (1974), pp. 539–50.

nothing else to change relationships between the Crusoes, I can see no reason to expect that they will begin to think of themselves as forming a community or to regard the redistribution as legitimate. The kind of ties we are looking for are not external and mechanical, but involve each person seeing his life as part and parcel of the life of the wider group, so that the question of how well his own life is going depends in some measure on how the community as a whole is faring. This brings in issues of common good, historical identity, and so forth which reach far beyond the scope of distributive justice. Rawls's notion that adherence to a shared conception of distributive justice could itself form a sufficient basis for community is quite implausible.[21]

I have not yet said anything about the idea of community that socialist proposals require, or about whether such an idea is feasible given the circumstances of an advanced industrial society. My argument so far is simply that a form of socialism which defines itself primarily in terms of distributive justice must still consider questions about the *quality* of social relationships if it wants to be something more than a nice intellectual construct. If socialism is to be politically feasible – if socialist arrangements once installed are to command the willing consent of the population – social relations generally must support the preferred conception of distributive justice. Even those who regard community as having no independent political value must rely on it in practice to underpin their distributive concerns. So at this point I turn to see whether there is anything in the recent communitarian literature that might be helpful to the socialist case.

II. The Ambivalence of Contemporary Communitarianism

I shall focus on the work of Alasdair MacIntyre, Charles Taylor, and Michael Sandel. Each of these writers would endorse the general argument I have just advanced: namely, that ideas of justice cannot be separated from a broader understanding of the community within which distributive practices exist.[22] It does not follow, of course, that the conceptions of justice and community they advance are socialist conceptions: indeed, in at least two out of the three cases, the evidence is rather to the contrary.[23] So our approach to their work must be a critical one. We can try to get clearer about socialist ideas of community, in part by seeing where they need to diverge from the ideas of MacIntyre, Taylor, and Sandel.

[21] Rawls, *A Theory of Justice*, section 79.

[22] See Alasdair MacIntyre, *After Virtue* (London: Duckworth, 1981), ch. 17; Taylor, "The Nature and Scope of Distributive Justice"; Sandel, *Liberalism*, ch. 4.

[23] Only Taylor seems in any way sympathetic to socialist views, and even he is mainly concerned to present socialism as trapped in the same modernist predicament as other outlooks: see Charles Taylor, "Socialism and Weltanschauung," eds. Leszek Kolakowski and Stuart Hampshire, *The Socialist Idea* (London: Quartet, 1977).

MacIntyre's understanding of community initially derives from his narrative view of the self. A person can only make sense of his actions, he argues, by placing them within a narrative structure – a self-told story which runs through the person's life from birth to death. The narrative I construct for myself, however, intersects with other people's narratives – I am a character in their stories and they figure in mine. This set of narratives, in turn, makes references to the wider communities within which the individuals in question bear social identities – say, as the occupants of kinship roles or as members of institutions. In particular, MacIntyre argues, moral activity itself depends upon an understanding of moral value which can only be provided within a particular community.

MacIntyre's claim, to sum up, is that people can only make sense of their lives by seeing themselves as members of large communities, which above all provide the preconditions of narrative unity. As to the *scope* of community, MacIntyre remains agnostic: he talks of "the family, the neighborhood, the city, and the tribe," and so forth.[24] What he does make clear, in contrast, is that the modern state is not an appropriate location for community. It cannot embody community, since in MacIntyre's view that would require a moral consensus at the political level which simply does not and cannot exist. Moreover, the mode of operation of the modern state tends to destroy such communal ties as still exist: bureaucratic procedures create individuals who are abstracted from any social identity, and whose residual sense of self is that of a pure chooser of ends. In his remarks on the Jacobins, MacIntyre does not exclude the possibility of an understanding of moral virtue that would give political participation a central place, but he argues that such an understanding is impossible to sustain in modern conditions. "The true lesson of the Jacobin Clubs and their downfall is that you cannot hope to re-invent morality on the scale of a whole nation when the very idiom of the morality that you seek to re-invent is alien in one way to the vast mass of ordinary people and in another to the intellectual elite."[25] So although patriotism – a special regard to the interests of my national community – remains a virtue for MacIntyre, it is no longer an idea which should inform my relations to the government of the day.[26] I should assess the state purely in instrumental terms: in terms of how effectively it keeps the peace between different communities, protects rights, and so forth.

It would be wrong to describe this outlook as politically conservative since,

[24] MacIntyre, *After Virtue*, p. 205.
[25] *ibid.*, p. 221.
[26] See *ibid.*, pp. 236–37 and Alasdair MacIntyre, "Is Patriotism a Virtue?", Lindley Lecture, University of Kansas, 1984.

as MacIntyre notes, it involves a complete rejection of "modern systematic politics, whether liberal, conservative, radical or socialist";[27] it can fairly be described, however, as morally conservative, in the sense that it defines moral virtue in terms of the traditions of such *de facto* communities as are salient for each particular person. Although MacIntyre, in his remarks on tradition, argues that living traditions always involve critical argument about the best way of carrying the tradition on, there is no wider forum within which the merits of different traditions might be debated – and, of course, MacIntyre rejects the idea that there are transcendent standards of justice which might be used to adjudicate between them.[28] From a socialist perspective, therefore, MacIntyre's view of community must appear dangerously tradition-bound, not so much in the sense that it starts with *de facto* communities as in the sense that it has no resources for getting beyond the notions of virtue embodied in each community except insofar as the community itself engages in critical reflection. I shall later connect this deficiency to MacIntyre's other view that political arrangements are irrelevant (in modern conditions) to communal life.

If we turn now to Taylor, we find once again that claims about the nature of personhood are advanced to underpin a (fairly unspecific) commitment to community. There is, however, this contrast with MacIntyre: whereas MacIntyre bases his account of the self on a pre-modern understanding of morality, Taylor assumes from the outset "the modern identity" – that is, a view of human nature which breaks decisively with the idea that human fulfillment can be understood as alignment with some given, cosmic order (as in older Christian views). Taylor accepts the modern idea that human self-realization involves choice as well as discovery; what he rejects are individualist accounts of that process of self-realization.

As far as I can discern, there are two major strands to Taylor's argument; I am not clear as to how these strands are supposed to be related. The first strand starts from a familiar liberal ideal, the ideal of personal autonomy. Taylor's claim is that individualist liberals fail to understand the preconditions for autonomy. They see it as unproblematically given and needing only protection against external constraints, whereas in fact it requires a certain kind of cultural background. People can only make authentic choices about their own lives against the background of a civilization in which, for example, moral questions are debated in public, certain aesthetic experiences are available, and so forth. Community makes

---

[27] MacIntyre, *After Virtue*, p. 237.
[28] For further reflection on the difficulties this entails, see my "Virtues and Practices," *Analyse und Kritik*, vol. 6 (1984), pp. 49–60.

its appearance here in the guise of a common culture, participation in which is a necessary condition of liberal aspirations to autonomy.[29]

The other strand in Taylor's argument moves further away from liberal premises. Taylor points to the importance, in the modern consciousness, of an attitude which he calls 'expressivism.'[30] This is the ambition to see the world around us as an expression of our authentic nature, an idea that was particularly prominent in the thought of the German Romantics and their followers. Now this attitude can take either private or public form, depending on whether the 'nature' to be realized is the essence of a particular individual or a nature common to the members of some collectivity. Taylor, however, regards private versions of expressivism as somehow deficient: he points to the nuclear family as the current embodiment of the Romantic ideal of a life according to nature, but claims that the family lacks the moral resources to contain narrow self-absorption.

> ... if the business of life is finding my authentic fulfilment as an individual, and my associations should be relativized to this end, there seems no reason why this relativization should in principle stay at the boundary of the family. If my development, or even my discovery of myself, should be incompatible with a long-standing association, then this will come to be felt as a prison rather than as a locus of identity.[31]

Hence, expressivist aspirations can only be fulfilled if we can discover some common identity that might be expressed in a public world. Where might such an identity be found? Taylor finds the answer in *language*, an institution that is necessarily public, and at the same time embodies a distinctive way of experiencing the world. The community here becomes the speech community. In talking to one another, we convey a shared view of the world: and this view is constantly open to modification as we change our language in order to express ourselves more adequately. Taylor summarizes:

> ... the expressive conception gives a view of language as a range of activities in which we express/realize a certain way of being in the world. And this way of being has many facets. It is not just the reflective awareness by which we recognize things as – , and describe our surroundings: but also that by which we come to have the

---

[29] See Charles Taylor, "Atomism," *Philosophy and the Human Sciences: Philosophical Papers II* (Cambridge: Cambridge University Press, 1985).

[30] See Charles Taylor, *Hegel* (Cambridge: Cambridge University Press, 1975), esp. chs. 1 and 20; "Legitimation Crisis?", in *Philosophy and the Human Sciences: Philosophical Papers II* (Cambridge: Cambridge University Press, 1985).

[31] Taylor, "Legitimation Crisis?", p. 283.

properly human emotions, and constitute our human relations, including those of the language community within which language grows.[32]

So we find two "communitarian" trains of thought in Taylor, one beginning with the liberal ideal of autonomy and ending with a view of community as common culture, the other beginning with expressivism and ending with a view of community as language-sharing. Rather than investigate the relationship between these conceptions, I want to point to three traits which they have in common.

First, on either view, the *scope* of the relevant community is exceedingly difficult to determine. How does one attempt to fix the boundaries either of a cultural or a linguistic community? On Taylor's first argument, there seems no reason to restrict the scope of community at all, since, presumably, the greater the cultural variety to which I am exposed, the more chance I have to develop my capacity for autonomous choice. The second argument does seem to imply a more particularistic view of community, but then we run into the familiar difficulties of individuating languages (is American-English the same language as English-English?). Taylor's communitarianism is unavoidably amorphous, and this immediately limits its power as a weapon in political philosophy.

Second, Taylor's view has the consequence of restricting the extent to which our communal relations are open to rational reflection. The ties that hold us together must, to some degree, remain opaque to critical investigation. Taylor makes this explicit when he describes languages as

> A pattern of activity . . . which can only be deployed against a background which we can never fully dominate; and yet a background that we are never fully dominated by, because we are constantly reshaping it. Reshaping it without dominating it, or being able to oversee it, means that we never fully know what we are doing to it; we develop language without knowing fully what we are making it into.[33]

Now it may turn out that communal relationships are indeed unavoidably opaque in the way that this view of language suggests; this is a matter requiring further investigation. But, *prima facie*, it undermines the belief held by some socialists, most notably Marx, that what we should be aiming for is a society in which human beings consciously and collectively control their destiny, and their relationships become entirely transparent. Community, on

---

[32] Charles Taylor, "Language and Human Nature," in *Human Agency and Language: Philosophical Papers I* (Cambridge: Cambridge University Press, 1985), p. 234.
   [33] *ibid.*, p. 208.

Taylor's view, is something that we are immersed in, but whose nature cannot be grasped fully and consciously, let alone shaped completely according to our will.

Anxieties about the potentially conservative character of Taylor's conception may be heightened when we notice that community has, for him, no necessary political dimension. It is true that he attempts to build a political argument onto his claim about the role of common culture in providing the conditions for autonomy. The logic of this argument must be that cultural forms and institutions are public goods, and it is unlikely that self-interested individuals will provide them voluntarily. That this is an empirical claim is made clear by Taylor's reply to the anarchist who thinks that these goods will be created spontaneously. "There is nothing in principle which excludes anarchism in the reflection that we owe our identity as free men to our civilization."[34] Political institutions, then, appear simply as instruments for protecting the elements of community by, for instance, subsidizing the arts. They are not part of the framework of community itself.

MacIntyre sees politics as irrelevant to community; Taylor sees it playing only an instrumental role. Sandel is, in contrast, more firmly set in the republican tradition. When he speaks of community, he appears to envisage a set of people engaged in, among other things, political deliberation. Corresponding to this is a stronger claim about the importance of community to personal identity. MacIntyre and Taylor both argue, in their different ways, that people's identities can't be satisfactorily defined without communal relationships in the background. Sandel's claim is that identity must, in part, be *constituted* by communal attachments. When people discover who they are (discover, not choose), part of what they discover is that they are members of this or that collectivity – a membership which they cannot relinquish without becoming different people in one important sense.

What is the status of Sandel's claim here? He presents it not as a description of present-day reality but as a presupposition of liberal theories of justice, especially the Rawlsian theory. His core argument is that the difference principle, which treats people's talents and abilities as common assets, can only be acceptable if we adopt the constitutive conception of community outlined above. He is far less sanguine about the practical feasibility of such a conception. In his brief remarks on the evolution of American politics, he traces a process whereby, starting with local political communities (which, by implication, were genuine communities), politics was progressively "nationalized" in response to economic pressures; but the

---

[34] Taylor, "Atomism," p. 207. Taylor later adds to his argument the claim that political deliberation forms an essential part of freedom, but this has the appearance of an afterthought. See *ibid.*, p. 208.

attempt to foster a new sense of community at *this* level was unsuccessful. "Except for extraordinary moments, such as war, the nation proved too vast a scale across which to cultivate the shared self-understandings necessary to community in the formative, or constitutive sense."[35] Hence what we are left with is a liberal politics of rights that lacks a coherent communal underpinning.

What lies behind this conclusion? Sandel must be assuming that a sense of community strong enough to foster constitutive attachments can only exist where people have face-to-face relationships (as in the traditional town meeting) or perhaps have strong cultural affiliations. Clearly, a large modern nation cannot expect to meet either of these conditions. So the upshot of Sandel's argument must be uncongenial to the socialist. Although the link between community and politics is forged, community is seen as a phenomenon of localities, and this cannot satisfy the socialist, who needs it to underpin distributive justice across whole societies.[36] By strengthening the conditions for community, Sandel at the same time precludes it from playing the kind of political role that socialists want it to play.

None of the three 'communitarians' we have considered advances a conception of community that seems well suited to socialist purposes. What lessons might we draw from this fact? For all three authors, the very idea of community is problematic in the modern world. MacIntyre sees us as clinging to fragments of community inherited from the pre-Renaissance period. Taylor sees communitarians as fighting a rear-guard battle against what he calls "Enlightenment naturalism" – a view of man as an agent who regards the surrounding world merely as an instrument to the optimal fulfillment of his freely-chosen desires. Sandel, as we have just noted, is pessimistic about constitutive community in the face of the scale of modern politics. Now one lesson we might draw is to take these authors' findings as confirmation of a certain negative view of socialism, a view which sees the socialist project as anachronistic from the very moment of its conception. On this view, socialism became a popular ideology precisely in response to the breakup of traditional communities under the impact of the industrial revolution. It became popular because it promised to restore the coherent

---

[35] Michael Sandel, "The Procedural Republic and the Unencumbered Self," *Political Theory*, vol. 12 (1984), pp. 81–96.

[36] If communal relationships foster a sense of justice that is relatively egalitarian, why shouldn't a society made up of small local communities develop a society-wide scheme of redistribution? Unfortunately, there is no reason to expect the *scope* of a practice of distributive justice to extend beyond the community that supports it. There is ample historical evidence of small communities (tribes, guilds, cooperatives) practicing quite radical forms of egalitarian redistribution internally, but dealing with outsiders on very different terms. Socialists must look for community at the level at which effective policies can be made for whole societies, which, in practice, means at the level of the nation-state.

moral life found in the disappearing communities, while at the same time providing all the material (and other) benefits of industrialization. But these two promises could never be fulfilled together. In industrial societies the appeal to community is always nostalgic and backward-looking, whatever its proponents may think.

This is not the lesson I want to draw, though I feel the force of the argument in the last paragraph which, as noted, reflection on the ideas of MacIntyre, Taylor, and Sandel tends to support. We see, once again, the attractions of a purely distributive view of socialism, which aims to discard community as an essential element in the socialist framework. On this view, particular communities may flourish under a socialist distributive regime, but this is, so to speak, an optional extra, not something that the regime itself requires. I have explained already why this attractive view cannot, in the end, be maintained. Socialists must take up the quest for community, but they should do so in a chastened spirit, in full realization of the obstacles that lie in their path. In the final part of the paper, I sketch in a socialist view of community which I hope meets these strictures.

III. A SOCIALIST CONCEPTION OF COMMUNITY

A socialist who wants to avoid the charge that he is merely nostalgic for pre-industrial forms of life cannot appeal to thick-textured, face-to-face community as the building block of his system. Where such communities still exist – as, for instance, in certain mining villages or other places where a fixed pattern of working life has persisted over decades – there is no reason to disparage them; equally, it would be wrong to make them integral to the socialist project, or in particular to suppose that the whole of a society could come to take on the character of these local communities. The tendency of an industrial economy is always to erode community in this strong sense, and, whether or not one thinks that economic policies should be designed to protect particular communities against such erosion, there is nothing here firm enough to support a socialist project.

It would be equally wrong to conclude that socialist community must comprise nothing less than humankind in general. Some socialists do seem to take it as their aim to extend fraternal sentiments to embrace all other human beings, and in the course of so doing to sweep away all local and particular attachments as relics of an unsavoury past. This aim is often thought to embody a certain idea of rationality. There is no good reason to treat our neighbors or our compatriots any differently from equally needy people elsewhere in the world, so any sense that we owe them special loyalties must vanish under critical scrutiny.

This view neglects the fact, evident enough in the writings of the communitarians we have considered, that communities just are particularistic. In seeing myself as a member of a community, I see myself as participating in a particular way of life marked off from other communities by its distinctive characteristics. Notions such as 'loyalty' and 'allegiance' make no sense unless there is an identifiable something towards which these attitudes are directed. Moreover, to say that such attitudes are necessarily irrational is to adopt a contestable view of rationality, one that presents it as a property of the deliberations of a detached subject reasoning entirely from universal principles. Socialists need not and should not take up the view of ethical rationality implied here. They are better served by a form of ethical particularism that allows existing commitments and loyalties a fundamental place in ethical reasoning – which does not entail that every commitment must be accepted uncritically.[37] They should, in short, prefer the Hegelian idea of ethical life to the Kantian idea of morality as an account of practical reasoning vis-à-vis other members of the community.

There is a further implication to be drawn here. A realistic form of socialism must start out from actually existing communities. It cannot hope to invent the communities that it might be thought desirable to have on abstract grounds. Communal relationships, for reasons already given, are inevitably fragile in the circumstances of a modern industrial society; they must be husbanded with care. Now if we take this point together with the earlier point that community is needed to legitimize practices of distributive justice, our conclusion must be that the relevant communities are nations. On the one hand, people do, in general, identify themselves with national communities in a way that they rarely do with wider constituencies. On the other hand, community at this level is normally broad-based enough to provide the conditions for an effective practice of distributive justice. The nation as a form of community must have a privileged position in socialist thought, at least in any future we can envisage.[38] And this, of course, runs directly counter to a well-entrenched tendency in socialist thought, which regards nationality less as a resource than as a problem to be overcome. For many socialists, the future has seemed to lie either with local community or

---

[37] I discuss ethical particularism more fully in "The Ethical Significance of Nationality," *Ethics*, forthcoming. See also Andrew Oldenquist, "Loyalties," *Journal of Philosophy*, vol. 74 (1982), pp. 173–93; John Cottingham, "Partiality, Favoritism and Morality," *Philosophical Quarterly*, vol. 36 (1986), pp. 357–73; Philip Pettit, "Social Holism and Moral Theory," *Proceedings of the Aristotelian Society*, vol. 86 (1985–86), pp. 173–97.

[38] There is no need, I think, to commit ourselves on the question of whether it is ultimately preferable to have a world order made up of distinct national communities or a global community. On one side stands the value of diversity; on the other, the problems of international distributive justice. The point is that the most extensive communal identities that people currently have are national identities, and there is no sign that this about to change. Insofar as there is any movement, it appears to be in the direction of smaller, more intense forms of nationality rather than towards internationalism.

with global community, or with some combination of these, but in any case not with existing nationalities.

Why is there such a resistance in socialist thought to the idea of national community? There is the belief in moral universalism which I have already discussed (national boundaries are morally irrelevant). There is also, of course, the horrific experience of "national socialism" in its German incarnation. But there is a further point. If one starts out by thinking of a community as involving a set of face-to-face relationships in which each person has full and direct knowledge of the qualities of the other members, then the idea of a nation as a community must indeed seem peculiar. Nations are, in Benedict Anderson's phrase, "imagined communities."[39] They exist only because of beliefs each of us have about our compatriots, beliefs not acquired by direct experience but culturally transmitted. As Anderson points out, nations can't exist without mass media (originally the printed word) to disseminate an understanding of national identity. But with this comes the possibility of distortion. The picture of national life that becomes embedded in the culture may not accurately reflect what is actually the case, both now and historically. The extreme version of this is, of course, Orwell's *1984*, where the telescreens project a version of events that bears no relation at all to reality. But even in societies that are much more open than Orwell's Oceania, we find that national identities contain a greater or lesser admixture of myth. And this apparently contravenes an idea of rationality that the socialist must find attractive – not the abstract idea of reason that I have already rejected, but simply the idea that, to be rational, I must regard all of my beliefs as potentially subject to critical scrutiny. It seems that if I adopt this policy with respect to nationality, I am bound to end up by rejecting a good part of my existing national identity.

I have elsewhere tried to assess how far national identities can survive the critical rejection of certain of their components.[40] Here I want to develop a different point. There may be built-in limits to the process of critical scrutiny itself. We may simply not be able to formulate everything that goes to make up our nationality in a way that makes rational scrutiny possible. Here we see the significance of Taylor's conception of language as "a pattern of activity ... which can only be deployed against a background which we can never fully dominate"; it is a conception which can, I think, be extended more widely to apply to many of the cultural phenomena which constitute nationality. Consider, for instance, the importance of symbols of various kinds – flags, emblems, festivities – in national life. When we respond to these symbols, as

[39] Benedict Anderson, *Imagined Communities: Reflections on the Origin and Spread of Nationalism* (London: Verso, 1983).
[40] See "The Ethical Significance of Nationality."

most of us do, we cannot spell out in propositional form precisely what it is we are responding to, although we may, of course, be able to say *something* about their significance. What passes through our minds as we stand before the Cenotaph to commemorate our war dead? Is it pride in the heroism of our soldiers, or horror at the carnage of war? Or perhaps both of these at once? If we can't be clear about what the ceremony means, how can we say whether it is rationally acceptable or not? Yet occasions such as these are an important component of national identity.

When assessing Taylor's view that communal relationships are unavoidably opaque, I pointed to its potentially conservative implications. Unquestionably, nationality is open to the same charge. If we define our community in terms of a spontaneously evolving national identity, we shall remain, to a large extent, the prisoners of our past. To avoid this implication, we must appeal to politics. The political forum must be the sphere in which we reshape our common identity through reasoned argument. A socialist view of community must therefore give a central place to citizenship. Not only should we be related as bearers of a common national identity, we should also be related as citizens, as co-determiners of our collective future.

Let me expand a little on this. It is important to see how nationality and citizenship are related in the view that I am outlining. Nationality is the identity we have in common, an identity in large measure inherited from the past, and not fully open to rational scrutiny. Citizenship is a political status which allows each of us to participate in reshaping that identity. For instance, we scrutinize our institutions and practices to see whether the meanings they convey (so far as these are determinate) are meanings we still want to endorse (to take a relatively trivial case, we may decide to abolish one public holiday and institute another); we decide which cultural activities are worthy of public support; more generally, our legislation may involve an attempt to influence future understanding of the meaning of membership in this society (consider the case of race-relations legislation). But this exercise never occurs in a vacuum. We take part in political debate already endowed with the shared understandings that come with a common nationality. Since critical reshaping starts with these understandings, we cannot get beyond them entirely, or certainly not beyond them all at once. Taylor's metaphor, borrowed from Neurath, of sailors rebuilding their ship at sea, seems to describe the case pretty well.

What must politics be like if it is to fulfill the function we are assigning to it? Socialists will certainly want to insist that citizenship must be a role available to everyone (or else the reshaping of communal identity won't be democratic), so we must envisage arrangements that permit everyone to be politically active. More significant for the present argument, people must engage in politics *as* citizens, that is, as members of a collectivity committed to advancing its common good. They cannot enter it in their capacity as private persons, each with a particular interest – say, an economic interest – to advance. This is a formidable requirement, as Rousseau understood in his pessimistic chapter on the silencing of the general will.[41] Socialism must draw on an ample stock of republican virtue. It must also become adept at what Michael Walzer has called the art of separation.[42] It must find ways of demarcating a person's role as citizen from other roles that he might perform, for instance, as enthusiast for a particular cause, or as spokesman for a sectional interest. A modern society will inevitably embrace a whole gamut of forms of private life (unless they are artificially suppressed), and these are bound to generate demands on public policy. There is always a danger that the force of these demands may obliterate citizenship. The sailors who are rebuilding their ship on the open sea may need to refurbish their tools at the same time.

This may indicate the distance between the form of communitarianism developed here, and the simpler view which sees community as a general, undifferentiated characteristic of relationships in socialist society. Community, on the present view, has a restricted character. It describes one respect in which members of a society may be related, but it does not exclude the possibility that they may also be related in other ways – say, as competitors in the marketplace. It also has an artificial character, at least to some extent.[43] I have argued that national identities will remain partially opaque to rational scrutiny; I have also argued that we may need devices – symbolic devices and so forth – to protect citizenship from invasion by private interests. This takes us very far from a view of community as the expression of natural sentiments, and of social relations as transparent to the participants. It is not clear to me, however, that socialists must disdain artifice, if that turns out to be the best way of achieving their essential goals. I draw comfort here from Jon Elster's recent discussion of the problem of constitutional choice, which takes up the idea that a constitution is a device for collective self-binding – a way of protecting ourselves from making certain kinds of decisions in the future – and applies it to the transition to socialism.[44] Socialists should discard the

---

[41] "In the end, when the state, on the brink of ruin, can maintain itself only in an empty and illusory form, when the social bond is broken in every heart, when the meanest interest impudently flaunts the sacred name of the public good, then the general will is silenced: everyone, animated by secret motives, ceases to speak as a citizen any more than as if the state had never existed; and the people enacts in the guise of laws iniquitous decrees which have private interests as their only end." Jean-Jacques Rousseau, *The Social Contract* (Harmondsworth: Penguin, 1968), p. 150.

[42] Michael Walzer, "Liberalism and the Art of Separation," *Political Theory*, vol. 12 (1984), pp. 315–30.

[43] I use "artifice" here in its neutral, Humean sense.

[44] Jon Elster, *Three Lectures on Constitutional Choice*, (mimeo) Oslo, 1981.

naive view that everything they want can be achieved by following majority opinion at each moment in time.

CONCLUSION

This paper began with the claim, made recently by several socialists, that socialism centers on the value of freedom – of ensuring that each person enjoys equal effective freedom. In pursuing the implications of that claim, we may seem to have turned a somersault, for there is a well-established view that sees the politically organized community as essentially totalitarian in its upshot. If we are to concern ourselves with our collective identity, and use politics as a means of remodeling that identity, what place is left for the freedoms that liberals characteristically cherish: artistic freedom, religious freedom, privacy, and so forth? How can socialism with a communitarian face possibly claim to be freedom-maximizing?

The argument for that claim, to recall, runs as follows. Freedom depends on the distribution of resources. To equalize effective freedom, we need a system of distributive justice. But such a system can't be legitimized unless people see themselves as tied together communally. Politics enters the picture to prevent communal ties becoming merely traditional, to honor socialist demands for rationality.

Such a view does not entail a rejection of liberal forms of freedom, or of practices such as the creation and enforcement of rights which protect those freedoms. Communitarianism, in general, may differ from liberalism more radically in its basic premises than in the practical policies it recommends;[45] this applies *a fortiori* to the streamlined version defended here. That is not to say that a socialist set of rights would have precisely the same content as the standard liberal set. Socialism requires the introduction of new rights, especially in the field of economics. Equally, it may require the abrogation of some liberal rights, particularly in areas in which forms of private culture threaten to have a destructive impact on the public culture which sustains a common identity.[46] So, for instance, a socialist society may wish to impose some limits on educational freedom, seeing the school as an important source of the political understandings that future citizens will bring to their public life. This may have implications both for the structure of the education system (should private schools be permitted?) and for the content of what is taught in certain fields (should teachers be permitted to transmit *any* version of the history and politics of their own country?). Where two sets of rights

[45] For an attempt at conciliation, see Gutmann, "Communitarian Critics of Liberalism." See also the brief discussion in Michael Sandel, "Morality and the Liberal Ideal," *The New Republic*, May 7, 1984, pp. 15–17.
[46] I have grasped this nettle in "Socialism and Toleration," ed. Susan Mendus, *Justifying Toleration* (Cambridge: Cambridge University Press, 1988).

intersect but neither includes the other, there is the familiar problem of deciding which is the more extensive – in the present context, the problem of aggregating liberties. Although I have not tried to show here that the solution to this problem must favor the socialist case, I can see no reason why it should not. In that sense, there is nothing incoherent in beginning one's intellectual trajectory as a socialist from a commitment to freedom and ending up at the circumscribed form of communitarianism I have been delineating in this paper.

Politics, Oxford University

A PUBLIC OWNERSHIP RESOLUTION OF THE TRAGEDY OF THE COMMONS*

By John E. Roemer

Introduction

Imagine a society of fisherfolk, who, in the state of nature, fish on a lake of finite size. Fishing on the lake is characterized by decreasing returns to scale in labor, because the lake's finite size (and finite fish stock) imply that each successive hour of fishing labor is less effective than the previous one, as the remaining fish become less dense in the lake. In the state of nature, the lake is commonly owned: each fishes as much as he pleases, and, we might suppose, calculates his fishing plan by taking the labor of the others as given, as he sees it. Each knows that the distribution of fish will be proportional to labor expended among the fisherfolk: if I fish twice as long as you, I will end up with twice as much fish as you. This is not due to some kind of concern with equity (or the labor theory of value) among the fisherfolk; it is a technological fact, implied by the assumption that fishing labor is homogeneous, and all are equally likely to catch a fish in a unit of time. An *equilibrium under common ownership* can be thought of as a Nash equilibrium of the game where each computes his optimal fishing plan, given the labor of the others and knowing what the consequent distribution of fish would be. (A Nash equilibrium is an allocation of labor and fish to each fisherman, with the property that no one can increase his utility by deviating in his choice of labor, given what the others are doing.)

When the fishing technology is characterized by non-constant returns to labor, the equilibrium under common ownership is not Pareto-efficient. This formalizes a tale known as the "tragedy of the commons." If the technology is characterized by decreasing returns, then the lake will be overfished, in this sense: the equilibrium under common ownership is Pareto-inferior to some other allocation of labor and fish in which the total expenditure of labor (and therefore the total catch of fish) is less than the labor expended (and fish caught) under common ownership. Everyone's welfare can be improved by exercising a restraint that no one has any interest in exercising in the state of

* I am indebted to Louis Makowski, Eric Maskin, and Joseph Ostroy for their discussions with me of implementation theory. I have used some material from my joint work with Joaquim Silvestre; I thank him for treating it as common property. I thank the National Science Foundation for supporting this research.

nature. The source of the inefficiency of common ownership equilibrium is that each fisherman imposes a negative externality on the others by his fishing, which decreases the productivity of the lake for everyone, the social cost of which he does not take account in his utility-maximizing calculus.

The tragedy of the commons is often put forth as an advertisement for private property. If the lake were run as a firm, a joint-stock company owned by some or all of the fisherfolk in various proportions, the market equilibrium would be Pareto-efficient (assuming the firm did not exercise any monopoly power).[1] But claiming that privatization of the lake is the necessary solution to the "tragedy" is false. There are other ways of arriving at a Pareto-efficient allocation of fish and labor. We might imagine the fisherfolk convening a meeting to collectively organize a plan that would solve the inefficiency of common ownership anarchy. They appoint a central committee empowered to restrain each fisherman in the interests of all. Under collective or *public ownership*, could efficiency be guaranteed, even though a different arrangement would prevail than under private ownership?

I argue that public ownership can bring about Pareto-efficient solutions to the tragedy of the commons, which are superior to private ownership solutions from a distributional point of view. Advocates of the market usually do not concern themselves with the distributional implications of private ownership.[2] I maintain that a concern with Pareto-efficiency need not crowd out a concern for distribution. Public ownership entails a property regime that addresses both issues.

I propose public ownership of the resource that was in common use as a response to those who argue for private ownership as the best (or only) resolution of the *inefficiency* of common use. But entitlement theorists also, or mainly, argue that a fisherman in the state of nature has a *right* to claim part of the commons as his private property under certain conditions. As G. A. Cohen argues, the existence of this right presupposes that, in the state of nature, the commons is unowned and therefore available for private appropriation. But what if, following Cohen, we believe instead that the commons need not be taken as unowned in the state of nature, but as owned by everyone, collectively? Then there is no obvious right to private ownership of pieces of it; instead, new uses of the commons must be approved by some compact among its joint owners.

---

[1] It is necessary for efficiency that the lake be run as a firm, and not simply divided up as private property among the fisherfolk. For in the latter case, if there are decreasing returns to scale in labor, there will be externalities in production: what happens on one section of the lake affects productivity of other sections. The firm internalizes these externalities.

[2] The 'Coase theorem', for instance, states that regardless of the distribution of (private) property rights in a heretofore commonly-owned asset, the allocation of the asset's productive uses will be the same after privatization if there are no income effects on demand. The criticisms one can raise against this statement are not my concern here.

Advocates of privatization argue that markets provide the best way of decentralizing economic activity, given privacy of information about preferences and endowments (such as labor capacity and skill). Central planning, associated with public property, is claimed to be an inferior institution for realizing an efficient allocation of resources. In Section IV, however, I show that the association of public ownership with planning is not always necessary: that is, some proposals for public ownership can be decentralized. Conversely, it is shown that a private property regime that must pass Robert Nozick's test for just acquisition cannot be decentralized: his modified laissez-faire regime requires, indeed, much more than a minimal state.

I. COMMON OWNERSHIP AND ENTITLEMENT THEORY

There are n fisherfolk, the ith one of whom has preferences over labor and fish represented by a utility function $u^i(L, Y)$, where L is the amount of labor she expends, and Y the amount of fish she consumes. Utility is decreasing in labor and increasing in fish. Fisherman i is endowed with ω^i amount of labor and no fish at the beginning. We allow different fisherfolk to possess different amounts of homogeneous labor (some are capable of working more hours in the day than others); alternatively, and equivalently, we could model the situation by assuming that each has 1 unit of labor, but that they work with different degrees of intensity or efficiency. The technology is represented by a production function $f(L) = Y$, which describes the conversion of labor into fish. If there are constant returns to scale in labor (CRS), then for some non-negative constant α, $f(L) = \alpha L$. If there are decreasing returns to labor (DRS), then $f(L)/L$ is decreasing in L. If there are increasing returns, then $f(L)/L$ is increasing in L.

A *feasible allocation* is $\langle (L^1, Y^1), (L^2, Y^2), ..., (L^n, Y^n) \rangle$ such that $f(L) \leq Y$, where $Y = \sum Y^i$ and $L = \sum L^i$ and $L \leq \sum \omega^i$. In words, a feasible allocation is a distribution of labor and fish that is technologically achievable for the given technology and labor endowments. A *Pareto-efficient allocation* is a feasible allocation that is dominated in utility by no other feasible allocation.

A Nash equilibrium of the common ownership game is a feasible allocation $\zeta = \langle (\hat{L}^1, \hat{Y}^1), ..., (\hat{L}^n, \hat{Y}^n) \rangle$ such that $(\hat{L}^i, \hat{Y}^i)$ is a best strategy for fisherman i, given the actions of the others. The tragedy of the commons is summarized by:

Theorem 1: A Nash equilibrium of the common ownership game, when f exhibits either decreasing or increasing returns to labor, is Pareto-inefficient.[3]

Inefficiency also results when there are increasing returns to labor, because in this case each fisherman bestows a positive externality on society

[3] The proofs of all theorems quoted are available, unless otherwise indicated, in John Roemer, "Public Ownership Resolutions of the Tragedy of the Commons," Department of Economics, University of California, Davis. Working Paper No. 295 (1987).

by his fishing, of which he does not take account, and so he does not fish "enough." (Increasing returns would occur if, for instance, the more lures there are in the lake, the more fish come out of the grottos.) Only under constant returns to labor is the equilibrium under common ownership efficient. (There are also mixed cases, where f exhibits different returns to scale in different intervals, which I shall not study.)

Assume, for the moment, that there are constant returns to labor: for some α, $f(L) = \alpha L$. Then each fisherman can safely ignore what the others are doing. He simply chooses that amount of labor L^i which maximizes his utility, knowing that $Y^i = \alpha L^i$. Under and only under constant returns, no fisherman bestows any production externality on the others, so none need take account of what the others are doing. One can imagine that constant returns only hold when the lake is infinitely large, at least for all practical purposes, relative to the number of fisherfolk. It is the unique case where each fisherman's action leaves "enough and as good in common for others,"[4] and hence where a strict reading of Locke allows private appropriation of the part of the lake which a person fishes. When there are decreasing returns, each person's action hurts the others, and when there are increasing returns each person's action helps the others, but each could adopt a different action which would make the lake even better for others.

Robert Nozick[5] would argue, based on his loose interpretation of Locke's proviso, that in the case of decreasing returns (for example) an entrepreneurial fisherman may appropriate the lake as long as he arranges a Pareto-superior allocation to the Nash equilibrium under common ownership. Nozick substitutes a criterion stated in terms of the respective welfares of the agents, rather than in terms of the physical availability of the good being appropriated: private appropriations of a resource previously in common use are justified, as long as they leave others at least as well off as they were when the resource was in common use.[6] Because the common ownership equilibrium is sub-optimal, such an action is possible. The entrepreneur grabs the lake, hires the other fisherfolk as laborers at a wage, and sells them the fish they catch at a price that leaves all better off than they were under common ownership. Or he designs a schedule of fishing, and rents the lake out to the fisherfolk in accordance with it. By designing an

---

[4] John Locke, *Two Treatises on Government*, ed. P. Laslett (Cambridge: Cambridge University Press, 1976), section 27.

[5] Robert Nozick, *Anarchy, State, and Utopia* (New York: Basic Books, 1974), chapter 7, section 1.

[6] Note that Nozick's proviso is weaker than Locke's because in the case of decreasing returns it is impossible to leave enough and as good in common for others. Thus, the substitution of a welfare criterion for a physical one is not innocuous. For an elaboration of this point, see G. A. Cohen, "Self-Ownership, World Ownership, and Equality. Part II," *Social Philosophy and Policy*, vol. 3, issue 2 (1986).

efficient use of the lake, the rent can be such that each fisherman is better off than under common ownership.

Although the grabber *could* arrange a Pareto-superior allocation to the equilibrium under common ownership, it is worthwhile to note that if he operates his lake as a competitive entrepreneur, the other fisherfolk will indeed all be worse off than they were under common ownership:

Theorem 2: Suppose the technology is owned by one or many agents, who operate it competitively, hiring the fisherfolk and selling the fish, or renting the lake to them at competitive rent. Then each fisherman is worse off than he was under common ownership.[7]

Note that Theorem 2 supposes that some outside entrepreneurs own the lake. If it is appropriated by some of our fisherfolk, and operated as a competitive venture, then the others will be worse off than they were under common ownership, and the appropriators may or may not be better off. (At least one of them must be better off.) Theorem 2 is a statement that the value of a fisherman's marginal product, which is what he receives in the competitive equilibrium when he owns none of the lake, is less than the share of the product he receives in the common ownership equilibrium.

A fortiori, if the appropriator of the lake prices as a monopolist, then the fisherfolk will be still worse off than they are in the common ownership equilibrium, because they will be worse off than in the competitive soluton. Thus, Nozick's scenario (that the grabber organizes production to render each at least as well off as before), while possible, would not result from normal market arragements. We shall study in Section IV whether there are more complex arrangements under which Nozick's project is not vacuous.

What are the results of appropriation when the fishing exhibits constant returns to scale? It is impossible to make anyone strictly better off without making someone else worse off (i.e., the Nash equilibrium under common ownership is Pareto-optimal). Thus, under Nozick's proviso, the appropriators cannot change things at all. Equivalently, if they operate the lake as a competitive venture, they will set a wage for fishing labor and a price for fish that leave each fisherman indifferent between this arrangement and the common ownership arrangement, and the appropriators will make zero profits. They will still have to fish themselves, exactly as they did under common ownership, in order to eat. If we take Locke's proviso, and we suppose that the constant returns are due to the lake's effectively infinite size, then anyone can appropriate the part of the lake he uses, without affecting others. He will not be able to eke any rent from his cove, for there are plenty

---

[7] This theorem is due to M. Weitzman, "Free Access vs. Private Property as Alternative Systems for Managing Common Property," *Journal of Economic Theory*, vol. 8 (1974), pp. 225–34.

of equally good coves for all. Only a monopolist who succeeds in excluding others from the lake can charge a monopoly rent for use of the lake: this renders all the others worse off than under common ownership.

Under decreasing returns to scale, it is possible to assign private property rights in the lake in such a way that each becomes better off than under common ownership. That scheme will be discussed below in Section III. In this section, I have aimed to show just that the kinds of appropriation that contemporary entitlement theorists deem permissible will not occur under laissez-faire. Although a lake-grabber *could* make others better off than they were in the prior sub-optimal allocation, he will not do so in competitive laissez-faire arrangements. And surely Nozick's acquisition proviso is appealing only if the compensation the appropriator could design for the others is in fact carried out. According to Theorem 2, it would seem that these lake-grabbers would have to be sharply regulated by a state agency set up by the fisherfolk for the grabber's appropriation to be justified by even Nozick's relatively lax proviso.[8]

II. Public Ownership: Proportionality Preserved

Suppose the fisherfolk convene to resolve the inefficient use of the lake that occurs in the state of common ownership. Their task is to decide upon a Pareto-efficient way of allocating labor and fish in their society. They respect the principles that each should earn returns proportional to the labor he expends (which is to say that there should be private ownership of labor), and that the lake should be public property. Their convention marks the transition from common to public ownership of the lake. While common ownership is clearly defined (free access to the commons), and private ownership is defined as well (allowing the owner of a thing to use or abuse it as he chooses, in particular, to exclude others from the use thereof), there is no clear conception of what public ownership of the lake requires. What does it mean for a whole society to own something?

For private ownership, we have both a political definition and an economic characterization of resource allocation. Politically, private ownership allows each to do what he wishes with his resources, subject, perhaps, to some rule against harming others. Economically, the paradigm of resource allocation in a private ownership economy is the Walrasian equilibrium allocation associated with the postulated property rights. With respect to public ownership, there is a political definition – the public has the right to decide what to do with their jointly-owned asset – but there is no agreed-upon economic characterization of the implied resource allocation. In this section,

[8] This result holds because the appropriators have no scarce talent, which they might otherwise use to increase, let us say, the productivity of the lake. Many of Nozick's examples refer to situations where the appropriators do have skills lacking in the rest of the population.

I outline a proposal for the public ownership resource allocation in the economy of fisherfolk, recently proposed and elaborated by J. Silvestre and myself.[9]

Public ownership perhaps requires that each should have free access to the lake. Only if the technology is one of constant returns to labor, however, does free access for some not impinge in any way on the opportunities available to others. So if the lake is of infinite size, the fisherfolk agree that public ownership of the lake, in conjunction with private ownership of labor, is implemented by the same solution that common ownership of the lake provides: each fisherman is allowed to fish the lake as he pleases. But under decreasing (increasing) returns to labor, free access must somehow be regulated to implement public ownership.

The common ownership solution, for *any* technology, has one aspect in common with the common ownership solution in the constant returns case: the distribution of fish is proportional to labor expended. It is proposed that this feature of proportionality is a desideratum of the general scheme the fisherfolk are searching for. That the output should be distributed in proportion to labor expended seems a natural way of respecting the differential efforts of the fisherfolk, their private ownership of labor, while using the lake to augment each fisherman's labor equally. It is an allocation that distributes output according to work, as the socialist principle calls for. Does there exist a way of allocating fishing labor and fish that is both (a) proportional, and (b) Pareto-optimal? Such an allocation, if there is one, would seem to be an attractive implementation of public ownership.

There is, indeed, always such an allocation. Formally, let an *economic environment*, which represents a possible society of fisherfolk, be represented as $\xi = \langle u^1, u^2, ..., u^n; \omega^1, \omega^2, ..., \omega^n; f \rangle$ or, for short, $\xi = \langle u; \omega; f \rangle$, where $u = (u^1, ..., u^n)$, $\omega = (\omega^1, \omega^2, ..., \omega^n)$. An economic environment is described by specifying the preferences of the n fisherfolk for labor and fish, u_i, their capacities for labor, w_i; and the lake technology, f.

Theorem 3: Given any economic environment ξ in which f exhibits constant or decreasing returns to labor, there exists an allocation of labor and fish, $\langle (L^1, Y^1), ..., (L^n, Y^n) \rangle$ that is

        (a) *proportional, that is,* $L^i/L^j = Y^i/Y^j$, *for all* i, j = 1, n

and   (b) *Pareto-optimal.*[10]

An allocation satisfying the conditions of the theorem will be called a *Proportional Equilibrium*. The Proportional Equilibrium has an interesting interpretation. Suppose we view the lake as being operated by a publicly

[9] John E. Roemer and Joaquim Silvestre, "Public Ownership: Three Proposals for Resource Allocation," Department of Economics, University of California, Davis, Working Paper No. 307 (December 1987).

[10] The proof is available in Roemer and Silvestre, *ibid.*, Theorem 8.

owned firm, which is owned by its members, the fisherfolk. The firm hires the fisherfolk at a wage, and sells them fish at a price. The firm is operated as a profit-maximizing venture, and its profits, which take the form of fish, are distributed somehow to the fisherfolk. Is there a way of assigning "shares" in the firm (or, what is the same thing, shares in ownership of the lake, which is the firm's resource) that will result in the distribution of labor and fish being exactly the allocation of a Proportional Equilibrium? It turns out this happens when *the ownership share of each fisherman in the firm is equal to the share of total labor expended that he provides* at the Proportional Equilibrium.

It is useful to give another example of this principle. Suppose there is a cooperative, which is publicly owned by its members. They do not work in the cooperative, but hire workers from outside the membership. The relevant input that the members contribute in this case is not their labor but their money: the revenue from purchases made at the cooperative is used to pay the outside workers. At the end of the year, there are profits which must be divided among the members in some way. They agree to the following rule: divide the profits among them in proportion to their purchases. This gives rise to the Proportional Equilibrium, a Pareto-efficient allocation of money and goods having the property that the value of a member's total consumption of goods (both purchased and received as his share of the profits) is proportional to the money spent at the cooperative.

This property of the Proportional Equilibrium is summarized by:

Theorem 4: Let $\xi = \langle u; f; \omega \rangle$ be an economic environment; let $\zeta = \langle (L^1, Y^1), ..., (L^n, Y^n) \rangle$ be a Proportional Equilibrium for ξ. Define the labor shares $\theta^i = L^i/L$, where $L = \Sigma L^j$. Let (w, p) be a competitive equilibrium wage-price pair for the economy in which agent i owns the share θ^i of the firm that operates the technology f, and in which he owns his own input ω^i. Then the allocation ζ is a Walrasian equilibrium allocation associated with these prices.[11]

The Proportional Equilibrium is an appealing realization of public ownership of the lake for several reasons besides its Pareto-efficiency. The proportional distribution of fish to labor attributes the economy's entire output to labor: the lake can be viewed as a common resource that benefits all, but does not "earn a return" itself. Taking a different viewpoint, the Proportional Equilibrium coincides with a perfectly competitive market outcome in which the shares of the publicly owned firm's profits are distributed among the members of the society in proportion to the labor they expend at this allocation.

In particular, the existence of a Proportional Equilibrium shows that there is no reason to rely upon privatizing the lake subject only to a Lockean or

---

[11] Theorem 9 in Roemer and Silvestre, *ibid.*

Nozickian proviso as the uniquely attractive way to resolve the tragedy of the commons. Thus far, I have not discussed how the Proportional Equilibrium might be achieved. One way, in principle, would be for a planner, who knows the preferences and labor endowments of the fishermen, to calculate the Equilibrium, and then to make labor assignments to fishermen, allowing each to keep his catch. In the Conclusion, the possibility of decentralizing the implementation of the Proportional Equilibrium is discussed.

III. PARETO-DOMINATION OF COMMON OWNERSHIP

In saying that the fishermen called a meeting to resolve the tragedy of the commons, I took an implicitly contractarian approach to the question of public ownership. One might insist that one condition for an acceptable resolution of the inefficiency of common ownership is that the scheme decided upon should render each fisherman at least as well off as he was under common ownership – that is, one might insist that any scheme of public ownership satisfy Nozick's proviso. This would be necessary, for instance, if every fisherman had veto power at the convention. As Theorem 2 states, private appropriations of the lake by only some of the fisherfolk in a competitive setting do not satisfy this criterion. It is notable, and perhaps surprising, that the Proportional Equilibrium does not, in general, Pareto-dominate the (Nash) common ownership equilibrium, either. This can be illustrated with the results from simulating the common ownership solution and the Proportional Equilibrium for a selection of 22 economic environments. Each environment, in the simulation, has 2 agents, with Cobb-Douglas utility functions $u^1(L, Y) = (\omega - L)^b Y^{1-b}$ and $u^2(L, Y) = (1 - \omega - L)^c Y^{1-c}$, where b and c are numbers between 0 and 1. The endowment of labor of the first agent is ω; the second agent's endowment is $1 - \omega$. The production function is of the form $f(L) = (.5 Y)^a$, where a is between 0 and 1. This specifies an economy with parameters (b, c, ω, a). In the simulations described, 22 different parameter vectors were chosen, and, for each one, the Nash equilibrium (characterizing common ownership) and the Proportional Equilibrium were computed. In Figure 1, the utilities of both agents are plotted for the 22 economic environments, at the common ownership and Proportional Equilibrium allocations. The circle- and square-studded lines represent the utility of the first agent under the Nash equilibrium and Proportional Equilibrium, respectively. The triangle- and diamond-studded lines represent the utility of the second agent under the Nash equilibrium and Proportional Equilibrium, respectively. Economy 12 represents a clear case where the Proportional Equilibrium Pareto-dominates common ownership; but in economies 15, 21, and 22, the second fisherman does worse under Proportional Equilibrium than under common ownership.

FIGURE 1

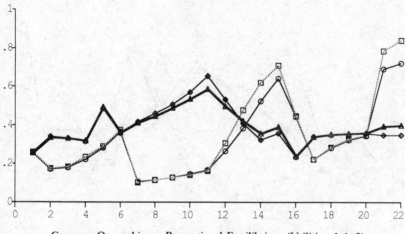

Common Ownership vs. Proportional Equilibrium (Utilities, 1 & 2)

○ utility of agent 1 in common ownership Nash Equilibrium (NE)
□ utility of agent 1 in Proportional Equilibrium (PE)
△ utility of agent 2 in NE
◇ utility of agent 2 in PE

If the economic environments of the simulations are possible worlds, the second fisherman would have reason to refuse to agree to the PE as the implementation of public ownership. Trying to address this deficiency, one is led to ask: Is there any equilibrium concept that (a) is Pareto-efficient and (b) always Pareto-dominates the Nash equilibrium under common ownership? The answer is yes.

Theorem 5 : Let (u, ω, f) *be an economic environment, and let* σ^i *be the labor share of the* i[th] *agent at a common ownership Nash equilibrium. Then the Walrasian equilibrium(a) associated with a distribution of the profits of the firm in which agent* i *receives share* σ^i *of the profits Pareto-dominates the Nash equilibrium.*

Call this solution the *Nash Dominator Equilibrium* (NDE). In Figure 2, the utilities of the two fisherfolk are plotted for the NDE and common ownership equilibrium. We verify the truth of Theorem 5 for these economies by noting that the diamond always dominates the triangle and the square always dominates the circle.

It is amusing to illustrate the "tragedy of the commons" by examining total labor expended and total fish produced under common ownership and the NDE. From Figures 3 and 4, note that more labor is expended and more

FIGURE 2

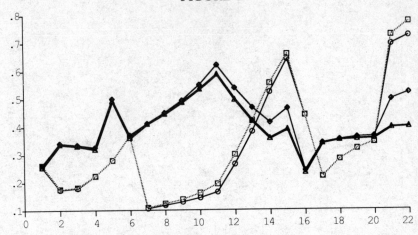

Common Ownership vs. Nash Dominator Equilibrium (Utilities, 1 & 2)

☐ utility of agent 1 in Nash Dominator Equilibrium (NDE)
◯ utility of agent 1 in common ownership Nash Equilibrium (NE)
◇ utility of agent 2 in NDE
△ utility of agent 2 in NE

FIGURE 3

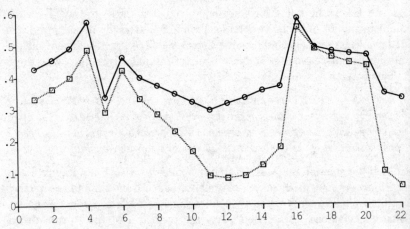

Total Labor: Nash Dominator Equilibrium and Common Ownership

◯ total labor expended in common ownership
☐ total labor expended in Nash Dominator Equilibrium

FIGURE 4

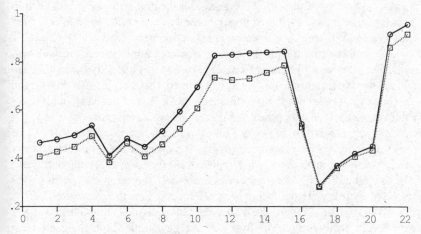

Total Output: Nash Dominator Equilibrium and Common Ownership

○ total output produced in common ownership
□ total output produced in Nash Dominator Equilibrium

fish are caught under common ownership than at the Nash Dominator Equilibrium. One might surmise from the figures that the gain in fish is not worth the extra cost in labor – which is, indeed, the case.

IV. THE DECENTRALIZABILITY OF PUBLIC OWNERSHIP

I have spoken of the Proportional Equilibrium as "implementing" an ideal of public ownership. In this section, I use "implement" in the technical sense that it has in game theory. Implementation, in the latter sense, has to do with the general issue raised by the planning-versus-market debate. An allocation rule, such as the Proportional Equilibrium, is said to be *implementable* if there is a non-cooperative game that the agents can play whose equilibria induce precisely the allocations chosen by the rule, as described below. One can think of allocation rules that are implementable as ones that can be decentralized, in the sense that the planner need only specify the rules of some non-cooperative game, but need not elicit information from the players about their preferences, skills, and endowments. The game is designed so that, whatever these preferences, etc., are, the equilibria of the game will trigger the allocation(s) that the solution concept – say, the Proportional Equilibrium – would propose, if all the information were known to the planner, who would in that case calculate the Proportional Equilibrium allocation directly and make labor assignments.

There are different kinds of implementation, depending upon the kind of non-cooperative game that is designed and the game-theoretic equilibrium concept that is used. I will first illustrate the concept of *implementation in Nash equilibrium*. We begin with an economic environment $\xi = \langle \omega^1, ..., \omega^n; u^1, ..., u^n; f \rangle$, and try to implement the Proportional Equilibrium associated with that environment. (There are one or, at most, several allocations that are Proportional Equilibria for ξ.) It is assumed that the planner knows the technology f (he knows about fishing, and the bounty of the lake), but he does not know ω or u. We propose a certain *game form*, G, consisting of $G = [S^1, ..., S^n, \varphi]$, where S^i is a strategy space for player i. Thus, an n-tuple $s = (s^1, s^2, ..., s^n)$ where $s^i \varepsilon S^i$ is an announcement by all players of their strategies. φ is a function that associates to each n-typle s of strategies an allocation of fish and labor to the players. With respect to each such allocation $\varphi(s)$, each player derives a utility, based upon his preferences. Say the allocation $\varphi(s)$ is $\varphi(s) = (\varphi^1(s), ..., \varphi^n(s))$, where $\varphi^i(s)$ is the allocation of labor and fish to player i. Then i's utility is $u^i(\varphi^i(s))$, if s is the strategy n-tuple. Thus the game form specified by the planner provides a way of transforming strategy announcements of players into allocations for the economy ξ.

We can now speak of the Nash equilibria of this game: a Nash equilibrium is an n-tuple of strategies $\bar{s} = (\bar{s}^1, \bar{s}^2, ..., \bar{s}^n)$ such that no player i can induce an allocation that is better for him than $\varphi^i(\bar{s})$ by proposing a different strategy from $\bar{s}^i$, assuming that the other players do not deviate from their announced strategies. The game form G is said to *implement the Proportional Equilibrium allocation mechanism in Nash equilibrium* if the Nash equilibria of the game described induce as their allocations under φ precisely the Proportional Equilibria of ξ, for *any* specification of the economic environment ξ.[12]

The problem of implementing the Proportional Equilibrium can be illustrated as follows. Suppose the strategy spaces S^i are taken, for each i, to consist of the set of all possible utility functions and all possible labor endowments that a fisherman might have. (Thus, each agent is assigned the same strategy set.) An agent announces, as his strategy, a utility function and a labor endowment. The game form consists of a rule that constructs the economy $\bar{\xi}$, from the utility functions and labor endowments that agents have announced, and assigns the Proportional Equilibrium allocation in $\bar{\xi}$ to the fishermen. The problem is that $\bar{\xi}$ may not correspond to the real economy ξ, because some fisherfolk may have lied about their preferences or endowments: indeed, they may have lied because it was in their interest to do so, knowing how the planner would decide upon the allocation. Does there

[12] The general theory of implementation of allocation mechanisms in Nash equilibrium is developed in E. Maskin, "The Theory of Implementation in Nash Equilibrium: A Survey," eds. Leo Hurwicz, David Schmeidler, and Hugo Sonnenschein, *Social Goals and Social Organization* (New York: Cambridge University Press, 1985).

exist some more complicated way (i.e., game form) of passing from the announced preferences and endowments to an allocation that provides the proper incentives for agents to tell the truth and has the property that a Nash equilibrium for the game involves a vector of announcements for the fisherfolk that implements the Proportional Equilibrium for the actual economy ξ?

If a proposal for realizing public ownership, such as the Proportional Equilibrium, is implementable in Nash equilibrium by a game form G, then G can be thought of as playing the decentralizing role similar to that played by the market in private ownership economies. G is an institution, which may be used by the fisherfolk, with no state intervention except to assure that the rules of the institution are followed (this is the function of a minimal state). There is, however, an important difference between the informational assumptions necessary to operate markets and the informational assumptions necessary to implement allocation rules in Nash equilibrium. Markets do not require that any agent know the characteristics of other agents. But to implement an allocation rule in Nash equilibrium requires that every agent know the characteristics (i.e., preferences and labor capacity) of the other agents. Thus, the degree of decentralization that implementation in Nash equilibrium achieves is considerably less than the degree the market purportedly achieves.

Theorem 6: The Proportional Equilibrium allocation mechanism is implementable in Nash equilibrium. The Nash Dominator Equilibrium is not implementable in Nash equilibrium.

Thus, from the point of view of implementability, the Proportional Equilibrium is preferable to the NDE. The failure of the NDE to be Nash-implementable, however, is not a defect of the NDE that can be remedied, given the contractarian concern that motivates it. I mean:

Theorem 7: There is no allocation mechanism that is Pareto-efficient, Pareto-dominates the common ownership equilibrium, and can be implemented in Nash equilibrium.

Hence, if the constitutional convention that the fisherfolk call to remedy the tragedy of the commons is committed to achieving an efficient allocation of resources, subject to the proviso that no member will veto it on the grounds that he would have been better off at status quo ante, then the convention must be satisfied with some degree of central allocation.

I do not view Theorem 7 as very damaging to a public ownership program committed to decentralization for the following reason. "Original-position contractarianism" does not require that a public ownership allocation Pareto-dominate the common ownership equilibrium, because in the morally appropriate original position there is no common ownership equilibrium that must be improved upon. In such an original position, it is not necessary to require that a satisfactory notion of public ownership produce an allocation that is better for everyone than the anarchical solution of common ownership, which has no historical significance. I said that Pareto-domination of the common ownership solution might be *politically* necessary if the convention of fisherfolk meets at a status quo of common ownership, and each member has a veto.

But Theorem 7 is quite damaging to Nozick's project of justifying private property in conjunction with only a minimal state. I have interpreted Nozick's Lockean proviso as requiring that any acceptable private appropriation must render every fisherman at least as well off as he was under common ownership. According to Theorem 7, no procedure that guarantees such Pareto-domination of common ownership and is Pareto-optimal can be implemented in a decentralized, competitive way, even under the assumption that each agent knows the characteristics of the others. Weitzman's Theorem 2 states that the competitive equilibrium associated with the privatization of the lake by some, but not all, of the agents will necessarily leave the disenfranchised ones worse off than under common ownership; Theorem 7 says that *no* decentralized, competitive procedure (i.e., non-cooperative game) exists whose Nash equilibria induce economic allocations satisfying Nozick's proviso for acquisition of property in an asset that was previously held in common.[13] Ironically, a powerful state (having the ability to assign allocations) is necessary to supervise the construction of a capitalist order with a Nozickian-approved history of private appropriation of the common resource.[14]

Finally, I will address the question of what allocation rules can be implemented by institutions that do not require any fisherman to know the characteristics of the others. The market is such an institution; proponents of laissez-faire champion it for its supposed ability to achieve an efficient allocation of resources when information on the characteristics of agents is private knowledge. To evaluate this statement at the level of abstraction adopted in this discussion, we need to formulate precisely what it means to

---

[13] There are other theories of implementation than Maskin's. Recently, a theory of implementation in sub-game perfect Nash equilibria by games in extensive form has been developed see John Moore and Rafael Repullo, "Implementation by Stage Mechanisms," *European Economic Review* (1987). For reasons beyond the scope of my discussion, I do not view this kind of implementation appropriate for solving the problem here.

[14] Joshua Cohen has questioned whether such an interventionist state might, nevertheless, not still be considered minimal by Nozick's definition, for the purpose of the interference is to learn the endowments of the population, not to tax their wealth. If privacy is a right which a minimal state must not transgress, then surely the state required to implement a mechanism that Pareto-dominate common ownership is not minimal.

say that "markets can implement an efficient allocation with only private information on preferences." This requires formulation of another kind of implementation. A game form $G = [S^1, S^2, ..., S^n, \varphi]$ is said to *implement an allocation rule* F *in dominant strategies* if there is a *dominant strategy equilibrium* of the game which induces just the allocations prescribed by F – that is, if there is a strategy $\bar{s}^i \, \varepsilon \, S^i$ for each player such that, no matter what strategies $s^1, s^2, ..., s^{i-1}, s^{i+1}, ..., s^n$ are announced by the other players, $u^i(\varphi^i(s^1, s^2, ..., s^{i-1}, \bar{s}^i, s^{i+1}, ..., s^n))$ is at least as big as it is for any other choice of strategy $s^i \, \varepsilon \, S^i$. (Each player should stick to his particular dominant strategy $\bar{s}^i$ regardless of what the other players announce.) If an allocation rule F is implementable in dominant strategies, then no player need know anything about what the other players are doing or what their preferences are. The allocation rule can be decentralized with complete privacy of information.

Now the claim that the market with private ownership is an efficient way of allocating resources in the presence of private information is stated formally as follows: that there is a game which implements a Walrasian Equilibrium allocation rule in dominant strategies. This claim is in general false, if economies are 'small'.[15] Indeed, there is no anonymous allocation rule that is implementatable in dominant strategy equilibrium for small economies.[16] Let us turn our attention to 'large' economies, which, after all, are the ones of interest if we are discussing societies with many agents.

The *type* of a fisherman is defined as the pair (u^i, ω^i) which specifies his preferences and his labor capacity. A *large* economy consists of fishermen of a finite number of types, but of an infinite number of fishermen of each represented type. We can represent such an economic environment as $\xi = \langle m^1, u^1, \omega^1; ...; m^n, u^n, \omega^n; f \rangle$, where m^i is the measure of type i fishermen in the economy. This means that, although there are an extremely large number of fisherman of each of the n types, their proportions in the

[15] This is so because, in a small economy, some agents (by definition of 'small') do not optimally behave by taking announced prices as given. An agent who has some market power will, strategically, set prices at what the market will bear; that he can significantly alter the supply of some good by withdrawing from the market enables him to manipulate prices. Because of this, the Walrasian equilibrium cannot be implemented by strategic players in a small economy playing a non-cooperative game, where dominant strategy equilibria are the rule.

[16] An anonymous allocation rule is one that distributes commodities according to the traits people have, but not according to their names or other extraneous identifying information. The class of allocation rules that are anonymous, Pareto-efficient, and implementable in dominant strategy equilibrium is characterized in a series of recent papers by Louis Makowski and Joseph Ostroy: Vickrey-Clarke-Groves Mechanisms and Perfect Competition," *Journal of Economic Theory* (1988); "Dominant Strategy Mechanisms in Nonatomic Transferable Utility Economies: Characterization and Existence," Department of Economics, University of California, Los Angeles, Working Paper No. 421 (1986); and "Efficient Dominant Strategy Mechanisms in Large Economies," Department of Economics, University of California, Davis (1987). There are no dominant-strategy-implementable, anonymous, Pareto-optimal allocation mechanisms on the class of economies with a finite number of agents.

population as a whole are given by the relative sizes of the numbers m^i. For such large economies, there is, in fact, an anonymous allocation rule which is implementable in a dominant strategy equilibrium, and it is unique among the class of anonymous allocation rules.

Theorem 8: There is a unique allocation rule which is anonymous, Pareto-efficient, and implementable in dominant strategies on the class of large economies. This rule assigns the Walrasian Equilibrium associated with the following distribution of property: each agent owns his own labor power, and an equal share in the profits of a firm which operates the lake.[17]

This result has the following two interpretations. Suppose there is a planner, who represents Nozick's minimal state. She will not overtly interfere in economic transactions, but will set up anonymous institutions, to be used by the fisherfolk, to arrive at an allocation of resources. The institutions should not require that any fisherman have knowledge of the preferences of labor capacity of any other. Each fisherman is presumed to act in his own self-interest, and all agree to respect the outcome which the institutions produce. (E.g., if the institution is the market, then all agree to respect the market outcome. This translates into the minimal state having the power to enforce market agreements.) Then the only efficient allocation of resources that can be achieved in all large economic environments by anonymous institutions is the allocation that is chosen by a market operating from initial property rights stipulated as follows: each fisherman owns his own labor power, and all have equal property rights in the firm that is set up to manage the lake.

The second interpretation does without the planner. Suppose society has evolved a set of institutions for allocating resources. We consider only institutions that provide minimal equality of opportunity, in the sense that no fisherman's name ever appears in the code that describes how the institutions work. (All that can be mentioned about a person are his preferences and his labor capacity – i.e., his announced type. Other characteristics of fisherfolk are irrelevant.) An institution is capable of decentralizing economic activity if no fisherman need know the type of any other fisherman. The only efficient allocation of resources that such an institution can achieve is the one that behaves like a Walrasian market, in which the property rights are assigned as described above. Or, equivalently, if an anonymous, decentralizing institution results in an allocation other than the "equal profit share" one then it cannot be efficient.

The "equal sharing of profits" allocation rule is different from the proposal for public ownership that I have made. I do not view it as implementing a satisfactory conception of public ownership (for reasons provided in "Public

---

[17] The proof, available in Roemer, (*ibid.*) is based upon Makowski and Ostroy (1986 and 1987 *ibid.*).

Ownership: Three Proposals for Resource Allocation"), but, perhaps more importantly, it is a far cry from what advocates of laissez-faire call for. Right-wing defenders of capitalism champion it as a system (1) whose institutions are anonymous (capitalism is a meritocracy, not an aristocracy), (2) that requires no interventionist state (markets require no commonality of information among agents concerning each others' characteristics), and (3) that achieves an efficient allocation of resources. Those certainly are desirable goals: and they can only be simultaneously achieved when the "lakes" are run as if they were joint-stock companies in which each person owns a per capita share![18]

Conclusion

The tragedy of the commons is often evoked as an argument for private ownership of resources in the external world. Laissez-faire advocates are frequently unconcerned with the distributional consequences of privatiza-tion. I have argued that a regime of public ownership provides an alternative to private ownership for resolving the inefficiencies of production and distribution in the state of nature.

When advocates of laissez-faire say that the tragedy of the commons can (or must) be solved by privatizing the commons, they mean that decentralized markets are capable of implementing an efficient allocation of resources after such privatization (or that only a decentralized private property system can achieve efficiency). Such advocates are, typically, relatively unconcerned with the distribution of property rights in the erstwhile commons. Coase, and the Chicago school generally, assert that any private property rights will do. Nozick is more discriminating, requiring that the privatization satisfy an acquisition proviso that compares the outcome of privatization with the outcome that attained when the property was held in common. (One might question whether the acquisition proviso does not violate Nozick's own attack on end-state, as opposed to process, rules. How can we decide if an appropriation is all right, without knowing the consequent outcome – that is, the new end state?) I have shown that if each

[18] This result is not so strong as it may appear, due to the assumptions of the model. It is assumed that (a) no one has any special technological knowledge – f is common knowledge, and (b) there is no prior private ownership of the technology (or the lake). Suppose, instead, it is assumed that there are two fisherman, A and B, each of whom knows a technology for fishing, f_A and f_B respectively, where f_A is slightly better than f_B. The rest of the fishermen know nothing about fishing. Then it will, in general, be possible to decentralize, using dominant strategies, an anonymous allocation mechanism in which A receives profits equal to the difference in total product from using f_A and f_B, and every other fisherman receives the marginal product of his labor plus a per capita share of the remaining profits. Only if some agents uniquely possess valuable knowledge will they receive special profits. (If, in particular, A and B each know the same technology, then neither of them will be able to appropriate any profits above their per capita share under a dominant-strategy-implementable, efficient mechanism.)

fisherman knows the preferences and labor capacities of the others, then there is an allocation rule that is decentralizable (in the sense of Nash implementation), and that implements a conception of public ownership (the Proportional Equilibrium). Furthermore, there is no allocation rule that can be so decentralized and satisfies Nozick's acquisition proviso. To implement an allocation satisfying the acquisition proviso requires a state that intervenes in more ways than simply policing the institutions that society has set up to coordinate economic activity. While this degree of central planning may be acceptable to those who advocate public ownership, it is not for Nozick-type libertarians.

If we require a more thorough kind of decentralizability – that economic institutions can operate in the case where no agent knows the type of another agent – then only one efficient allocation can be implemented by institutions that provide minimal equality of opportunity. This allocation is quite egalitarian. It requires that technologies in which there are decreasing returns be run as joint-stock companies, owned in equal shares by every member of society.

Thus, if proponents of laissez-faire are committed to minimal equality of opportunity, efficiency, and decentralizability in a world of private information, they must accept a distribution of income that is highly egalitarian. If they are commited to a clean history of the appropriation of private property (the acquisition proviso) and efficiency, then they must be content with an interventionist state. At least in the model of fisherfolk economy, the libertarian program in toto is an impossibility.[19]

Economics, University of California at Davis

---

[19] The model of fisherfolk with different endowments of labor is a limited one for evaluating the claimed virtues of private property. The Austrian school advocates private ownership as the unique institution that elicits scarce talents and entrepreneurship from members of society. To study this claim requires a model in which there are several kinds of labor and many (potential) commodities. The concept of Proportional Equilibrium extends to such economies; see Roemer and Silvestre, *ibid*. The implementation theory of public ownership for such economies is a project for future work.

FROM HERE TO THERE;
or, If Cooperative Ownership Is So Desirable, Why Are There So Few Cooperatives?

By Jon Elster

Introduction

In this paper[1] I want to discuss a well-known but poorly understood problem: how can socialists reconcile the observed paucity of cooperatives in capitalist societies with their alleged superiority on normative grounds? If cooperatives are so desirable, why don't workers desire them? If one's ideal of socialism is central planning, it is clear enough that it cannot emerge gradually within the womb of the capitalist economy. If instead it is something like market socialism, it is not clear that a discontinuous transformation of society is required. If workers want (market) socialism, they can start up here and now. If they don't, doesn't it prove that they do not want it?

I shall proceed as follows. Section I argues that the usual explanation – that cooperatives are not economically viable or that workers prefer working in capitalist firms – is not necessarily correct. The explanation may lie elsewhere, in endogenous preference formation, adverse selection, discrimination, or externalities.

Section II is concerned with the variety of cooperative arrangements. Only rarely do we find cooperatives in their pure form, with all workers and only workers having equal ownership rights. Non-working owners, non-owning workers and unequal distribution of shares are frequent. When the deviations become sufficiently large, the firms cease to become cooperatives in any meaningful sense.

Section III extends the argument of Section I by surveying the causes of cooperative failure. Some fail by success: profitable cooperatives often attract or turn into private ownership. Others fail outright, partly because they tend to be established under unfavorable circumstances and partly because of intrinsic difficulties of management.

Section IV considers the issues of optimality, stability and accessibility. First, workers' preferences are taken as homogeneous and exogenous. Later, issues of heterogeneity and endogeneity are introduced.

[1] This article draws heavily on the Introduction in eds. Jon Elster and Karl O. Moene, *Alternatives to Capitalism* (Cambridge: Cambridge University Press, forthcoming).

I. WHY ARE THERE SO FEW COOPERATIVES?

On any definition of a cooperative, there are very few of them in contemporary capitalist societies. If we do not count the Israeli kibbutzim, the Mondragon group in Spain is the only large cluster of worker-owned firms.[2] In other countries there are worker-owned firms in many industries, but, with a few exceptions, they are small taken individually and insignificant in the aggregate. My guess is that if a moderately stringent definition is adopted (see II below), they represent less than 1 percent of the total work force of these countries. Many of them are short-lived, being desperate attempts by workers to save firms in adverse market circumstances.

I shall briefly mention some frequently cited explanations of the paucity of worker-owned firms. Some suggest that cooperatives will not be set up in the first place, others that they tend to be driven out of business by more competitive capitalist firms.

(i) Workers do not want to participate in the decision-making of the firm. They prefer a life of private consumption over one of active participation. (ii) "[W]orking men prefer to work where they can obtain the best wages and the most comfortable place, while at the same time they also prefer to invest their capital where they think it will bring the greatest interest or dividend, whether that place be the one in which they are employed or elsewhere."[3] Risk-averse workers, in fact, would prefer not to invest their savings in any single firm, but to have a diversified portfolio.[4] Moreover, *if* they invest all their capital in their own firm, their risk-aversion will make for inefficient behavior. (iii) Workers lack the technical competence and market expertise which are required for successful management in a complex and constantly changing environment. (iv) Participatory decision-making is inherently costly and inefficient, not because bad decisions are made (this was argument iii), but because horizontal integration is more time-consuming than vertical.[5] (v) Cooperatives generally wait too long before they lay off workers during recessions, generating bankruptcies that would have been avoided by a capitalist enterprise. (vi) Cooperatives have bad incentive properties. Workers have no motivation to work hard unless supervised by a manager who is motivated to make them work hard. A manager has no motivation to

---

[2] Around 1980, the Mondragon system included 70 cooperative factories with a work force of more than 30,000 cooperators, and a credit cooperative bank with 93 branches and 300,000 deposit accounts. See Henk Thomas and Chris Logan, *Mondragon* (London: Allen and Unwin, 1982), p. 1.

[3] Letter from William Nuttall to Auberon Herbert (1877), cited after Benjamin Jones, *Co-Operative Production* (London, 1894, reprint New York: Augustus Kelley, 1968).

[4] Jacques Drèze, "Some Theory of Labour Management and Participation," in his *Essays on Economic Decisions under Uncertainty* (Cambridge: Cambridge University Press, 1987), p. 375ff.

[5] Oliver Williamson, *Markets and Hierarchies* (New York: The Free Press, 1975), ch. 3.

make workers work hard unless he is also the residual claimant.[6] For similar reasons, the incentive for investment and innovation is much weaker in a cooperative than in a capitalist firm.

My main task here is not to refute or question these explanations, but to suggest some alternative lines. Let me, nevertheless, comment briefly on each of them, not to argue that the cited obstacles have no explanatory power, but to suggest that they need not be insuperable.

(i) It is true that participation can be strenuous and be shunned for that reason. It can also, however, be very rewarding. Collective decision-making can be a form of self-realization which, like all such activities, is rewarding *because* it is strenuous.[7] (ii) The argument against putting all one's eggs in one basket points to a serious problem. In a cluster of interlocking cooperatives, like the Mondragon one, it can to some extent be alleviated by some balancing-off between successful and less successful firms.[8] (iii) Competence and expertise can be hired. The expertise necessary to identify the experts differs by orders of magnitude from the expertise of the latter. (iv) Participatory mechanisms can be more or less time consuming, depending on whether they take the form of direct or representative democracy. Ultimate control is fully compatible with delegation or abdication of current authority. (v) The same argument can be used to counter the objection from reluctance to layoffs. The cooperative can authorize a manager to decide when and how many workers shall be laid off, the selection criteria having been chosen ahead of time by the cooperative itself. (vi) Disincentives for work can be reduced by mutual monitoring of workers by each other. Disincentives for investment can be overcome by a combination of individual shareholding and collective investment decisions. Disincentives for innovation present a more serious problem. If the lure of entrepreneurial superprofits is indispensable for innovation, as Schumpeter argued, cooperatives might be expected to be rather sluggish. Against this it must be said that corporate capitalism, with its highly routinized innovative procedures, does not seem to be less dynamic than entrepreneurial capitalism.[9] Finally, as a comment on all the efficiency-

---

[6] Armen Alchian and Harold Demsetz, "Production, Information Costs, and Economic Organization," *American Economic Review*, vol. 62 (1972), pp. 777–95.

[7] See my "Self-Realization in Work and Politics," *Social Philosophy and Policy* vol. 3 (1986), pp. 97–126.

[8] Hugh Thomas and Chris Logan, *Mondragon* (London: Allen and Unwin, 1982), pp. 155–58.

[9] The studies surveyed in Morton I. Kamien and Nancy L. Schwartz, *Market Structure and Innovation* (Cambridge: Cambridge University Press, 1982), pp. 76–84, indicate that there are clear economies of scale in innovation, at least up to a certain point. The patterns are complex, however, and there are many exceptions.

related arguments, empirical studies suggest that cooperatives are at least as productive as their capitalist counterparts.[10]

Any serious discussion of cooperative ownership would have to face these problems in much greater depth than is possible here. I set them aside because I want to focus on another possible source of problems for the cooperative. It could be that the isolated cooperative in an otherwise capitalist economy suffers difficulties that would not arise within a fully cooperative context.[11] This could happen in four ways: by endogenous preference formation, adverse selection, discrimination, and externalities.

Endogenous preference formation could be an obstacle to cooperatives if the presence of this type of firms is a necessary condition for the desire to have them. The mechanism might operate at two levels. First, it might influence the desire of the worker to join a cooperative. Secondly, it could affect his desire to live in a cooperative economy. The former might block individual moves towards socialism; the latter might block political movements to the same goal.

Adverse selection is somewhat related to endogenous preference formation. As noted by Louis Putterman, "reform experiments might attract unstable individuals, excessive risktakers, and people lacking in pragmatic orientation."[12] The easy reply would be to say that such people would be attracted only to inherently unviable enterprises. But there is an alternative explanation. In any society, going against the current in any endeavor requires qualities which do not always make for success in it. As Tocqueville pointed out: if people who marry for love in aristocratic societies tend to have unhappy marriages, it is not because marriage founded on love is inherently

---

[10] Cooperative firms usually have lower turn-over rates than capitalist firms. See Thomas and Logan, *Mondragon*, p. 48; Michael Conte, "Participation and Performance in U.S. Labor-Managed Firms," eds. Derek Jones and Jan Svejnar, *Participatory and Self-Managed Firms* (Lexington: Lexington Books, 1982), pp. 213–38. They have lower rates of absenteeism – see Thomas and Logan, *Mondragon*, p. 49ff; Christopher Gunn, *Workers' Self-Management in the United States* (Ithaca: Cornell University Press, 1984), p. 143 – and virtually no production losses from strikes. Other things being equal, all of these should increase productivity. Since other things may not be equal, we must turn to direct studies of productivity. Both the Mondragon cooperatives and the well-known American plywood cooperatives have an excellent record, superior to conventionally organized firms, over a long period (Thomas and Logan, *Mondragon*, ch. V; Conte, "Participation and Performance"). Similar but more ambiguous findings with respect to Britain are given in Derek Jones, "British Producer Cooperatives, 1948–1968: Productivity and Organizational Structure" in Jones and Svejnar, eds., *Participatory and Self-Managed Firms*, pp. 175–98.

[11] Conversely, it could be that a cooperative performs *better* in a capitalist environment than in a cooperative one. It may be able to attract exceptionally motivated workers. It may receive assistance from ideological support groups. And it may be able to take a free ride on the innovative activities of capitalist firms. I neglect these possibilities here, not because I think they are unimportant, but because they cannot help us understand why there are so few cooperatives.

[12] Louis Putterman, "Some Behavioral Perspectives on the Dominance of Hierarchical over Democratic Forms of Enterprise," *Journal of Economic Behavior and Organization*, vol. 3 (1982), pp. 139–60, at p. 152.

unstable, but because it takes a certain stubbornness to go against social conventions and because two stubborn people are not likely to form a happy union.[13]

Discrimination is a more important problem.[14] In the present context, the problem is one of unfair competition – by underselling cooperatives or by blocking their access to credit. Robert Nozick states categorically that the latter obstacle will not arise: "[D]on't say that it's against the class interest of investors to support the growth of some enterprise that if successful would end or diminish the investment system. Investors are not so altruistic. They act in their personal and not their class interests."[15] This statement, while plausible in part, is too strong. The plausible bit is that investors, or capitalists in general, do not act in their class interest. The less plausible claim is that they act out of their purely personal interest. One hundred years ago, another political philosopher supported a cooperative lockmaking firm which was the victim of collusive underselling and similar practices by its capitalist rivals:

> I beg to enclose a subscription of £10 to aid, as far as such a sum can do it, in the struggle which the co-operative platelock makers of Wolverhampton are sustaining against unfair competition on the part of the masters in the trade. Against fair competition I have no desire to shield them ... but to carry on business at a loss, in order to ruin competitors, is not fair competition. In such a contest, if prolonged, the competitors who have the smallest means, though they may have every other element of success, must necessarily be crushed through no fault of their own ... I am now convinced that they ought to be supported against the attempt to ruin them.[16]

Local group interest can override personal interest, as abstract class interest cannot be expected to do. The Wolverhampton employers did not fear the abstract principle of worker ownership: they were afraid of losing their workers, or of having to pay them more. It is impossible to assess even approximately how much such discrimination, or the anticipation of it,[17] has contributed to the difficulties of cooperatives. My conjecture is that it has been quite important.

[13] Alexis de Tocqueville, *Democracy in America* (New York: Anchor Books, 1969), p. 596.

[14] To pursue the analogy, Tocqueville also notes that people who marry for love in societies where this is rare tend to attract hostility, which in turn generates bitterness and unhappiness.

[15] Robert Nozick, *Anarchy, State and Utopia* (New York: Basic Books, 1974), p. 252–53.

[16] John Stuart Mill, as quoted in Jones, *Co-Operative Production*, p. 438.

[17] If a supplier believes that the bank will discriminate against the cooperative, he will accept only cash on delivery. If the bank believes that suppliers discriminate, it will offer credit on less favorable terms. What a firm may not do out of ill-will, it may do out of (possibly unfounded) suspicion of the ill-will of others.

Finally, isolated cooperatives could be disadvantaged (i) by the negative externalities created by capitalist firms or (ii) by their failure to internalize positive externalities generated by themselves. An instance of (i) is the set of "opportunistic externalities" created by the presence of wage labor and investment capital in the economy. In a capitalist environment, successful cooperatives will be tempted to employ some workers on a wage basis in order to increase their ability to adjust flexibly to changes in market conditions. In so doing, however, they may end up losing both the intangible benefits from working in a democratic enterprise and any tangible productivity benefits that may arise from the intangible ones. Also, cooperatives might be tempted to issue outside shares to attract new investment capital, wrongly believing that this will not threaten their identity as cooperatives. These are *opportunistic* externalities because they arise through the permanently available opportunity of hiring labor and capital. They are opportunistic *externalities* because they are negative side effects of the activities of capitalist firms. One might argue that creating opportunities cannot harm anyone, as long as there is no compulsion to use them and as long as other options are not foreclosed. Against this, it seems clear to me that we often refrain from making available to people (including ourselves) opportunities that they might want to exploit out of a desire for short-term gain, although doing so is sure to harm them in the long run.[18]

Another example of (i) is the "collective bargaining externality" identified as follows by Peter Jay: "Insofar as the crucial advantage urged for the labour-managed economy is that it would cause collective bargaining ... to wither away, so dissolving the catastrophic dilemma of high unemployment or accelerating inflation, that cannot be tested by examining the experience of individual co-operatives in a capital-managed economy where the general need for trade union organization and collective bargaining is bound to be strongly felt."[19]

An example of (ii) could be the "entrepreneurial externality" created by cooperatives. In a democratically-run enterprise, entrepreneurially gifted individuals will not just make good decisions: they will also educate their fellow workers. If the workers who have benefited from the education leave the firm and take a job in a capitalist enterprise, their training is made available to other firms free of charge. Even if the cooperative is driven out of business because the private return to its activities is below that of the typical capitalist firm, the social return may be higher for the cooperative than for the capitalist firm. True, capitalist firms are also vulnerable to leakages of this

[18] See my "Weakness of Will and the Free-Rider Problem," *Economics and Philosophy*, vol. 2 (1985), pp. 231–66.
[19] Peter Jay, "The Workers' Cooperative Economy," ed. Alasdair Clayre, *The Political Economy of Co-Operation and Participation* (Oxford: Oxford University Press, 1980), pp. 9–45, at p. 40.

kind, but the problem is more serious for cooperatives because the workers they train are, on the average, more valuable.

Another suggested example of (ii) is the "political externality" created by cooperatives.[20] If members of cooperatives make better political citizens and if civic spirit is a public good, cooperatives generate diffuse benefits not captured by the price mechanism. Against this, one may object, first, that for many people economic participation will reduce, rather than enhance, their participation in political affairs. To paraphrase Oscar Wilde, there are only so many evenings to go around. Second, it is doubtful whether participation in economic decision-making will have these positive effects in other arenas unless it is regarded as valuable in its own right. The spill-over effects of participation are essentially by-products.[21]

Of these, I believe the opportunistic and the entrepreneurial externalities to be the most important ones. The former is illustrated in III below. The latter is somewhat speculative, but I believe it could be quite important. Cooperatives may have a leavening effect in the economy that, precisely because it is not internalized, detracts from their economic success.

I do not claim to have demonstrated that the observed paucity of cooperatives is due to endogenous preference formation, adverse selection, discrimination, or externalities. I have indicated, albeit very briefly, why the explanations usually put forward are not watertight – at least in their present form. It is not proven that cooperatives fail because they are less attractive to workers or less efficient than capitalist firms. And I have tried to make a case for the prima facie plausibility of a different explanation, which emphasizes interaction with the environment rather than intrinsic features of the cooperative. Further implications of that argument are examined in IV below.

II. Varieties of Cooperative Production

What is a cooperative? The answer might seem obvious: a cooperative is a firm in which the workers own the means of production and have full control over all economic decisions. Yet the answer, as it stands, is ambiguous and incomplete. It fails to capture the variety and complexity of existing cooperatives. I shall not here propose a formal definition, but only point to some ways in which cooperatives can differ.

A basic problem is whether to define cooperatives in terms of ownership or in terms of control over decisions. These do not always go together. In Yugoslavia, self-managing enterprises do not have full ownership of their means of production. In particular, they are legally forbidden to disinvest, i.e.,

---

[20] Carole Pateman, *Participation and Democratic Theory* (Cambridge: Cambridge University Press, 1970).

[21] See ch. II of my *Sour Grapes*.

to sell capital goods or let the capital stock run down.[22] In a study of British cooperatives, Derek Jones found that, even in firms in which workers did not own a majority of the shares, they had a majority on the governing board of the firm, because elections follow the principle "One man, one vote," rather than "One share, one vote."[23] Jaroslav Vanek has argued that the optimal arrangement for a cooperative is to be financed fully by outside non-voting equity capital, so that income accruing to workers would come to them *qua* workers and not *qua* capital owners.[24] Conversely, the formal conditions for worker ownership may be fulfilled without effective workers' control. In some of the American firms in which workers have gained a majority of the shares by employee stack ownership plans (ESOP), the unequal distribution of shares among employees prevents the great majority of workers from having any effective influence on decisions. (These firms follow the principle "One share, one vote."[25]) Empirical studies of cooperatives and participation have explored both ownership and control as independent variables, the main dependent variables being productivity, job satisfaction, and earnings.

To consider the ownership problem more closely, we may distinguish between several different structures. The firm can be based (i) wholly on leased capital goods, (ii) on outside non-voting shares, (iii) on voting shares with the principle "One shareholder, one vote," (iv) on voting shares with the principle "One share, one vote," (v) on collective ownership of the firm's assets by the workers, or (vi) some combination of the above. Of these (i), (ii), and (v) are uncontroversially and unambiguously worker-controlled. To assess (iii) and (iv), which are the more frequent forms, we first define the ideal cooperative as one in which all workers and only workers hold equal shares in the firm. The ideal can be subverted in three ways. First, workers may own unequal amounts of shares. In type (iii) firms this is not a source of unequal influence on decision-making, but it can be a source of unequal incomes if workers receive interest on their capital holdings. Second, some shares may be held by outsiders who don't work in the firm. Third, the firm may employ some workers who are hired for a wage and who do not hold shares in the firms. The more one (or several) of these obtain, the more the firm differs from the ideal cooperative type and approaches the capitalist firm.

[22] Stephen Sacks, *Self-Management and Efficiency: Large Corporations in Yugoslavia* (London: Allen and Unwin, 1983), p. 76.

[23] Jones, "British Producer Cooperatives," p. 179.

[24] Jaroslav Vanek, "The Basis Theory of Financing of Participatory Firms," ed. Jaroslav Vanek, *Self-Management* (Harmondsworth: Penguin Books, 1975), pp. 445–55.

[25] For details about ESOP, see Keith Bradley and Alan Gelb, *Worker Capitalism: The New Industrial Relations* (Cambridge: M.I.T. Press, 1983) and Note, "Worker Ownership and Section 8(a)(2) of the National Labor Relations Act," *Yale Law Journal*, vol. 91 (1982), pp. 615–33.

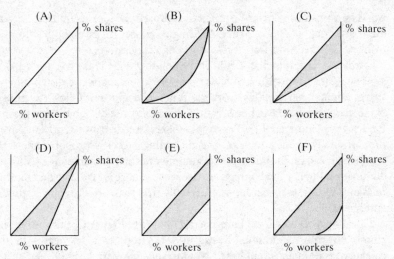

These distinctions can be stated more vividly by constructing a Lorenz curve for cooperatives.[26] In the diagrams above the percentage of workers is shown along the horizontal axes and the percentage of shares in the firm along the vertical. A point (x,y) in the coordinate system indicates that the x percent of the workers with the smallest number of shares have a total of y percent of the shares. The heavily drawn lines represent the Lorenz curves for different types of cooperatives. Figure A represents the ideal system, where all and only workers hold shares and the distribution of shares among them is absolutely equal. Figure B represents a "deviation of the first kind." Here all and only workers hold shares, but some hold more shares than others ("skewed ownership"). Figure C represents a "deviation of the second kind," in which all workers hold shares, but there are some non-working shareholders ("diluted ownership"). Figure D represents a "deviation of the third kind," in which only workers hold shares but there are some non-shareholding workers ("restricted ownership"). Figure E represents a combination of the second and the third type. In Figure F all three deviations occur.

I shall give some examples of these deviations, drawn partly from contemporary practice and partly from nineteenth-century British experience as summarized in Benjamin Jones's monumental *Co-Operative Production* (1894). The first thing to note is that the ideal form, corresponding to Figure A, is relatively rare. Jones asserts that he knows virtually no cooperatives in which all workers are members and all members

[26] This diagrammatic device is taken from N. Mygind, "Are Self-Managed Firms Efficient? The Experience of Danish Fully and Partly Self-Managed Firms." Mimeo, Copenhagen School of Business, January 1985.

workers. Some of the firms he refers to approach the ideal condition, without quite attaining it. Today, the Mondragon cooperatives embody the ideal form, as do the American forest workers' cooperatives.[27]

Deviations of the first kind, corresponding to Figure B, are hard to ascertain, since most sources have no information about the distribution of shares among shareholding workers. When cooperatives follow the rule of "One man, one vote," such inequalities affect only the distribution of income. Under the American ESOP system, shares are distributed to employees proportionally to their salaries, and the voting power is proportional to the number of shares. In practice, this amounts to the management retaining a dominant influence in all important decisions. There is evidence that internal relations in these firms are more conflictive than in ordinary capitalist enterprises.[28]

Deviations of the second kind, corresponding to Figure C, exist but are not among the most common. Benjamin Jones reports a few cases in this category, as does an unpublished Norwegian survey by Karl O. Moene and Tone Ognedal.[29] In his study of British cooperatives, Derek Jones writes that "only in exceptional cases do current workers own a majority of the share capital. In many cases, though, the vast majority of workers are members, and often a majority of members are workers."[30]

Deviations of the third kind, corresponding to Figure D, are quite common. They represent the formation of an aristocracy of labor – of cooperators hiring other workers without admitting them to their ranks. The best-known American cooperatives, the plywood firms of the Northeast, employ hired workers quite extensively.[31] Although some of these are well-paid specialists who are hired for specific jobs, many apparently perform the same jobs as the coop members. Consistently with this practice, the attitude of the members is reported to be individualistic and non-ideological. In nineteenth-century Britain, this organizational mode was quite common and a source of many conflicts, some of which are reported below.

A very frequent case combines deviations of the first, second, and third kind, corresponding to Figure E and Figure F. In nineteenth-century Britain, if we are to believe Benjamin Jones, this was the most common type of cooperative. The main shareholders in most production cooperatives were retail and wholesale cooperative societies. Workers in the cooperatives sometimes had a few shares, but often none at all. Instead, they might get a

---

[27] Gunn, *Workers' Self-Management*, ch. 3.
[28] Note, "Worker Ownership," p. 620.
[29] "Utbyttedeling og medarbeidereie" ("Profit sharing and employee ownership"), Department of Economics, University of Oslo, 1987.
[30] Jones, "British Producer Cooperatives," p. 179.
[31] Gunn, *Workers' Self-Management*, ch. 4.

bonus from profit-sharing schemes.[32] In addition, there were often some individual non-working shareholders. These firms were thought of as cooperatives because they were owned by cooperatives, not because they were operated as cooperatives.

It might appear desirable to be able to say when ownership of a firm has become so skewed, limited, or diluted that it ceases, for all practical purposes, to be a cooperative. For explanatory purposes, this is probably the wrong question to ask. This being a matter of degree rather than of black and white, we should look for a way to measure the distance from the ideal of different firms. One proposal is to use the Lorenz Curve to construct a "Gini index" of the degree of cooperativeness, as the ratio of the shaded area to the area under the 45° line.[33] This has the advantage of allowing us to rank all deviating types along a single dimension. It is doubtful, however, whether this index is correlated with anything else of much interest. In the diagram, firms B, C, and D have approximately the same Gini index, yet we would expect them to behave in very different ways. The quantitative degree of deviation as measured by the Gini index cannot be expected to have much explanatory power. We must consider the qualitative nature of the deviation from the ideal type, as well as the extent of the deviation.[34] The distance is a vector, not a scalar.

Nevertheless, for normative purposes a stipulative definition may be useful. Minimally, in a cooperative the workers must have a majority of votes at the general meeting, whether it is because they hold a majority of the shares, because they are in a majority among the shareholders, or because outside shareholders lack voting rights.[35] Successively stronger definitions

[32] In light of the current interest in proposals for profit-sharing, I list here some of the practices reported by Benjamin Jones. A fixed dividend to shareholders, ranging from 5 percent to 10 percent, was always paid before any further sharing. The remainder was often split three ways: between shareholders, workers and purchasers. Sometimes it was split two ways, between any two of these three groups. The split could be in equal absolute amounts (one-third or one-half of the dividendum to each group) or in proportion to the amounts represented by each group. In the latter case, a stock-flow confusion was often found: shareholders got the same percentage on their capital as workers on their wages. Sometimes, however, shareholders received the same percentage on their dividends as workers did on their wages or workers received the same percentage on the capitalized value of their labor as shareholders did on their capital. Bonuses could be distributed equally among the workers, or proportionately to their wages. In multi-plant cooperatives, the bonus was sometimes calculated on the cooperative as a whole, sometimes on each plant separately.

[33] Mygind, "Are Self-Managed Firms Efficient?"

[34] This is the practice followed by Jones, "British Producer Cooperatives."

[35] The last possibility might seem strange. Why would outside investors be attracted to a firm over which they have no control? For all they know, the cooperative might pay zero dividends year after year. A counterargument (Jay, "The Workers' Cooperative Economy," pp. 14–15) is that the cooperative would be kept in line by the knowledge that it may need to attract capital in the future. Unless present shareholders are paid satisfactory dividends, future investors will not be forthcoming. Knowing this, present investors will not be deterred by the fact that the cooperative is formally free to reduce dividends to zero.

would require that all workers who want to buy shares are allowed to do so, or that all workers are required to be shareholders. My intuition suggests that a firm cannot claim to be a cooperative if it employs, on a permanent basis, some workers who are not allowed to buy shares in the firm. A firm in which labor exploits labor is not a workers' cooperative, but a partnership of small capitalists.[36] This is the criterion I shall adopt in the following section.

III. Obstacles to Cooperative Production

For this survey I shall have to go over again some of the ground covered in I and II above, but from a different perspective and, I hope, without too much repetition. I rely heavily on Benjamin Jones's *Co-Operative Production*, since most other writings focus, understandably enough, on surviving firms that have not (yet) been worn down by attrition or metamorphosed by success into something else.

(*i*) *Legal obstacles.* In Britain, cooperatives were not allowed the – decisive – advantage of limited liability before 1862.[37] In the United States, the National Labor Relations Act, based on an adversarial conception of labor-management relations, poses an obstacle to employee participation and ownership.[38]

(*ii*) *Free-rider problems.* Reading Benjamin Jones, one is struck by the absence of a clear understanding of the free-rider problem in cooperative production among the writers he cites. Advocates of the cooperative system (here, taken in a wide sense that also includes profit-sharing) argued that "they must interest a workman in his work, and they could not do that in a better way than by giving him the result of the extra care, skill and energy he threw into his work" (p. 233); that "it was a right thing to do to give bonus, in order to encourage workers, and get them to feel that in proportion to the amount and quality of their work they would receive benefit" (p. 224); and that profit-sharing was a means of "giving the workmen employed an immediate interest in the progressive extension and security of the undertaking" (p. 574). It is assumed throughout that the workforce behaves like one body, being sensitive to collective rather than to individual incentives.

The reality of the free-rider problem is not in doubt, however. It shows itself most clearly in multi-plant cooperatives. Here, the issue was whether the bonus should be calculated for each plant separately, so that only the workers actually responsible for good results should benefit from them, or whether the same bonus should be paid for the whole concern. The advocates

---

[36] For the idea behind this intuition, see John Roemer, *A General Theory of Exploitation and Class* (Cambridge: Harvard University Press, 1982).

[37] Jones, *Co-Operative Production*, chs. XI–XII.

[38] Note, "Worker Ownership."

of the latter scheme are motivated by a conception of fairness. "You may get an efficient class of workers in the productive departments, and each man do his best; yet through a mistake in the management, they will turn out no profit? Is it fair to give no bonus when this occurs?" (p. 249) Those who argue for a separate bonus, on the grounds of efficiency and proper incentive structures, seem oblivious to the fact that the problem can arise within as well as across divisions. Although the force of collective incentives is larger in small groups that allow members to monitor each other's performance, it takes quite special circumstances for the free-rider problem to disappear altogether.

(*iii*) *Lack of work discipline*. The horizontal structure of decision-making in cooperatives has often been perceived as a weakness. Benjamin Jones (pp. 257–58) quotes from a speech by Sir James Kay Shuttleworth to the Social Science Congress in 1863, where he refers to a cooperative which failed because of

> a desire to introduce into the concern the principle of co-operation to this extent, that the shareholders should have the advantage of the employment of their families in the mills. The immediate effect of that was this, that instead of producing stricter discipline and that close attention to the working of machinery, which was so necessary in cotton mills (and he might mention that the discipline of a regiment was inferior in strictness to that of a cotton mill), at their quarterly or half-yearly meetings most vexatious complaints were made by the workers against the overlookers, and an overlooker who had dared to discharge a worker who was a shareholder, was in extreme danger of being dismissed at the next meeting.

Similar complaints were made by the managing director of the Ouseborn Co-Operative Engine Works Company, to explain the failure of the company:

> The times rules of the Ouseburn, including the rule that each day counts its own overtime, the excessive restrictions upon labour from a section of our men, the small proportion of our apprentices, the frequent discussions and deputations, the excessive amount of overtime required to enable us to finish our contracts, and generally, the want of discipline resulting from the impression that every man was his own master – all contributed to increase the cost of production.[39]

Cooperatives took measures to counteract these tendencies, often bending over backwards to avoid anarchy and nepotism. In some firms, a shareholder

---

[39] Jones, *Co-Operative Production*, p. 454.

could not, while he was a director of the firm, have any relatives employed in it. In many others, workers could not be on the board of directors. More generally, the problem of control has been solved by having indirect rather than direct accountability. Workers "should remember that, although a shareholder, each would have to be subject to a manager as much as if he had not a farthing in the place. All work must be done under the direction of the manager for the time being; there must be one hand, one eye, and one mind. The proper place to complain of a bad manager was to the directors."[40] Admittedly, these solutions were imposed rather than self-imposed. In the nineteenth century, we do not find workers taking steps to prevent themselves from interfering destructively with day-to-day management. In recent cooperatives, including the Mondragon group, constitutional self-binding has been widely used.[41]

   (*iv*) *Organizational problems.* The organization of cooperatives can create problems for their functioning. In the Ouseburn cooperative, the rule was that every employee must be a shareholder. Quite probably, this explains the small proportion of apprentices in the firm, and the subsequently higher costs of production. Another recurring difficulty is well described in the following account of the downfall of the Woverhampton Plate-Locksmiths:

> The main business of the society during the time of its prosperity was, as its name implied, the manufacture of plate-locks, which were large and rather costly articles, yielding a net profit to the society . . . of from 18 percent to 32 percent. A society which had succeeded in obtaining a considerable business of this character easily made large profits; but, with the period of commercial depression which followed the coal famine, the demand for these costly articles ceased. There remained to the society, as a source of income, only the manufacture of common locks, which did not yield more than about 9 percent on the turnover. If the business had been carried on by a private manufacturer, he would probably have discharged the workmen for whom, from the falling off of the demand for plate-locks, he could not find profitable employment, and applied himself to develop the trade that remained. But this would have involved on the body of workers who formed the society an amount of self-sacrifice for which they were not prepared. Instead, they worked for stock, in the hope that the demand would revive. As it did not revive before their resources were exhausted, they inevitably came to grief. Debts multiplied upon them: the best workers fell away.[42]

---

[40] Cited after Jones, *ibid.,* p. 284.
[41] Thomas and Logan, *Mondragon*, p. 28.
[42] Jones, *Co-Operative Production*, p. 443.

The locksmiths, who had survived unfair competition from capitalist firms, were brought down by their inability to adapt to bad times. The converse problem is just as serious: the inability of cooperatives to remain worker-controlled in good times. Successful cooperatives are permanently vulnerable to restriction or dilution of ownership.

An example of dilution is provided by the Rochdale Co-Operative Manufacturing Society, a cotton mill. Although not a cooperative in the full sense, it had a profit-sharing scheme which was very favorable to workers. "[T]he success of the society . . . attracted to it persons who only cared for the eternal 'divi'. These persons brought into the society their money very rapidly for shares, thus raising the number of shareholders from 200 or 300 to 1,400. It was the new shareholding element that swamped the original promoters of what was then called 'Bounty to labour'."[43] After the bonus on wages had been abolished by the new shareholders, a critic wrote that "Working men, in public meetings or elsewhere, must speak with bated breath in denouncing the oppression and tyranny of capitalists, else someone will point to the rapacity of certain working men in Rochdale, who, on becoming employers of labour, took the bounty off their work-people at the so-called co-operative mill . . . Nearly all the anti-bountyites are persons who joined the society after it had become a prosperous and paying establishment . . . It appears to me to be wrong for persons to enter (invade) a society with whose principles they disagree, and then destroy its constitution."[44]

Cooperatives in the full sense of the term run a similar risk if there is a substantial minority of outside shares and if shares are freely traded. Some worker-shareholders might be tempted to sell at the high price which pivotal shares in a successful enterprise would command. It may be difficult to get access to outside capital without inviting takeovers. On reflection, this is not surprising. One can rarely expect to have one's cake and eat it too.

The problems of restricted ownership are illustrated in a number of boot and shoe cooperatives in Northamptonshire.[45] In the original society, all shareholders were workers, but not all workers who wanted to could become members. The frustrated workers set up two new societies, which in turn began to refuse admission to non-members working for them. These non-members promptly formed new societies, one of which stated that "Our object is to give every competent man a chance who is willing to join, which is not the case with the existing society." With this exception, it is quite clear that the members knew they were onto a good thing, which they did not want to share with others. Differences in bonus between members and non-

[43] ibid., p. 262.
[44] ibid., p. 263.
[45] ibid., p. 402ff.

members can have the same result. In the Co-Operative Padlock Society, "members refuse to elect other workers as shareholders, as it would to some extent reduce their bonus, for half the non-members' bonus is retained and added to the reserve fund."[46]

IV. ACCESSIBILITY, STABILITY, OPTIMALITY

I now return to my central question: could it be that the relative absence of cooperatives in capitalist societies is due to obstacles that arise precisely because there are so few of them? I shall focus on the problem of externalities and of endogenous preference formation, but many of the arguments also apply to obstacles created by adverse selection and discrimination.

The main externalities I have in mind are the entrepreneurial and opportunistic ones. Cooperatives are less competitive because they cannot internalize the benefits from training. The presence of investment capital and wage labor in the economy can transform cooperatives by leading, respectively, to dilution or to restriction of ownership. To overcome these externalities, collective action and state intervention may be required.

Let us first assume that all workers have identical preferences, which are, moreover, independent of the economic organization of society. I also assume that a fully cooperative economy is collectively superior to capitalism, in the sense that all individuals would be better off if all worked in cooperatives than if all worked in capitalist firms. Yet workers in an individual enterprise might not find it in their interest to take the first step from capitalism towards market socialism. In addition, they might find it in their interest to take the first step away from market socialism towards capitalism. If the externalities have the first of these effects but not the second, we are in the presence of an Assurance Game: both the inferior and the superior system are stable. The superior system is not, however, accessible through actions taken by individual firms acting out of self-interest. If the externalities have both effects, the situation is that of a Prisoner's Dilemma: only the inferior system is stable.[47] Of the externalities identified above, the problems of training costs and of wage labor would not arise in a fully cooperative economy. The risk of ownership dilution could be more real. Workers might want to invest some of their income in other firms than the one in which they work. Firms might welcome outside capital. As a result, capitalist ownership structures could be reestablished, and the cooperative economy gradually unravel.

If the inferior system is stable, one might want to legislate in favor of the superior alternative, by forbidding or taxing capitalist firms or by subsidizing cooperatives. If the situation has the structure of an Assurance Game, such

---

[46] ibid., p. 481.
[47] David Miller, "Market Neutrality and the Failure of Cooperatives," *British Journal of Political Science*, vol. 11 (1981), pp. 309–29.

legislation could be a temporary measure. After a while, one might reintroduce the freedom to create capitalist enterprises. If the situation has the form of a Prisoner's Dilemma, permanent legislation would be required. Specifically, legal restrictions on trade in shares might be necessary.

Let us now assume, more realistically, that one system is preferred by most but not all people. Assume that a majority of the workers prefers market socialism over capitalism, while the minority has the opposite preference. We also assume, as before, that nobody wants to make the first move away from capitalism. A pertinent question is whether the majority would prefer a mixed system in which they worked in cooperative enterprises and the minority in capitalist enterprises over an all-capitalist economy. Assume, for specificity, that 70 percent prefer a fully cooperative system and 30 percent prefer a fully capitalist one. There are several possibilities.

(1) The members of the majority prefer a system in which 70 percent work in cooperative firms and 30 percent in capitalist firms over a fully capitalist system. This amounts to saying that the cooperative sector is collectively stable.

(1.1) It might also be individually stable, in the sense that once it has reached 70 percent, no members of the majority are tempted to defect. In this case temporary measures would be sufficient to overcome the externality.

(1.2) If the cooperative sector is individually unstable, a universal and permanent ban on capitalist firms might be necessary, unless the members of the cooperative majority could somehow agree to refrain from steps that would reintroduce capitalism.

(1.2.1) The assumption that members of the majority would defect from the cooperative sector is consistent with the notion that in a fully cooperative economy no members of the majority would be tempted to defect. The presence of the capitalist minority would nevertheless, in the absence of legislation, make the situation unravel: the minority would defect, and thereby create an incentive for the majority to defect.

(1.2.2) The assumption is also consistent with the opposite possibility, that capitalist firms are always individually preferred, regardless of the number of cooperative firms in the economy.

(2) Finally it might be the case that the majority does not prefer a mixed economy over the fully capitalist one. It would then have to force its will on the minority to get rid of the externalities. It might do that in case (1.2) as well, since in that situation members of the majority would, in the absence of universal legislation, have an incentive to present themselves as members of the minority. It might want to do so even if there were no incentive problem, since the majority would always be even better off in the absence of the minority.

Consider finally the problem of endogenous preference formation. It is a truism, but an important one, that workers' preferences are to a large extent shaped by their economic environment. Specifically, there is a tendency to adaptive preference formation, by which the actual mode of economic organization comes to be perceived as superior to all others. There are two distinctions to be made here. First, the object of the adaptive preferences could either be the kind of firm the worker wants to join or the kind of society in which he would want to live. Second, the cause of the adaptive preferences could either be the actual economic organization or the set of feasible economic organizations.[48] It might happen, for instance, that in a socialist regime workers would prefer socialism as long as there was a ban on capitalist firms, but cease to do so as soon as capitalism became legalized. A more robust preference for socialism would survive the legalization of capitalist firms.

The presence of externalities, taken by itself, could reconcile the observed paucity of cooperatives with the theoretical superiority of the cooperative form. Endogenous preference formation, taken by itself, could also reconcile the two. The two mechanisms could also interact, to drive in an even bigger wedge between what workers choose and what would be good for them. Initially, the paucity of cooperatives might be due to externalities. If workers' preferences are shaped by what they observe to be the actual economic arrangement, the values of self-realization, participation, and community will be downgraded, making the formation of cooperatives even more unlikely. Conversely, if these values are not strongly held, the ability to resist temptations from the capitalist environment will be correspondingly weaker.

CONCLUSION

The main argument of this paper is apparently inconclusive: we just don't know whether the observed lack of cooperatives is due to their inherent inferiority or to interactions with the non-cooperative environment. From this many will argue as follows. Given our ignorance of the efficiency properties of cooperatives, there is no reason to experiment with this mode of ownership. There are, after all, many reforms that *might* have good properties in the large even if they work out badly in the small – but society cannot go ahead and try them out on the basis of a mere possibility. A strong probability of success would be required, to offset the inevitable costs of transition. I would, however, draw exactly the opposite conclusion.[49] The basic argument for cooperatives is one of economic justice. Unless it can be shown that the

---

[48] For this distinction, see my "Sour Grapes," pp. 121–23.
[49] For an elaboration of the following argument, see my "The Possibility of Rational Politics," *Archives Européennes de Sociologie* XXVIII (1987), pp. 67–103.

cooperative mode is inherently inefficient, it ought to be vigorously pursued. The introduction of universal suffrage provides a useful analogy. Nobody could prove that extension of the suffrage would result in worse decisions, any more than it could be demonstrated that political decision-making would be improved. In consequence, the arguments from justice carried the day.

Political Science, University of Chicago

SOCIALISM AS CLASSICAL POLITICAL PHILOSOPHY*

By Loren E. Lomasky

I. Socialism: Economics or Politics?

A small puzzle: the terms 'capitalism' and 'socialism' initially present themselves as contraries, the one affirming what the other rejects. However, once removed from the dictionary, they function otherwise. The theory of capitalism is very much contained within the science of *economics*. The positive theory of capitalistic institutions, but also its normative superstructure, rest most easily within the language and methodology of the economist. What distinguishes the free market? It is *efficient*; allocation of factors of production are *optimized*; individuals *maximize their utility*; and so on. These are the terms with which justifications of capitalistic production typically begin – begin, and often end.

Socialism is different. Its legitimation is overwhelmingly sought within a discourse proper to *politics*. Proper socialistic organization of the means of production will, one is told, banish *exploitation* and thereby transcend *class conflict*. Socialist society is fundamentally more *democratic* than whatever bourgeois society holds forth because it is a more *egalitarian* order. (And the contemporary identification of the *bourgeoisie*, whatever its origins, has become an act of political classification.) These entirely familiar locutions can hardly be misidentified: they advance political arguments. It is erroneous to view capitalism and socialism as theories in conflict. That cannot be so, because they occupy substantially different domains. The puzzle is why that should have come to be the case.

During the previous century, the divergence in domain was neither so marked nor so thoroughgoing. Marx and his immediate followers appealed to many of the same standards of evaluation that were courted by the classical economists. The failure of capitalism that Marx chronicles in *Capital* was fundamentally an economic failure. In virtue of features endogenous to capitalist production, surplus value would become inexorably more elusive, thus causing the rate of profit to fall and workers to experience increasing immiseration. This process, at its crescendo, would usher in revolutionary

* I have benefited from the comments of Roger Fischer, Richard Hudelson, the editors of *Social Philosophy & Policy*, and participants in the "Capitalism and Socialism" conference (Key Biscayne, November 1987) at which an earlier version of the paper was presented. I am especially grateful to Philip Kain for extended discussion of many of the issues addressed.

change in which the bounds of the old order would burst asunder and a new one take its place. Once the new order had emerged, production would be rationalized on a stable base of workers enjoying the fruits of the value generated through their labor. To speak anachronistically, the failure of capitalism and the success of socialism were traceable to the fact that the latter enjoyed the presence of equilibrating conditions that the former decisively lacked.

Here, perhaps, it is possible to identify a part of the reasons why socialism and capitalism no longer share a ZIP code. The particularly economic argument for socialism has not weathered the past century well. The understanding of *value* on which Marx's analysis rested was being rendered obsolete by the new marginalist economics even as the early editions of *Capital* were rolling off the presses. Men such as Walras, Menger, and Marshall generated analyses intended to demonstrate that market-based economies could prove to be not only stable but, indeed, optimific. Although the followers of Marx remained unconvinced and managed to generate a rival tradition of theoretical economics, they were relegated to a peripheral position of permanent opposition. Within the universities, it was Marshall and not Marx who carried the day. From the perspective of academic economics, the marginalists had rendered socialism marginal.[1]

Unkinder yet than theory was practice. Capitalist institutions obdurately declined to implode in the manner prescribed for them. Instead, they displayed an embarrassing capacity to increase wealth. From time to time, to be sure, depressions depopulated the factories and led to bank runs, and these downturns in the business cycle occasioned new predictions of the death of capitalism. Each obituary notice proved premature. Their authors began to resemble the wearers of sandwich signs who proclaim the imminent end of the world. Nor did the process of capital accumulation coincide, as Marx had predicted, with the impoverishment of the proletariat. Just the reverse: first in England, and then in Europe and the United States, workers experienced increasing standards of living that lifted them into the middle class. This was

---

[1] The debate over the possibility of rational economic calculation within socialism is a late entry into what was once a vigorous contest. Mises and Hayek deny economic rationality to socialism, and Oskar Lange defends it by suggesting that the socialist economy can simulate market structures, and so derive for the planners information equivalent to that which market prices afford. Note the extreme defensiveness of Lange's position: socialist economies achieve rationality only to the extent to which they succeed in replicating a feature intrinsic to capitalism. Although the socialist planning debate still surfaces in the literature, it is the ring around the bathtub, indicating the former presence of a live body. See Ludwig von Mises, "Economic Calculation in the Socialist Commonwealth," and F.A. Hayek, "The Nature and History of the Problem," ed. Hayek, *Collectivist Economic Planning* (London: Routledge and Sons, 1935); and Lange's 1938 response, "On the Economic Theory of Socialism," ed. Benjamin F. Lippincott, *On the Economic Theory of Socialism* (New York: McGraw-Hill, 1964).

not supposed to be, and socialist theorists sought for an explanation. Borrowing from J. A. Hobson, Lenin found it in imperialism. In his revised Marxian account, the exploited workers of Western liberal society were transformed into co-exploiters of a newly-discovered global working class. Duly revised too were scenarios for capitalism's *Gotterdammerung* ; the names of the players were changed, but the final inning of the game was to be the same.

These expectations also proved to be wide of the mark. In the aftermath of World War II, the great colonial empires were dismembered – all, that is, except the Soviet empire. Dozens of newly-minted nations in Africa and Asia were released from the alleged shackles of imperialism. The results did not follow Lenin's recipe. Western Europe and America not only avoided the predicted paroxysm, but instead enjoyed sustained economic growth in excess of that experienced during any previous period in their history. The record for the new nations was mixed. Among those that adopted market institutions, the usual result was strong economic expansion. Capital investment from the industrialized West fueled much of that growth. Economies such as those of Singapore, Taiwan, South Korea, and Hong Kong moved from the realm of the "have-nots" to the "haves." And, of course, the release of Japan from feudal institutions generated the most noteworthy of all the post-war successes.

Concurrently, a different course predominated in Africa, Soviet-"liberated" Eastern Europe, and much of Southeast Asia. Following hard upon the final lowering of the colonial occupier's flag, indigenous rulers proclaimed the establishment of "democratic socialist" regimes. The democratic character of one-party states in which rule was transferred by coup rather than the ballot box is doubtful. But the disdain in which free markets were held is beyond all doubt. Control over the means of production was centralized within state bureaucracies. Some of these regimes took their marching orders from Marx, while others followed prescriptions first penned at the London School of Economics. Although many resisted foreign investment as a recrudescence of the old imperialism, they typically received sizeable capital transfers in the form of low-interest loans and outright gifts. And, despite vast diversity among these new nations, economic results were surprisingly similar. National product, when not actually in decline, was stagnant. Agricultural productivity especially lagged, and countries pos-sessed of some of the world's richest farmland experienced devastating famine. Nor was it noticeably the case that efficiency had been traded off for enhanced equality. Quite the reverse: forced transfers from the countryside to the city, from those who labored with their hands to a "new class" who directed that labor, and from the populace at large to those of the ruling party exacerbated pre-existing inequalities. And, of course, those who starved or were liquidated experienced the ultimate inequity. If the success of socialist economics were to be judged by the performance of those societies that explicitly labeled themselves as "socialist," its credentials would be slim indeed. It is understandable, then, why socialist advocates would seek other territory for their energies than the narrowly economic.

It can, of course, be objected that not all – and perhaps not *any* – of the self-proclaimed socialist societies genuinely instantiate the model of Marx or the Webbs, or whomever is deemed to be authoritative on such matters. The objection has considerable merit. It is doubtful whether countries such as Ethiopia, Cambodia, Guyana, and Tanzania can even be said to *have*, in other than an purely honorific sense, a national economy; in no sense can they be deemed models of anything. However, the objection undercuts itself by prompting the further question: for what reason do regimes whose economies surely come out of no textbook and that are mired in a financial morass adamantly persist in classifying themselves as "socialist"? One presumes that it is not the consequence of a self-conscious decision to seek inclusion among the global economy's most conspicuous under-achievers. Rather, this preferred self-identification demonstrates that, whatever its economic vagaries, socialism possesses a political cachet. For petty tyrants as well as for faceless functionaries of the *nomenklatura*, there evidently is mileage to be gained through espousing a political socialism. And that is to return to the puzzle with which this essay opened: why should what is ostensibly a design for economic order instead present itself under the guise of political theory?

It was suggested above that the practical and theoretical failures of socialist economics is what has prompted the change of address. That, however, does not satisfy as a full explanation. For, to judge by usual standards, socialism is hardly to be reckoned as a political success either. True, half the world's population lives in regimes that are, at least nominally, socialistic. That is not an inconsiderable achievement. But is is not the sort of achievement that one would expect intellectuals to prize. And they are the ones who, far more than a semi-mythologized proletariat, display a notably socialistic class consciousness. The academy remains a venue within which socialism presents itself as a live option and, more specifically, as an option that embodies distinctively political aspirations. One suspects the existence of a deep-seated rationale.

The remainder of this essay suggests that there is such a rationale and that it grows from roots planted deep in the Western tradition of political philosophy. Briefly: socialism incorporates motifs central to the study of politics that germinated in Greece and were preserved throughout the Middle Ages, but which were superseded by the modern revolution in political theory. That is, there is an important sense in which Marx is more truly the legitimate heir of Plato and Aristotle than are Machiavelli, Hobbes,

Smith, and Kant.[2] Whatever the achievements of the modern political scientists – and they surely were many – the rock that they discarded served well the socialist builders of a restored classicism.

II. CLASSICAL ROOTS

The view of politics born in Athens and nutured in various hybrids of Rome and Jerusalem is, of course, far too rich to be neatly pinned down in any brief synopsis. Still, one can identify at least three significant themes that are pervasive within that tradition, that inform its understanding of the nature of the good political order, and that become increasingly attenuated in the modern era. They are:

- A. The attainment of political order is an exceedingly difficult, indeed heroic, task, and requires the full exercise of deliberative wisdom.
- B. Political order flows from the top down.
- C. The making of the polity, both for good and ill, is a making of its citizens in some fundamental sense.

The three themes are too intertwined to present as independent strands within the tradition. The degree to which they so appear in the remainder of the section is an artifact of the exposition, rather than an accurate representation of their status within classical political theory.

A. Politics and Deliberation

Even prior to the emergence of philosophy, the political problem was commonly held to be one so difficult to solve, so rife with prospects of disruption and decay, that the work of designing a constitution was deemed to be fitting labor for a city's god. When men such as Lycurgus or Solon presented to the *polis* a design for political order, they did so in virtue of a wisdom that was more than merely human, and they thereby bequeathed to their compatriots a bounty that entitled them to the veneration of posterity. This conception of the political task survived the transition from *mythos* to *logos*. Nowhere is it more visible than in Plato's *Republic*.

In *Republic* II, Socrates is challenged, abortively by Thrasymachus and more resolutely by Adimantus and Glaucon, to persuade them that the just man's excellence is more than the quasi-voluntary assumption of a yoke of conventional restraints so as to avoid the ire of other men: that is, to show that justice pays. For many bright freshmen, one of their first triumphs in philosophical scrutiny is to notice that Socrates conspicuously fails to meet that challenge – at least during the early hours of the conversation at the house of Cephalus. Instead, Socrates leads his interlocutors into a facsimile of the heroic enterprise: the construction of a constitution for the city. The

---

[2] And with appropriate academic credentials: Marx's doctoral dissertation was on *The Difference Between the Democritean and the Epicurean Philosophy of Nature.*

rationale he provided for the detour is that justice is to be better perceived in the large, as embodied in the city, than as it may exist in men's souls. The bright freshman will see this to be a transparent ruse, but Glaucon's seduction proves to be painless. A well-brought-up youth will naturally be somewhat ill at ease in questioning the rationale for just living, but he will rise to the challenge of taking what is literally a god's-eye view in designing the fabric for a city. Even Socrates's later admission that this is a city that exists in thought – and that very likely can exist *only* in thought – does not stifle Glaucon's ardor. Instead, he is sucked into the philosophical enterprise, drawn into and out of the cave, even brought to the verge of acknowledgment that the political life may not necessarily be the most noble for a man such as himself. It may have a worthy competitor: the philosophical life as represented in Socrates. Some of our bright freshmen reach that position too.

The process of construction of the city's laws is consonant with the tone established in the early books of the dialogue. In pursuit of the supremely good order, established practice repeatedly comes a cropper. When men and women doff their clothes to test each other in the *gymnasium*, they also remove associational patterns that seem to be as deeply rooted in nature as any that characterize human relations. Similarly radical is the rejection of property acquisition by the guardians, including, of course, acquisition of property in a mate and children that are decisively one's *own*, in favor of a communism of the elite. And Socrates's 'third wave', the one that threatens completely to engulf the party in a sea of derision, is enthronement of the paradigmatically impractical philosopher as the city's king. By the time the wave crashes, the party not only tolerates but enthusiastically embraces it. That circumstance reveals, perhaps, more about the conception of political construction motivating the *Republic* than do the various details of the design. The acceptability of turning a settled human order topsy-turvy presupposes the existence of an enterprise unchecked by quotidian restraints, presupposes that the enterprise is, in a fundamental sense, more than human. Socrates enthrones philosophical reason where formerly Athens's gods sat. The tradition he establishes proves to be enduring.

One does not expect to encounter such flights of fancy in Aristotle, and that expectation is fulfilled. Nonetheless, the aspirations of an Aristotelian politics are hardly less lofty than those encountered in the *Republic*. Political science is, Aristotle avers, the architectonic science, the one that orders all other pursuits. Its object is nothing less than the full good for man in society, insofar as it is subject at all to choice. The proper credential for rule is knowledge of the good, coupled with fixed habits of behavior and emotion conducive to effective realization of that which is known.

Aristotle does not endorse the candidacy of philosopher-kings for a position atop the political pinnacle. (Nor does Plato in the considered work of his older, less heroic years, the *Laws*.) However, the qualities of character and intellect that define the philosopher are to be embedded in the political order. For reasons as cogent now as then, Aristotle declines to locate these qualities in one outstanding individual or dominant class; instead, they are to be given effect in the constitution of the city as a whole. In a sense, he follows Plato in taking justice to be more adequately sought on the macro level than in a single human soul. The well-ordered city is one that incorporates the perceptions of its various classes. Within the frame of that mixed constitution, partial visions of the good stand a decent chance – Aristotle is no utopian – of being amalgamated into something genuinely synoptic.

One should also take note of that which is *not* deemed by Aristotle to be sufficient as a source of political authority. Aristotle often displays deference to that which is traditional, and he maintains that longstanding structures possess at least a presumptive claim on citizen's allegiance. If this is to be conservative, then Aristotle is of that persuasion. However, his is not the conservatism of a Burke or Oakeshott who embed the authority of tradition on a time-immemorial fixity that defies rational analysis.[3] Quite the reverse: established practice is said to have weight because it can be supposed to encapsulate the wisdom of great men of previous generations. The supposition is, though, defeasible. To the extent that practices are unable to give a decent account of themselves, they are replaceable by practices that can. Error is not sanctified by age. That is why the most venerable political imprimatur of all, that given by the city's gods, finds so little scope in Aristotle. Philosophers may not be qualified to be kings, but priests do not even enter the political arena.

The classical tradition of politics long survives the demise of Greece and Rome. The priests, to be sure, exact a measure of revenge over the philosophers, but some priests were also philosophers. Despite stormy sessions and even trial separations, the marriage between faith and philosophy proves enduring. In one of the earliest reports of Hellenism's encounter with the Jews, Moses is depicted as a supremely wise lawgiver much on the model of Solon; Clearchus reports that Aristotle himself meets, and is favorably impressed by, a philosophical Jew. Relations do not remain idyllic for long, but the impulse philosophically to square the monotheistic circle remains strong. Tertullian professes an irremediable antipathy between Athens and Jerusalem, but he is branded a heretic by the Church before he dies.

Augustine fares better, and his politics are both Christian and Platonic. The contours of the City of God are, in this life, only dimly to be seen, and the

---

[3] These are thinkers who deliberately set themselves in opposition to the claims of an extreme rationalism in politics. For that reason, it is anachronistic to place Aristotle in their company.

City of Man embraces both the saved and the damned. Despite (or possibly because of) that fact, the statesman's science is not to be despised. Augustine possessed considerable talent for venting his displeasure, and he directs a good measure of it at those who would abandon political order for an anchorite's anarchy. Although no salvation of the world was to be achieved through secular strategies, it was nonetheless critical for God's people that they enjoy the benefits of a stable polity whose *telos* was the full human good. While this good was unlike Aristotle's in possessing a supernatural dimension, it could be realized only in a well-designed social order that kept a tight rein on an only partially redeemed human nature. So, just as much as for Plato and Aristotle, ruling required the exercise of wisdom. The Church possessed authority because the divine *logos* was permanently present in it, and secular powers would establish harmony only insofar as they too partook of a wisdom that transcended the merely human.

During the Middle Ages, it is the classical political tradition more than the Church that is genuinely "catholic." Three warring faiths nurtured philosophers who displayed remarkable similarity to each other and to their ancient philosophical forebears. Maimonides's *Guide of the Perplexed* is dedicated to the "one in a thousand" who possesses the intellect to understand the deepest truths revealed by Scripture: that is, who can understand them in their proper philosophical sense. Since Maimonides holds to the traditional rabbinic view that authority to judge is vested in those learned in Torah, it follows that the few who are philosophers are the legitimate rulers in Israel. The inference is not made explicit in his writings, but its validity does not escape the attention of Maimonide's distinguished rabbinic contemporaries, some of whom would have had his books summarily burned.

Al Farabi, and his philosophical successors in the Arabic world, similarly advocate that philosophical doctrine should be revealed only to the very few who would be capable of properly plumbing its meaning; the remainder were to be fed some version of a noble lie. The Koran was the proper constitution of the nation, but the Koran can be understood on many levels, the deepest of which was the exclusive possession of the philosophers. Consequently, the politics that emerges as a consequence of that epistemological theory is one in which philosophers again are seen as the proper kings.

Medieval Christian philosophy does not, for the most part, issue so striking a brief for rule by the (philosophically) wise, nor does it display as pronounced an esoteric aspect. Nonetheless, Christians too subscribed to the classical ideal of political constructivism mediated by a controlling *logos*. A large component of Christian philosophy was Augustinian, and through him the classical tradition gained considerable currency. To the extent that men such as Aquinas, Dante, Ockham, and Marsilius of Padua venture beyond

Augustinian precedent, they do so within the framework of the classical standards. Though they were not of one party, it is impossible to conceive any one of them invoking a divine right of kings simply in virtue of being king, or maintaining that unquestioning deference should be shown to bishops merely because they sit in a seat once held by Peter. Rather, it is the ability to cognize and give effect to a genuinely common good that most fully establishes the claims of an institution to possess authority. The authority of both kings and bishops is derivative.[4]

B. Top-Down Politics

If construction of a political order requires the deliberate activity of truly exceptional men, it follows as a corollary that a regime's shape is impressed from above. The task of political science is, therefore, to supply to rulers the principles by means of which design can most appropriately be imposed on the raw material of recalcitrant and obdurate human beings. In one notable version, the roles of political scientist and ruler are vested in the same individual. A less iconoclastic version presents the philosopher as tutor and advisor to those whose pedigree qualifies them for rule, but who are not themselves philosophers.[5] Without any wish to minimize the extent of differences between the strategies of Plato and Aristotle, one may emphasize their basic similarity. On both accounts, it is clear that change is to be effected by decree from above.

It is, of course, one thing to decree, and quite another to realize the intended design. Classical political theory very much occupies itself with the task of determining appropriate means for the implementation and enforcement of the regime's chosen policy. Some policies will predictably founder because of unfriendly external circumstance or resistance in the will of human beings, and so political theory is charged to be practical: to determine not only what is the best in some abstract, removed sense, but also what can be implemented. Still, the craft of the architect of regimes is much like the craft of the architect of buildings: it is the builder and not the stones who conceives and carries out the design, even though the nature of the materials constrains what can be achieved.

This conception of a political intelligence that proceeds from above is reinforced by philosophy's encounter with the scripturally-based religions. Israel's law is Torah, and it is received by Moses from God and then brought to the people for their acceptance. Jesus is also deemed to bring a law, a New

---

[4] The influence of Maimonides and Al Farabi within Christian Europe is considerable too, although it was not always politic to acknowledge that influence.

[5] It also is the version more successful in practice. Philosopher-kings are few and far between, but from Aristotle to Henry Kissinger, students of statesmanship have taken it upon themselves to instruct present and aspirant officeholders.

Testament, to those who will constitute a New Israel.[6] God's entitlement to rule is absolute and beyond all question. Those to whom he gives the custodial prerogative to bind and to loose inherit that authority. The political flow-chart is thoroughly hierarchical and unidirectional. This is not to deny that rule can be conceived to be in the service of the ruled. The various scriptures each press that point, and the legitimacy of a regime can quite consistently be held to be a function of the extent to which the people are well-served by their guardians. Nonetheless, the question of *in whom* authority is vested is not the same as that of *on behalf of whom* that authority is to be directed. Just as Plato was aware of the distinction between the shepherd and the sheep, so too were the rabbis and Church fathers.

C. *Remaking human beings*

As noted above, the success of a statesman hinged on the wisdom of his design, and that, in turn, rested on taking an appropriate view of the nature of the raw material at hand. However, it is not a part of the classical conception to concede that the quality of that raw material is fixed. The brazier's material has been refined and processed, and the fineness of the artifacts he produces is consequent upon the extent to which that material has been rendered suitable. Similarly, the artifact that the statesman undertakes to construct will be better or worse, insofar as its components are well- or ill-honed. That means that a political order will represent the order of its citizens' souls. A regime cannot be made good unless men are made good, and it is the end of the state to generate such goodness.

Therefore, Plato's strategy of exploring for justice within the individual by means of finding it in the constitution of the well-ordered city is less extravagant a conceit than it might appear to contemporary readers. We are the recipients of a heritage of liberal politics that conceives things quite differently.[7] For liberals, the excellence of the state is more like the excellence of an umpire of a game than that of the players, or even their coach. The conception of a neutral state apparatus is not, however, easily achieved, and it is quite foreign to the classical political theorists. Socrates does offer an apology for the practice of philosophy in which he urges the regime to allow the philosophers to go unimpeded about their business of examination, but he bases that plea on the proposition that philosophy does not corrupt the citizenry, but rather improves it. That is why he merits a lifetime pension from the city, and honors on the scale of those accorded to Olympic victors. The Athenian jurors see things differently and condemn

---

[6] That Moses receives the Law on Mt. Sinai and that Jesus's most involved sermon is delivered from a mountain are nice realizations of the top-down metaphor. Nor does it seem likely that the topography is purely coincidental.

[7] This receives further discussion in Section III, below.

him to death. Both sides, however, take it for granted that it is the proper business of the city to see to the quality of the moral instruction afforded its young, and, more generally, to protect the city from the rot that necessarily must follow upon any worsening of the character of the individuals of which it is constituted.

In the *Republic*, Socrates promises to respond to Glaucon's challenge to demonstrate that justice pays, but he precedes that demonstration with an extended episode of city-building which, in turn, incorporates a lengthy discussion of the proper curriculum for its citizens. Education is important for all, but the pedagogy is not one of "mainstreaming." Those who are inherently less educable are fed a diet of myth. The myth lies, but is also noble in virtue of preparing its receivers to accept the rule of the portion of the city that is most fit to exercise that capacity.

The regimen for future guardians is spelled out in far more detail. It includes attention to physical exertions that will harden the soul and the musical modes that will allow it, nonetheless, to remain gentle. Instruction in mathematics informs the intellect of a realm of being higher than that to which the senses afford entry, and the capstone of the educational process is immersion in philosophy itself. That, however, is to come only when the individual has attained sufficient maturity to be benefited rather than harmed by it. Socrates thus concedes that the Athenian jury is indeed correct when it judges that philosophy is not an innocuous thing, but is rather entirely capable of corrupting the young. He also concedes that it is the proper business of the regime to ensure that its citizens do not suffer such injury.

The paramount significance to politics of character development is demonstrated by the remarkable extent to which customary practices are to be disrupted for the sake of improving souls. Poetry possesses the capacity to move and inspire people, but poetry does not contain within itself knowledge of the good toward which persons should aspire. The poet, therefore, is potentially a subversive figure, and so Homer and Hesiod are exiled beyond the city's walls. The gods and heroes of the *polis* must serve to edify. To the extent they do not, they also are banished. Love for the particular spouse and children that are one's own powerfully motivates individuals to act on behalf of a good that is personal rather than common; therefore, mating of the guardians is manipulated by an arcane formula rather than being allowed to respond to natural erotic pulls, and children become the common patrimony of the city. Similarly, private property intrinsically erects a barrier between that which is *mine* and that which is the possession of *others*, and so its acquisition is banned. Finally, the construction of the ideal city is proclaimed to be unattainable unless the raw material can be processed in mint condition so all persons above the age of ten are discarded.

Aristotle, like Plato, views politics as an educative science. His quarry is the good regime rather than that which is ideal, and the methods he commends are correspondingly more modest than those of the *Republic*. He insists, however, that candidate-students of political science must be well brought up, else their subsequent instruction will be in vain. They must already have been habituated to temperance, courage, moderation, high-mindedness, and the other virtues requisite to the proper exercise of rule. And though, unlike the *Republic*, the family remains as the arena within which primary education is carried out, it is the task of the city to ensure that conditions necessary for its general success obtain.

The higher education of bright scions of good families builds on this base. They are supplied the theory which will enable them to act efficiently to bring about the good that they have already been conditioned to prize. Political deliberation is over means to ends that, in turn, are grounded in the nature of human beings as both rational and social animals. There exists a natural end for man and, more particularly, for men in society, but human beings do not mechanically gravitate to their *telos* in the unthinking fashion of the lower organisms. Because they possess the capacity of voluntary choice, they must be directed to prize that which is good and to shun that which is inferior. Political science incorporates both the study of means conducive to appropriate ends and, more fundamentally, the study of how to develop in persons right beliefs and emotions concerning just what the appropriate ends are.

Christian philosophy entirely subscribes to the educative function of civil society, but it superimposes on this base distinctive theories of the nature of the transformation required and the means requisite to its attainment. Human beings have a nature that dictates their proper end, but it is a fallen nature. Thus, the regime's task becomes more modest than that envisaged by Greek philosophy, and also more audacious.

It is more modest in that no radical transformation of the soul is attainable via natural means. Contra Pelagius, Augustine declares that though man has fallen through the exercise of his free will, he cannot rise by it. No human politics or educative program is more than superficially efficacious; only the supernatural infusion of God's grace affords a fundamental improvement of the individual's condition. And it is through individuals rather than nations or the human race as a whole that grace is operative – at least in this in-between time. People can achieve redemption, but states can never be more than mediocre.

It is audacious in that the ultimate transformation envisaged by the theologians is more radical even than that contemplated by Plato. Human beings are to be made truly whole, thus triumphing over all the infirmities to which they are heir, including death itself. Politics cannot effect that transformation, but it can supply the backdrop within which the grace-conferring sacraments are extended. There is something to be rendered *both* to God and to Caesar, because the temporal power provides an order and stability within which God's Church can proceed about its proper business. Providence affords a place to priests and also to princes. In this manner, the nexus between transformation of the individual and the maintenance of proper political order is preserved within the tradition of Christian political philosophy.

Neither Judaism nor Islam adopts a view of human nature as fallen. However, each acknowledges the fundamental importance of education as transformation of character. Their philosophers, not unexpectedly, supply a philosophical twist to the conception. As noted previously, Al Farabi adopts the Platonic picture of the ideal ruler as philosopher, and, as such, the ruler serves in an educative capacity. Maimonides develops a theory of prophecy in which the prophet's enlightenment is the natural fruit of completeness in body and spirit, rather than an extraneous supernatural gift that contravenes nature. That is, prophetic enlightenment is literally an *ordinary* rather than an extraordinary state of man. It is, though, a state to which only a few attain – just as only a few achieve genuine philosophical reflectiveness. And as the prophet educates and thereby shapes those less gifted, so too does philosophy mold the intellect of those who can receive it. Correspondingly, politics is the science of providing doses of instruction measured to the capacity of the individual who is to receive it, with the goal of maximizing the potential of each to be governed by that which is truly highest. Neither Plato nor Aristotle would demur.

III. The Modern Turn

From the perspective that hindsight affords, the early modern political philosophers may be judged to have erred on a number of points great and small. However, their self-understanding as having turned sharply from their classical predecessors is not to be denied. Where modernity differed is a vastly complex matter that cannot be reduced to a few pages of description. Still, it is apparent that each of the three bases for political theorizing described above is, in one way or another, profoundly modified or decisively rejected by Machiavelli, Hobbes, and their successors.

Nowhere is the shift more marked than in their understanding of what it is to found a state. That which for the Greeks is a supremely heroic act is, in the telling of the moderns, born of desperation, and motivated by a tightening in the belly rather than a vision to stir the imagination.

The state of nature varies in its loveliness among Hobbes and Locke, Rousseau and Kant, but for each it is the problem for which civil society is the solution. Escape requires a certain elemental calculative skill, but no great wisdom or vision of a transcendent good. That is why all together can contract themselves out of the state of nature, and need not wait for a god or god-like person to rescue them. Political constructivism acquires a democratic veneer that it never enjoyed even in democratic Athens. Within it, there is little place for the heroic temperament. Nobility is transformed from solution to snare. It is the universality of the threat of violent death as the strongest human motivator that provides for Hobbes the basis of the departure from nature into civil society. The classical conception of the hero was, of course, the man whose love of honor leads him to scorn death.[8] Because war holds out prospects of glory that peace does not, he will not easily be induced to renounce his prerogatives so as to secure from the commonwealth an equal share of physical protection. Accordingly, Hobbes banishes honor from political constructivism, and this banishment becomes an enduring feature of liberalism. From the sixteenth century onward, the erection of political structures is portrayed as stemming from man's animal instinct for survival, rather than an urge for transcendence.

A corresponding sea change is seen in the conception of the rationality that will provide the instrument for political construction. Without rationality, no progress can be achieved; fortunately, its attainment is no great thing. To be rational is no more than to be prudent, and the goods that define the domain over which prudence is to operate are themselves drastically pared down from the listing that standardly would have been supplied by the ancients. To be prudent becomes, in essence, to act to avoid death, and items are categorized as goods or bads insofar as they conduce towards survival. Peace is the *sine qua non* for human beings, and a regime that effectively ensures the maintenance of peace thereby possesses rightful authority. All accouterments to civil society that do not bear directly on the statistics entered in mortality tables are strictly irrelevant to the legitimacy of the regime.

A Form of the Good or Aristotelian natural human end have been left far behind. Their place has been usurped by instinctual desire and calculative cunning. This modest basis for political stability may lack the luster of the picture drawn by Plato in the *Republic*, but for Machiavelli and Hobbes modesty is indeed a virtue. The loftiness of the classical vision ensured its unattainability, and in politics practicality is everything. Constructing and perpetuating even the modest state is not an easy thing. Not everyone calculates well, and the usually prudent person can be swayed by a forceful present desire. The problem is basically one of imaginative vividness: that which is distant presents its claims less forcefully than that which is at hand. One pressing task for politics is to make long-term bads appear as more to be

---

[8] The philosophical counterpart to an Achilles is a Socrates who will not be dissuaded by threats of death from the life he takes to be highest and best.

avoided than short-term goods are to be pursued. This can be done if the
majesty of the sovereign is impressed on the mind of the subject, so that the
sovereign's justice inspires awe and fear. Fundamentally, then, the faculty
that holds desire in check and molds it appropriately is imagination, not
intellect. Political order requires only a minimum level of calculative skill
coupled with vivid present apprehension of future prospects. What it does *not*
require is directedness by apprehension of an external standard of value.
That is why, summarizing two centuries of modern theory, Kant can claim in
Perpetual Peace that

> It only remains for men to create a good organization for the state, a
> task which is well within their capability, and to arrange it in such a
> way that their self-seeking energies are opposed to one another, each
> thereby neutralizing or eliminating the destructive effects of the rest
> . . . so that man, even if he is not morally good in himself, is
> nevertheless compelled to be a good citizen. As hard as it may sound,
> the problem of setting up a state can be solved even by a nation of
> devils (so long as they possess understanding).[9]

Constraining one's vision is prescribed not only for the ruled but also for
the ruler. Princes, Machiavelli explains, can fail for any number of reasons,
not all of which are under their control. *Fortuna* is not so much a cruel
goddess as one who is indifferent. However, their failure becomes predictable
if they are distracted from the business of rule by standards external to that
task. Princes can be cruel and they can be kind. If they are to keep their
regime intact, however, they must dispassionately utilize cruelty and
kindness as instruments appropriate to that end, rather than from any
independent attraction to cruelty and kindness for their own sake. Successful
princes will amass glory and power and riches (not inconsiderable fringe
benefits) but if they make the pursuit of glory, riches, and power their chief
aim, the riches will be forfeited along with the domain. Most notoriously,
Machiavelli counsels that preoccupation with the good of the philosophers or
the revealed Word of God is inimical to successful governance. A prince must
choose: either to *be* a prince or to dedicate himself to the sacred. The point is
that it is a genuine choice, and one is guilty of self-deception – as well as
destruction of the regime – should one act as if it is not. The revisionary
tradition for which Machiavelli is so notable a spokesman has little truck with
a politics of philosophical star-gazers; it is rather firmly rooted in the dirt.

It is not remarkable, then, that the second standard of the classical
tradition, the conception of top-down political order, also comes under

---

[9] In *Kant's Political Writings*, ed. Hans Reiss (Cambridge: Cambridge University Press, 1970), p.
112.

attack. As previously noted, the seeds of that attack are sown by Hobbes when he hypothesizes political origins as emerging from the combat of all against all. It is to miss the point to ask who in the state of nature is the prime actor in creating civil society; the various struggling egos are interchangeable, and each is motivated in parallel with all others to devise a means of egress. The sovereign emerges as the capstone and guarantor of the primal compact, not as its initiator. The Lockean covenant reflects an individualism more bound up with accumulation and safeguarding of property than with a concern for simple physical security, but it too explains politics as emerging from below, from elemental desires common to all men, rather than as the fruit of revelation or a stunning triumph of intellect.

Subsequent developers of the liberal tradition go further. Mandeville explains in *The Fable of the Bees* how private vices become public virtues. Needless to say, the transformation is not the product of any deliberate intervention by men or God, but rather exhibits the sort of order-conferring mechanism that the natural philosophers were busy finding in matter. Hume criticizes the social contract theorists for their naiveté in supposing that deliberate concern to better one's condition could culminate in a political convocation in which the Articles of Peace are fully formulated, signed, and notarized. Rather, justice is an artificial virtue (though no less a virtue for that) whose particular conventional expressions in society are not the product of any anterior design, but that persist because of their functionality.

Adam Smith extends his friend's insight to a considerable portion of the phenomena encountered by the political economist. In the *Theory of Moral Sentiments*, Smith reflects that the beggar sunning himself by the side of the road enjoys a happiness equivalent to that of the lord of the manor. The quest for opulence as a means toward happiness is almost entirely vain, but its unintended consequence is the provision of a livelihood for thousands. The best-known expression of this theme is his statement in *The Wealth of Nations* that the investor in domestic industry

> neither intends to promote the publick interest, nor knows how much he is promoting it. By preferring the support of domestick to that of foreign industry, he intends only his own security; and by directing that industry in such a manner as its produce may be of the greatest value, he intends only his own gain, and he is in this, as in many other cases, led by an invisible hand to promote an end which was no part of his intention.[10]

Despite the obtuse remarks of several critics, Smith is not suggesting the existence of some spectral intervener. Quite the reverse: the argument

---

[10] IV.ii.9, p. 456, in the Glasgow Edition (Oxford: Oxford University Press, 1976).

clearly is that deliberate intervention is unnecessary for the generation of many social desiderata. Moreover, as he proceeds to note, such intervention will often yield the opposite of its intended object: "I have never known much good done by those who affected to trade for the public good." The "system of natural liberty" receives a hearty (though not exceptionless) endorsement, because the disorderly anarchy of uncoordinated behavior by a multiplicity of self-interested individuals is capable of generating a higher degree of social order than can a deliberate quest for that order. The idea has a flavor of paradox, and Smith enjoys displaying that paradox in a host of different contexts. The technique probably served the schoolmaster well in a classroom of easily distracted boys. However, from the perspective of the modern science of politics, emergence of an unintended and undesigned social order is no more paradoxical than is the observed order of the astronomical bodies.

Kant is fully aware of the turn that has been taken by the moderns and here, as elsewhere, he attempts to effect something of a synthesis. The mechanistic processes of nature are, he writes in *Perpetual Peace*, the guarantors of peace. Man's inhospitable drives play themselves out on a stage of discord, but their ultimate product is international harmony. The term we are drawn to apply to this goal-orientated and functional nature is *providence*, but, for reasons developed at length in the First Critique, providential design can neither be observed nor inferred. Practical reason may be driven to postulate such noumenal agency, but its existence lies strictly outside of science. So for the human sciences, the status of emergent order is fundamentally the same for Kant as it is for Smith. The irrationality or non-rationality of war, birth, death, the carrying of wood by ocean currents to unforested Arctic coasts, and so on combine to populate the entire earth, create the exigency from which civil society arises, and, ultimately, achieve the goal that would have been the anterior will of a supreme moral consciousness. There is, however, no such supreme consciousness – at least not within the purview of political science. In its place, we find mechanism.

It is not that private vices have become public virtues; for Kant, virtue is intrinsically private. However, mechanistic nature and virtue intersect on the plane of history and, in somewhat Mandevillean fashion, it is vice that catalyzes the evolution of the conditions under which virtue can most fully be realized. Conflict is the motivating engine of a pacific civil society, and it is only within such society that the naturally necessary human desire for happiness finds harmony with the Good Will. A conception of moral grandeur thus enters Kant's political philosophy, but from the rear (so to speak). Rather than being the premise from which political order is derived as the conclusion, it is the (unintended) consequence of political processes that are themselves without any moral standing. Despite Kant's inclination toward synthesis, the distance he has traveled from the classical theorists is apparent.

No extended examination is needed to provide evidence that the third standard of the classical tradition is also abandoned by the moderns. It is abundantly clear from a reading of Machiavelli and Hobbes that the fixity of human nature is taken as a given. Rather than standing as an obstacle to the political constructivist, it makes possible the development of a genuine political science. Because humans are what they are and not some other thing, careful observation and reflection will make possible the discovery of universal and general laws of behavior that can serve as grist for the regime's mill. For such a conception of political science, protean man would be an embarrassment. So it is not surprising to observe Locke's primitive accumulators motivated by entirely the same principles that inform the activities of the seventeenth-century London bourgeoisie.

The moderns are not fazed by the fact that the human nature whose constancy is postulated would have appeared unlovely to the Greeks. Fear of death and desire for wealth admit of easier manipulation in the service of a public good than do the love of glory or an obdurate quest for salvation. That is not entirely to abandon the case for virtue, but the virtues deemed by the moderns appropriate for a political order take on a distinctly middle-class flavor, and they serve antecedently-given desires. Reason, Hume tells us, is not a faculty for the discovery of an independent good, but is and ought to be the slave of the passions. As such, it can do real service for the good.

Virtue may be in short supply, but the predominant response of the liberals was not to place all one's political chips on a major augmentation of the stock, but rather to economize on the amount of virtue demanded by political order. We do well in erecting political institutions, Hume suggests, to operate on the assumption that each man is a knave and proceed accordingly to neutralize their knavery. This is a lesson taken to heart by the framers of the American Constitution. Madison emphasized that they were neither legislating for angels nor possessed the power to transform men into angels. What wise legislation could accomplish, however, was the setting of faction against faction on a plurality of levels; this way, the common good would not be entirely dissolved by the victory of any one party.[11] And Kant, as noted above, believed that the political problem was solvable even by a race of intelligent devils – provided, that is, that they were intelligent. Given this consensus, the classical concern for the transformation of rude man seems very distant.

[11] In other respects, of course, the framers self-consciously saw themselves as heirs of a classical republicanism. Nor are they the only creators of modern liberalism with a foot in the camp of the ancients. The argument of this section is that modernity displays a decisive break with the classical political tradition, not that classical themes are entirely and in every respect spurned by all successors of Hobbes.

The consensus, though, was not complete. Here, as elsewhere, Rousseau stands as the conspicuous exception. In his writings, both the descent into civil society and the ascent from its current pathology entail the reshaping of man (and woman – here, too, Rousseau is distinctive). The political story as he tells it is, at the same time, a morality play and a tale of transfiguration. Its plot is not, however, simple. The noble savage is indeed noble, but is also savage. Civil society puts a blot on natural nobility, but it is also the antidote to savagery. Therefore, Rousseau's account of the emergence from the state of nature is not an unalloyed triumph as it is in Hobbes, Locke, and Kant, but neither is it a secularized rendition of the Fall. There is a tension here between the natural self and the civil order, and there is a related tension between the individual and the general will. Rousseau is, however, too thoroughly a modern to adopt Plato's solutions – or, that is, too thoroughly a modern to embrace them entirely.[12] He prefigures, though, a reaction to modernity that incorporates many strands of the classical conception.

IV. Marx's Classical Politics

There are many socialisms, and there are even many Marxes: each commentator has one. It would be foolhardy to claim to have detected the *real essence* of the socialist persuasion. Still, if one finds in Marx, and those directly or indirectly under his spell, significant passages in which the modern liberal conception of a political science is decisively rejected, and if one finds other passages (or the same ones) which seem to offer a reprise of themes continually played within the classical tradition, that circumstance will itself be suggestive. What it may suggest is that the capital on which socialist theory draws its annuity was laid up by the ancients. Because that capital is fundamentally political, one is able to understand why socialism today survives, and even thrives, as a mode of political discourse.

The suggestion may appear to be a non-starter. Marx, it will be objected, is thoroughly to be placed among the moderns; indeed, he belongs there on grounds sketched out in the previous section. Whether via the mediation of Hegel or through some other means, he learned well the lessons of Smith and Kant concerning the workings of the invisible hand. His rendition of the history of the accumulation of capital does not feature feudal and then capitalist villains whose exploitation of the working class is deliberately contrived. Instead, the main actors are material forces of production that exhaust each possibility latent in themselves before being superseded by the subsequent historical stage. Further, the laws that govern material production are laws of *matter*, not statements of the intention of individual

[12] The Rousseauian bringer of the constitution bears striking resemblance to the philosopher-king, and also to Greece's legendary law-givers.

holders of property. The beauty of *Capital* is its intricate construction of an array of forces which, when let loose, play themselves out to a denouement displaying the inevitability of a Greek tragedy. How can *this* Marx – reference in the previous sentence aside – be seen to bear any affinity to the political philosophers of Athens?

The answer is not to maintain that there are two Marxes – that's old hat – but to disentangle two divergent strands in his expositions. One frames the tale of the rise and fall of capital, and is very much at home within the disciplinary structure of a science of political economy arising from modern philosophy. If this were the extent of his contribution, however, the visible presence of Marx today would probably be roughly the same number of textbook footnotes enjoyed by other defunct nineteenth-century economists of similar stature – Nassau Senior, for example. The other strand runs through Marx's epistemological and cultural analyses, rendering them important political documents. Indeed, this second strand is nowhere absent from his work and stands, for example, as the grand finale to the story told in *Capital*. It has enlivened socialist advocacy, and continues to animate it despite the demise of nearly all the economic pure theory that Marx himself regarded as his truly important scientific contribution. The second strand is classical in its pedigree.

Nowhere is the classical flavor more pronounced than in Marx's discussion of *ideology*. An ideology is, of course, political: it is the congeries of myths that the ruling element creates in order to justify its dominant position. But it also contains an epistemological element; or rather, it is the epistemological component that lends the concept the distinctive political bite it possesses. Crucially, an ideology *falsifies* nature; it represents what is not real as being real in order to afford sanction to a social order that is, in a clearly pejorative sense, unnatural. The deception that an ideology incorporates need not have been constructed with malice aforethought. Unlike Plato's tellers of the Noble Lie, the propounders of the regnant ideology may be, and typically are, as much in the grip of the image it presents as are its recipients. The essential point, though, is that an ideology (i) functions to disguise nature and (ii) does so in the material interest of the dominant class.

There exists no more graphic depiction of the ideology-governed society than that provided by Plato at the beginning of *Republic* VII. The prisoners within the cave are chained to a shadow-world distant from the natural order. One is tempted to say that they are *alienated* from both their own human nature and the natural world of which they are properly part. They are, however, unaware of this divorce. Were they compelled to abandon the familiar chains and forced into the light, they would suffer pain. They have been conditioned to be comfortable with their shadows, and to take delight in charting their course on the walls. An attempt to release the captives from this condition of epistemological deformity would elicit resistance from both the prisoners and their shadow-casting masters. Nothing less than a *revolution* would suffice to bring about the destruction of the regime of the cave. That revolution would be simultaneously political and epistemological, because release from the cave is release from the grip of its shadows.

For Marx, the sway of ideology is the reign of the cave or, more exactly, the reigns of successive versions of the cave. Each cavern differs, to be sure, in notable ways from the one from which it proceeds, but all are exactly alike in segregating man from the reality proper to his species. Therefore, atop the historical progression of the journey from cavern to cavern, there stands the pivotal last step of ultimate emergence from the cave, of the transition from earlier forms of society to communism.

It is important to note that the transition is, for Marx, truly epochal and not merely another variation on a tired theme. Escape from capitalist exploitation is not merely the escape to higher wage levels or full employment; it is the escape from ideology itself. All previous systems of production justified themselves on the basis of a falsehood; with the coming of socialism, man will finally return to the light and see himself and his world for what it really is. Communism is not another but better – i.e., more humane, more egalitarian, fairer – ideology, but rather represents the ultimate vanquishing of ideology. Capitalism is to communism not as less attractive is to more attractive, but rather as myth is to science.

The ideologist's claims lack epistemic weight because they are informed by interest rather than by correspondence to what is the case. Were Marx to identify himself as the propounder of some other, perhaps more "progressive," ideology, then he would have rudely hoisted himself on his own petard. Marxian doctrine would be one more shadow on one more wall. Clearly, that does not represent his self-conception. Rather, he claims on his own behalf a liberation of truly heroic proportions. Prometheus was unable to release himself from Zeus's chains, although he retained his defiance as the eagle tore at his flesh. Marx too enjoyed a goodly quota of defiance, but he possessed more than defiance and thus did Prometheus one better. By *understanding* the nature of ideological chains, he slipped their bonds. "The philosophers have only *interpreted* the world, in various ways; the point, however, is to *change* it:" yes, but to construe Marx as hereby rejecting the philosophical quest for enlightenment is widely to miss the mark. The philosophers' interpretations were impotent because they were refracted through ideological spectacles they unwittingly wore. *The point* is to change the world by eliminating the distortions that hide from one's view a clear perception of what that world is and what it can be. Plato, Aristotle, Locke, Kant, Hegel: each had conspicuously failed to achieve the clarity of vision necessary to the task. Marx, however, had finally succeeded in removing the flawed lenses. That is why his was a *scientific* doctrine rather than ideology, a light that shone where previously only shadows reigned.

For Marx as well as for Plato, the shift from politics-as-usual to a regime grounded on accurate apprehension of that which is true is the crucial step that lies before man. And like Plato, he held that governance by informed reason was the *telos* of man in society. However, it would be a mistake to conclude that Marx is to be accounted a nineteenth-century Platonist. They are separated by many factors, not least of which is Marx's prodigiously greater optimism. For Plato, the likelihood that a king would become philosopher or (less likely still) that a philosopher would become king was a small chance indeed. And that is why he has Socrates confess to Glaucon that the city they had laboriously constructed might well have its only existence in their minds' eye. That may not be the solution to the political problem, but imagination has its charms too. Those charms are, however, insufficient for Marx. Rather, he claimed for his version of the regime of unchained reason the force of historical necessity. Perhaps he did so because he had clear evidence in hand that at least *one man* (two, if Engels can be counted) had escaped the cave. Or perhaps it was the conviction that human history is as much the object of causally deterministic science as are the motions of particles in a vacuum that inspired his confidence. Whichever, the outcome that Plato held (Sicilian false steps aside) to be only the noetic consolation for imperfect material existence Marx took to be the inevitable consequence of the operation of the laws of matter.

For Marx, therefore, as for Plato (here taken only as an especially pure case of the classical tradition in politics), the possibility of constructing a regime that genuinely enjoys legitimacy is also the possibility of having genuine knowledge of a legitimacy-conferring natural order. To know the truth is to set oneself free, because knowledge is the bursting of ideological shackles. Such a politics of liberation is something quite other than the careful accountancy prescribed by Machiavelli, Hobbes, Locke, and their successors. It is, rather, the stuff of which heroes are made. *Marx Agonistes* is the propaedeutic to mankind unchained.

It is easier to establish the proposition that socialist politics evinces a heroic leap into instantiation of an order that reason commends than to demonstrate that it is also a top-down politics. Marx, for reasons that are evident, is precluded from advancing any such conception.[13] If the historical processes

---

[13] At least not in explicit fashion. One juncture at which the usually voluble Marx is strangely reticent concerns his own role in the unfolding of the historical drama. Would events have transpired toward the same end if he, himself, had fallen under the wheels of a runaway carriage? The logic of the doctrine suggests the affirmative, but Marx surely does not press the point. Indeed, the vigor with which he advances his own claims to be the proper expounder of socialist writ suggests rather the opposite.

that proceed from Asiatic despotism to advanced capitalism possess genuine inevitability rooted in the nature of material existence, the transition from capitalism to communism must also proceed from a material floor upwards (or so the logic of the argument seems to indicate). Accordingly, Marx mostly espouses a socialism free of philosopher-kings.

It is, then, well worth observing the extent to which this aspect of the doctrine of the Master is honored more in the breach than in the observance. Marx himself does so when he alternately thrills to the defiance of the Parisian communards and dismisses their building of barricades as premature. The disciples are even less constrained. If the proletariat displays insufficient zeal to set itself on the course that history dictates, is it not appropriate for those possessed of history's road map to set themselves apart as the proletariat's vanguard? Had Lenin not done so, he would now be safely interred in some Swiss graveyard, while Russia would be continuing on a slow progress from feudalism to capitalistic modes of production. When a dictatorship of the proletariat displays internal tension, it is the proletariat that comes a cropper.

Those socialists not firmly committed to a metaphysics of Marxian materialism are even more prone to request the emergence of a vanguard – and to nominate themselves for that status. The Webbs *et al.* were not loath to suppose that an enlightenment sufficient to move Britain (and the world?) might filter down from Fabian redoubts. Frankfurt critical theory saw itself as performing a catalytic function by irritating the soft tissues of the dormant masses with Marxist (and Freudian) insights until they would be spurred to relieve the itch with a mighty scratch. Habermas criticizes advanced capitalistic society precisely for its tendency unreflectively to accept the deliverances of bottom-up economic and technological processes:

> In the face of research, technology, the economy, and administration – integrated as a system that has become autonomous – the question prompted by the neohumanistic ideal of culture, namely, how can society possibly exercise sovereignty over the technical conditions of life and integrate them into the practice of the life-world, seems hopelessly obsolete. In the technical state such ideas are suited at best for "the manipulation of motives to help bring about what must happen anyway from the point of view of objective necessity."[14]

Against this working of "objective necessity," Habermas commends a dialogic structure designed to substitute rational reflection on each aspect of the warp and woof of technological society. For society to be rational and

---

[14] Jurgen Habermas, *Toward a Rational Society*, trans. J.J. Shapiro (Boston: Beacon Press, 1970), p. 59.

humanistic, it must embody deliberate design, and each citizen must enjoy full and equal status as co-participant. This may not be Marx, whose personal practice featured little commitment to dialogic co-participation, but it has thoroughly infused the contemporary socialistic critique of a "mindless" capitalism. The Habermasian inference seems validly to follow from socialist premises. If socialism represents the long-delayed ascendancy to conscious- ness of that which has been disguised by ideology, then what could represent a fuller or more satisfactory consummation than an ascendancy that is appropriately democratic and universal? It is the image of sociality in which *everyone* cohabits at the top, *everyone* pronounces the dictates of reason. The power of this ideal is exhibited by its endurance in the face of a distinctly contrary socialistic practice.

Finally, it is easy to identify within socialist thought the classical theme of a politics committed to the personal transformation of the individual. Marx tells us that man's species-nature, surrendered to the division of labor, will be reclaimed with the coming of socialism and the concomitant transcendence of division. Man will no longer be one small thing but many things, perhaps everything:

> the division of labor offers us the first example for the fact that man's own act becomes an alien power opposed to him and enslaving him instead of being controlled by him . . . In communist society, however, where nobody has an exclusive area of activity and each can train himself in any branch he wishes, society regulates the general production, making it possible for me to do one thing today and another tomorrow, to hunt in the morning, fish in the afternoon, breed cattle in the evening, criticize after dinner, just as I like, without ever becoming a hunter, a fisherman, a herdsman, or a critic.[15]

This, commentators are quick to note, is the young Marx; his more mature offspring eschews such romantic soliloquies. And so he does – for the most part. But Marx's considered views are not to be equated with preponderant socialist tendencies, as Marx himself acknowledges when he grumpily declares, "All I know is that I am not a Marxist." Whether because of the early Marx or despite the later Marx, socialism typically embraces a view of transformed man.[16] The order of precedence is not always clear: is it

---

[15] *The German Ideology*, in *Writings of the Young Marx on Philosophy and Society*, trans. Lloyd D. Easton and Kurt H. Guddat (Garden City, New York: Anchor Books, 1967), pp. 424–25.

[16] If preceding arguments are correct, one need not cite such passages to demonstrate that Marx conceives of socialism as entailing radical human transformation. The overcoming of ideology and alienation from one's real being is itself a momentous transformation, and these are not themes restricted to writings of the young Marx.

socialism that breaks down the walls of alienation, or do initial triumphs over alienation knock the linch pins from under the capitalist order and usher in socialism? It may matter to socialist theorists – what does not? – but from the perspective of this essay, precedence is peripheral. How much can it really matter whether philosophers become kings or kings philosophers? The point is that we now have a wondrous hybrid, and the life of man in society is thereby transformed. Not even Plato managed to characterize the transformation more glowingly than did Trotsky:

> [Under communism] man will become immeasurably stronger, wiser and subtler; his body will become more harmonized, his movements more rhythmic, his voice more musical. The forms of life will become dynamically dramatic. The average human type will rise to the heights of an Aristotle, a Goethe, or a Marx.[17]

Assuming that no sly swipe at Aristotle, Goethe, and Marx is intended, it represents an epitome of the classical vision of man raised to his natural grandeur, or the Christian vision of fallen man made whole.

Conclusion

It has been argued that socialism is fundamentally the conveyance of a political vision, and that the vision it presents is familiar from the classical tradition. Somewhat more speculatively, it has been suggested that much of the currency that socialist theory enjoys is consequent on its having successfully tapped a vein that still carries riches. The modern political science that depicts men possessed by desires rooted in their lower faculties, men who generate outcomes neither intended nor foreseen but which are none the worse for that, and who are destined to retain their present visage of self-interested acquisitiveness evidently fails to address some inclination to see politics as the stage on which grand things are done. Because socialism in its contemporary guise does address that inclination, it retains a currency impervious to the misadventures of a properly economic socialism. Just as Socrates captured Glaucon for a night of political adventure, so too does socialistic politics capture this century's Glaucons.

It would, of course, be an egregious overstatement to claim that the only feature lending socialism an enduring attraction is its expropriation of classical motifs. Other factors are surely at work too; they include the lure of a millenarianism phrased in "scientific" language, envy of the rich, gravitational pull exerted by a socialist superpower, intellectuals' desire to be "in opposition" to the settled order, the inertia of ideas – even the imperfections undeniably lodged in liberal democracies. Nor is it maintained

---

[17] *Literature and Revolution* (New York: Russell & Russell, 1957), p. 256.

that the thesis applies with equal force to all socialist theorists. Marx is not Lenin, nor is either Trotsky, the Webbs, Gramsci, or Habermas. Any attempt to ascribe some one tendency to so variegated a collection of thinkers is necessarily to paint with a broad brush. The same broadness will necessarily attach to general characterizations of ancient versus modern political theory. Nonetheless, the picture is distinctly recognizable – certainly more so than the myriad of tortured attempts to exhibit a "true socialism" through one after another modification of Marx's economics. Establishment of a likeness between classical political theory and contemporary Marxism does not explain everything one would like to understand, but neither is it without force.

That is to advance neither an argument for rejecting socialism nor one for adopting it. It is neither because, as Marx and many other philosophers have taught, the theory whose appeal is strong may nonetheless fail to correspond with any reality. Neither, though, is the preceding analysis strictly irrelevant to the appraisal of socialist theory. In order to establish the criteria by means of which socialism is properly to be evaluated, one must first categorize it accurately. If the foregoing has been correct, to evaluate socialist claims as economic doctrine is to misappraise.

Socialism is, quite literally, reactionary. "Reaction" is typically used as a term of condemnation, but is not so employed here. It is intended in a purely analytical capacity. By no means has it been presupposed that the tradition running from Plato and Aristotle through to Al Farabi and Maimonides is inferior to that espoused by the moderns. It would be rash to declare a winner in the combat between the gods and the titans. The foregoing is meant to label the contending parties, not to take sides.

Nonetheless, it may not be inappropriate to close with a cautionary note. The classical tradition was fueled by a metaphysics adequate to serve its politics. It featured a robust natural order that defined a natural end for man and could speak in a prescriptive voice. That natural end was variously rooted in the will of God, a Form of the Good, or a world of substances each directed toward its *telos*. Because value was taken to be objective and scrutable in the natural order, a politics constrained by a good both external and anterior to transient human designs is at least coherent. It may be that only a few are situated so as to be able to cognize that good, and so it may be that only a few are naturally fit to rule. However, the conception of an objective normative hierarchy provides the metaphysical framework within which philosophers can consistently attempt to determine those conditions necessary and sufficient for the attainment of human good within civil society.

Contemporary classicists of the socialist persuasion retain the prescriptivity, but rarely locate it in a nature fit to speak in teleological cadences. Prescriptivity is, rather, internalized to correspond with some alleged human need or longing. The politics may be classical, but the metaphysics is much more locatable among the moderns. Machiavelli claimed to have established that which eluded the ancients: a political science. Socialists from Marx to the present have rejected the politics but accepted the science. One may justifiably doubt whether the compromise is viable.

Philosophy, University of Minnesota, Duluth

REVIVING THE SOCIALIST CALCULATION DEBATE: A DEFENSE OF HAYEK AGAINST LANGE*

By Daniel Shapiro

The socialist calculation debate is a debate about whether rational economic decisions can be made without markets, or without markets in production goods. Though this debate has been simmering in economics for over 65 years, most philosophers have ignored it. This may be because they are unaware of the debate, or perhaps it is because they have absorbed the conventional view that one side decisively won.[1] This is the side represented by economists such as Oskar Lange and Fred Taylor who, in opposition to free-market economists like Fredrich Hayek, allegedly showed that their version of market socialism is, in principle, as efficient as capitalism.

Allen Buchanan's recent book, *Ethics, Efficiency, and the Market*,[2] is an exception to the prevailing philosophical ignorance of the socialist calculation debate. However, Buchanan ends up arguing for something close to the conventional view. My aims here are to defend Hayek against Lange by way of criticizing Buchanan's account. But before this can be done, something should be said about why we should *care* if it turns out the conventional view of this debate is wrong.

First, setting the intellectual record straight on such an important matter is obviously worthwhile. Second, any political philosopher concerned with comparing socialism to capitalism should be interested in questions of efficiency, as this is one important sort of comparison. Third, almost all philosophers sympathetic to socialism are interested in some form of market socialism;[3] indeed, outside of the Soviet Bloc there are few defenders of central planning. So if some form of market economy is the only real

* A shorter version of this paper was read at the Pacific Division meeting of the American Philosophical Association in March 1987. I wish to thank Paul Lyon for his comments at that meeting, and Christopher W. Morris for written comments on the APA version. I would also like to thank N. Scott Arnold, Eric Mack, and referees for this journal for comments on the longer version. The Earhart Foundation of Ann Arbor, Michigan provided me with support to do research on the socialist calculation debate, for which I am most grateful.

[1] For a representative sample of the conventional view, see Joseph Schumpeter, *Capitalism, Socialism, and Democracy* (New York: Harper and Brothers, 1950), pp. 172–86.
[2] Totowa: Rowman and Allenheld, 1985.
[3] Though not necessarily the Lange-Taylor model. See note 52.

alternative, then the debate over the relative efficiency of market socialism is central to the larger debate of capitalism versus socialism. Fourth, as we shall see, the socialist calculation debate raises important issues about the appropriate standards for intersystemic comparisons of efficiency.

This paper contains four sections. Section I sets out Buchanan's view of the dispute between Hayek and the Lange-Taylor model of market socialism (henceforth called the LT model). In Section II, I show that Buchanan misrepresents Hayek's arguments, as most people have done who have written on the socialist calculation debate, and that Hayek's arguments look quite plausible when they are set out correctly. In Section III, I discuss what standard of efficiency Hayek was or should have been using in his argument against the LT model; Hayek's views on this matter turn out to be rather unorthodox. Once Hayek's views have been correctly set out, and his standard of efficiency explained, there remains an important question: how could a defender of the LT model respond? I discuss some replies in Section IV, and show that Hayek's arguments have established that the burden of proof is upon the defenders of the LT model.

I. BUCHANAN ON HAYEK

In order to understand Buchanan's arguments, some background is necessary. The beginning of the socialist calculation debate is usually attributed to Ludwig von Mises, who in 1920 argued that, without markets, economic calculation would be impossible.[4] If Mises is interpreted as making a logical point,[5] then it is widely believed that he is wrong. About 20 years earlier, Barone and Pareto had shown that, given complete knowledge of all the relevant economic data, it is possible to solve the millions of simultaneous equations which would be necessary to make rational economic decisions.[6] Hayek's contribution, says Buchanan, was to argue "that the more plausible interpretation of Mises's argument was *epistemological*, rather than logical."[7] Even if, in principle, the equations could be solved, the amount of information that would have to be fed into the equations could not be

[4] Ludwig von Mises, "Economic Calculation in the Socialist Commonwealth," ed. Friedrich Hayek, *Collectivist Economic Planning* (New York: Kelly, 1967), pp. 85–130.

[5] I believe that this interpretation of Mises is wrong, but a discussion of Mises's views would take us too far afield. See Don Lavoie, *Rivalry and Central Planning: The Socialist Calculation Debate Reconsidered* (New York: Cambridge University Press, 1985), pp. 48–77. Lavoie's book is valuable for combating the conventional view of the socialist calculation debate.

[6] Eugene Barone, "The Ministry of Production in a Collectivist State," *Collectivist Economic Planning*, Appendix, and V. Pareto, *Cours D'Economie Politique*, Volume II, 1897.

[7] Buchanan, p. 110.

absorbed by any individual or group of planners. According to Buchanan, Hayek provides the following arguments.[8]

First, there is the problem of the staggering amount of information that must be fed into the equations. In order to make rational economic decisions, the planners must be able to estimate, with some degree of reliability, the costs of producing X amount of good A as opposed to Y amount of good B for all the types of goods under consideration – and this requires estimating the least costly method of production for each producing unit in each line of production. And if one wants to take into account the preferences of the individuals who are consuming the goods, then the planners must know what goods consumers want, in what amounts, and at what cost in foregone opportunities for enjoying other goods, etc. This problem is compounded once one realizes that the *type* of information that is required for rational economic decisions is very particular and concrete, and could not be adequately represented in the statistical type of information that the planners would necessarily rely on. What is relevant, for example, concerns not machines of a certain general or abstract type, but machines of a certain age, in a certain stage of wear and tear, in a particular locale or space, etc.

Hayek calls this the problem of divided knowledge. He means by this that knowledge is scattered throughout society. Different people know (or believe) different things, and most people have a kind of "specialty" vis-à-vis local, concrete, specific knowledge. Thus, no one mind or group of planners has all the economic knowledge that is dispersed throughout the system.[9]

The second problem that Hayek raises is that the information that must be acquired and utilized by the planners is constantly changing on both the producers' and consumers' side. I shall call this the problem of continual and continuous change. Hayek stresses something Buchanan does not, which is

---

[8] Buchanan, pp. 16–17, 110. In what follows, I shall add to Buchanan's account where I think he has neglected some important aspects of Hayek's views. One reason Buchanan has done so is that his account relies for the most part on "The Present State of the Debate" [henceforth called PSD] in *Collectivist Economic Planning*, Hayek's 1935 article on this topic. Hayek's view is not fully appreciated unless one also looks at his 1940 article, written specifically in response to Lange, "Socialist Calculation III: The Competitive 'Solution'," [henceforth called SCT] in *Individualism and the Economic Order* (Chicago: University of Chicago Press, 1948), pp. 181–208, as well as some later articles which illuminate Hayek's general framework. Two articles that are valuable in this regard are "The Use of Knowledge in Society," in *Individualism and the Economic Order*, pp. 77–91 [henceforth called UKS] and "Competition as a Discovery Procedure," in *New Studies in Philosophy, Politics, Economics and the History of Ideas* (Chicago: University of Chicago Press, 1978), pp. 179–90 [henceforth called CDS].

[9] See UKS in particular. Hayek tends to use "knowledge" sloppily, not distinguishing it from true belief, where one's beliefs may not be justified, or even from justified belief, where one's beliefs may not be true. To avoid such problems, I shall generally use the term "information." It should be assumed, unless otherwise stated, that such information is true.

that the consequence of this is that virtually all economic decisions involve some anticipation or hunches about the future.[10]

Though these two problems can be separated conceptually, in reality they are connected. If economic realities were unchanging, the problem of dispersed knowledge would be manageable. (Conversely, the problem of continual and continuous change might not be troubling if information were not dispersed.) For Hayek, what makes something an economic problem is that it involves dispersed knowledge about constantly changing conditions.[11]

Buchanan fails to notice that these two problems that Hayek raises in his discussion of non-market planned socialism are rooted in Hayek's overall philosophy of economics. As we shall see, the idea that economic problems are, in large part, problems that arise because of dispersed knowledge about continually and continuously changing conditions plays a crucial role in Hayek's criticism of the LT system as well.

Hayek's epistemological argument against non-market socialism only has force if one can show that the market can accommodate the division of knowledge and continual change. According to Buchanan, Hayek argues that, in contrast to the amount of information required to be fed into the equations needed for the planners to run the economy efficiently, the amount of information that a successful producer or consumer requires in the market is fairly narrow. They need to know if certain goods or a certain number of goods can be bought or sold at certain prices; they don't need to know how many goods of that type the economy must produce or consume, or how many it must produce relative to other goods that need to be produced or consumed. Not only does each individual participant have no need for a great deal of knowledge about the whole economic system, but the market encourages people to gather and utilize their own specialized knowledge. Indeed, exchangers are specialists in limited, concrete information of various sorts.

Buchanan is correct that Hayek argues that the successful individual producer and consumer in the market requires relatively little information, and that the market encourages people to specialize in the concrete, very particularized information that one needs. However, Buchanan fails to notice that Hayek's comparison of markets and non-market mechanisms isn't just a comparison which concerns the relatively small amount of information successful participants in the former need as compared to how much information is needed by planners attempting to completely supplant

---

[10] *ibid.*, pp. 81–83.

[11] *ibid.*, pp. 81–82. Of course, this is not meant as a definition. The point is that these are two very important necessary conditions for something being an economic problem. (It's worth noting that Hayek's arguments in what follows can probably go through with the weaker claim that economic problems *typically* involve dispersed knowledge about constantly changing conditions.)

markets; Hayek's argument also concerns how markets adapt to *changes* that are dispersed throughout the system.[12] Hayek stresses that changes in prices register or reflect the changes in economic realities that are or will be occurring and communicate the result of these changes to those who need to be aware of them.[13] An individual may not be aware that the demand for a certain good has increased or that a significant source of that good has dried up; but if at least some of those who are aware of and specialize in such information do act on this information, the price of that good will rise, sending a message to those that use that good: "Use less." In this way, changes in production occur throughout the system: not only will uses of that good be affected, but so will substitutes for it, the substitutes of those substitutes, the supply of all those things made from the good, etc. What makes the market quickly adapt to or anticipate these changes is (in part) that those who have the foresight or luck to recognize that production is discoordinated relative to changes that are or will be occurring tend to make profits and avoid losses (which give signals to others to follow suit).[14] In this way, present prices tend to reflect changes in future economic realities.[15]

Buchanan thinks that "Hayek's epistemological argument may be a decisive objection to planned non-market socialism,"[16] but that it "is less than decisive against the Lange-Taylor model."[17] In the LT model,[18] there is a market for consumer goods and a market in labor, but there is no market for production goods: a central planning board (CPB) fixes prices of

[12] At one point Buchanan says "in the market enormous amounts of complex information are utilized in the emergence and adjustments of prices over time ..." (p. 16), but he really doesn't say much more than this.

[13] UKS, pp. 85–87.

[14] My use of "coordination" and related terms throughout this paper is different than the "coordination problem" of which game theorists speak. For game theorists, a coordination problem occurs when two or more people can get what they most prefer only if they choose the same course of action; the coordination problem arises in that there is no unique action that will produce what they most want. For example, in order to get a smooth flow of traffic, it doesn't matter whether we drive on the left or the right, but we must all drive on the same side of the road. The use of "coordination" in this paper concerns whether opportunities for mutually beneficial exchanges are grasped or recognized, or whether exchanges are made on the basis of misinformation about economic realities. See Section III for more detail.

[15] Of course, those who make pricing and production decisions will make errors, and these will cause prices to be somewhat mistaken relative to changing economic realities. The structure of the argument does not require the assumption that prices will communicate and disseminate information perfectly. Rather it requires that a system which allows people to act on their beliefs about changing economic realities, and which tends to reward them if those beliefs are more often than not correct, will be more coordinated than a system which lacks such features. A similar point arises in Section IV in the discussion of business cycles.

[16] Buchanan, p. 110.

[17] *ibid.*, p. 111.

[18] I rely here on Lange's account, since his is more thorough. See Oskar Lange, "On the Economic Theory of Socialism," in *On the Economic Theory of Socialism*, ed. B.E. Lippincott (New York: McGraw-Hill, 1964), pp. 57–144.

production goods and plans investment. In order to determine if the relative values the board places on production goods are accurate, the board uses the trial-and-error method of successive approximation: it raises and lowers the prices of such goods at the end of a specified production period, depending on whether or not there is shortage or surplus of such goods. Also, the CPB directs the managers of the plants and factories to minimize the average cost of production, and to produce at a scale of output at which the marginal cost of the product equals the price of the product. Following these rules will enable the managers to produce efficiently, since they are the same rules followed in a perfectly competitive market. A perfectly competitive market is an efficient market, because when it is in equilibrium[19] its outcomes are Pareto-optimal. To say that a perfectly competitive market in equilibrium is Pareto-optimal is to say that there is no feasible alternative state of that market in which at least one person is better off and no one is worse off.[20] (There will be more discussion of Pareto-optimality in later sections.)

Buchanan argues that the trial-and-error method overcomes the problem that non-market planning has concerning the need to accumulate and communicate concrete, very particularized economic information. The CPB doesn't need to ferret out such information, since it just looks at the results of interactions, that is, whether there are shortages and surpluses. Furthermore, the CPB is engaging in the same kind of trial-and-error method that producers in a perfectly competitive market do; as such producers notice shortages and surpluses, they raise and lower their prices accordingly. So the CPB is using the same kind of information that the producers do in a market that produces efficient outcomes. If one is worried about the CPB's initial prices being set arbitrarily, this can be avoided by originally setting the prices at historical levels or copying them from a currently existing free-market economy.[21]

Buchanan does concede that the CPB will need a larger amount of information than any individual producer needs on a market (since the former has to monitor shortages and surpluses in all of the producer markets), but he doubts that this is "an insurmountable problem, given anticipated advances in computerized technology for data processing."[22]

Concerning the problem of continual and continuous change, Buchanan does not claim that the LT scheme can adapt to change as flexibly as market capitalism. However, I suspect that he would be skeptical that an argument

[19] In this paper, I employ an intuitive and common-sense notion of equilibrium where it means, roughly, a stable outcome where there are no endogenous disturbances. Hayek's conception of equilibrium will be discussed in Section III.
[20] Any standard introductory text in economics will show why a perfectly competitive market in equilibrium is Pareto-optimal.
[21] Buchanan, pp. 110–11.
[22] *ibid.*, p. 111.

denying that the LT model is less flexible than market capitalism could be successfully made. When discussing a similar argument, he says that there seems to be no "theoretical" way of demonstrating this point, and there are no empirical studies available, as no present socialist systems even come close to emulating the LT model.[23]

So Buchanan's argument comes to this: the trial-and-error method in the LT model can overcome the problem of the division of knowledge, and it's doubtful one can show that it will have a serious problem adapting to continuous and continual change. Hence, Hayek's arguments do not succeed.[24]

II. BUCHANAN'S MISUNDERSTANDING OF HAYEK

Buchanan's arguments against Hayek rest largely on two comparisons. First, Buchanan compares the informational requirements of the CPB in the LT system with the individual producer on the market, and argues that they both use and require the same kind of information (though perhaps the CPB needs some more information). In this regard the LT system is in far better shape, Buchanan claims, than non-market planned socialism, since the former, unlike the latter, does not need to accumulate and communicate enormous amounts of very particularized information. Second, he compares the CPB's method for discovering the information it needs with the method used not just by individual producers in a market, but with the method used by producers in a *perfectly competitive* market. Both comparisons involve mistakes. Once we see these mistakes, we shall see that Hayek's arguments are more powerful than Buchanan realizes.

The first comparison is mistaken because the analogous role to the individual producer on the market is the individual manager in the LT model; the CPB's informational role is analogous to the informational role of producer prices on the market. In both systems there is specialized knowledge or hunches that the *individual* economic agent has about changes which are or will be occurring, and some *systemic* mechanism that is needed for accumulating information about the result of these changes, and then communicating such information to those who may be affected by such changes. If we are to fairly compare the two systems, we should compare the way in which this need is met in both systems by the price system. Hayek's argument – which Buchanan does not really discuss – is that that the LT

---

[23] *ibid.* The argument that Buchanan discusses is that, in the LT model, price readjustments would have to be so frequent and the cost of constantly accumulating data would be so high that the system would be less efficient. This is in effect an argument that, were the LT model to try to mimic market capitalism's flexible adaptation to change, it would be so costly as to be inefficient.

[24] It should be noted that Buchanan also discusses what he takes to be a motivational objection that Hayek raises against the LT model. I discuss this in Section II.

system's fixed prices cripple the communication function of prices and the way in which price changes accumulate scattered information.

Consider the relationship between the managers and the CPB. Managers don't have the authority to change prices when they recognize or anticipate changes in economic realities during a period when prices are fixed; they have to get permission from the CPB and, even if it is granted, it may be too late.[25] And contrary to Buchanan's claim, the CPB *does* need to utilize very particularized, concrete information, for to make rational price-fixing decisions, it needs to take into account local differences in quality, place, etc. For example, the CPB will need to decide whether steel in plant A in industry B in state of wear and tear C is to be placed in the same category and thus priced the same as steel in plant D in industry E in state of wear and tear F, etc.[26] As we already noted, the CPB lack such information. The move by Lange (and Buchanan) at this point – that the initial prices can be set at historical levels or can mimic an existing capitalist economy – is off the mark. Historical levels quickly become irrelevant, given changing conditions, and copying a capitalist economy will not help that much given that *local* conditions of quality, place, etc., will be different.

Thus, the fixed prices of the CPB can't contain as much or as up-to-date information as producer prices can on the market. Since Buchanan brought up the issue of advances in data processing, it is worth stressing that this does not vitiate the argument. The data in question here concern changes in economic realities which are scattered throughout the system. If advances in data processing are to make a difference, it must be the case that those who are aware of or anticipate these changes can almost instantly communicate them to the CPB and almost instantly get permission to change the prices of their inputs or outputs. But if this occurred, then there wouldn't be CPB price-*fixing*, but *de facto* price-setting by the managers.

What about Buchanan's argument that the CPB's trial-and-error method is just what a producer does in a perfectly competitive market? This is also the wrong comparison, since Hayek is not comparing a perfectly competitive market, but real markets, to Lange's scheme.[27] In order to understand Buchanan's error – which is unfortunately all too common – we must take a brief tour through the model of perfect competition.

The model of a perfectly competitive market has been developed and refined over the last 115 years or so of neoclassical economics. It originated in

[25] SCT, pp. 188–89, 192–93. Hayek also notes that for goods made to order the notion of price fixing from above makes no sense.

[26] *ibid.*, p. 193.

[27] Hayek wasn't as explicit about this as he should have been when he discussed the LT model, but remarks in PSD, pp. 212, 226–27, and SCT, pp. 188, 191 show that his benchmark of comparison is not a perfectly competitive market. UKS and, most importantly, CDS, pp. 179–86, give a systematic account of the misuse of the perfect-competition equilibrium model.

an attempt to describe that state of affairs where no one has any control over price: this requires that there be an indefinite number of undifferentiated sellers and buyers who are all price-takers. It was further analyzed as an economy where there was complete or perfect knowledge.[28] No real markets are perfectly competitive; the main interest in perfect competition is that, with the addition of a few other assumptions,[29] one can show that it leads to an equilibrium state which is Pareto-optimal. In fact, saying it "leads" to an equilibrium state is a bit misleading; as any elementary economic textbook will demonstrate, given the complete economic knowledge and maximizing aims of the agents in a perfectly competitive model, the system logically must be in equilibrium.[30] The trial and error that exists in perfect competition is merely postulated to show how if there was a shortage or surplus, it would be eliminated by the undifferentiated buyers and sellers reacting by raising and lowering their price. In this sense, whatever change exists in the perfectly competitive model is purely exogenous; it is a static model where there are no changes in economic realities other than price changes, and these are built into the model merely to show why perfect markets must reach equilibrium.[31]

The CPB's trial-and-error method is closely analogous to trial and error in perfect competition. Just as the producers in a perfectly competitive market are all price-takers, i.e., treat prices as given, and can only react identically to a shortage or surplus, so the managers in the LT model treat prices as fixed. There is a slight distinction: the managers don't react in unison to the existence of shortages and surpluses; the CPB tells them how to react. However, this seems to be a distinction without a difference. There is no significant difference between equilibrium being achieved by *many* (undifferentiated producers) *reacting* identically to the existence of shortages or surpluses in just the right way so as to achieve equilibrium, as opposed to

---

[28] For a history of the concept of perfect competition, see George Stigler, "Perfect Competition, Historically Contemplated," in *Essays in the History of Economics* (Chicago: University of Chicago Press, 1965), pp. 234–67.

[29] Some of the more important ones are: (i) Each agent is a utility maximizer. For consumers, this turns out to entail that they obtain the same marginal utility per monetary unit for every product they purchase. For producers, it turns out to entail the rules we discussed earlier: e.g., that output should be maintained at the point where price equals marginal cost. (ii) All goods are privately owned. (iii) There are no externalities. (iv) All utility functions are independent.

[30] There may be multiple equilibria in a perfectly competitive market, but this issue isn't important for the topic at hand.

[31] In Walras's model of how perfectly competitive markets reach equilibrium, which Lange alludes to, the static nature of trial and error is particularly clear. An auctioneer calls out a set of tentative prices and the economic agents indicate precisely what they would supply and demand at those prices; if there is a shortage or surplus, the auctioneer calls out a different set of prices, and so on until the equilibrium set is found. No trading or exchange occurs while the tentative prices are called out; this occurs only when the right prices are found.

one (the CPB) *ordering* the many how to react in just the right way so as to achieve equilibrium.

So Buchanan, following Lange, is correct in his claim that the CPB's trial and error is using the same method that is used in perfect competition by individual producers. But clearly Hayek was not using the model of perfect competition as his standard for criticism of the LT model. Since Hayek viewed economic problems as arising due to the division of knowledge and continual and continuous change, he would not use a model that banished both of these as a way to criticize the LT model. If we are to compare trial and error in the LT model with trial and error in Hayek's framework, we need to compare it with real markets, where there is a division of knowledge and continual and continuous change. In such markets, trial and error means experimenting with different mixes of factors and production techniques, since the producers do not know which "mixture" will turn out to be most profitable nor for what period of time; in so experimenting, producers bid prices up and down. Thus, the division of knowledge and continual and continuous change produce in real markets product differentiation and, (partly) in virtue of this, price competition – the very *opposite* of perfect competition. Price and product competition are the vehicles which force real competitive markets towards producing things at the cheapest discoverable cost; producers must continually struggle to discover cheaper combinations of factors of production, for they may always be threatened by a competitor who discovers how to produce in a different and cheaper manner. These vehicles are absent in the LT model. No manager has to contend with price competition from a rival. With prices fixed, the managers' ability to try different production techniques and different mixes of factors is severely limited; they can't induce suppliers to supply more or different inputs or purchasers to purchase more or different outputs by changing prices.[32] Thus, fixed prices also limit product competition among managers.

Buchanan recognizes that the LT model provides no account of what compels the managers to produce cheaply, but he thinks that this is primarily a *motivational* problem: how, asks Buchanan, can the managers have incentive to follow the rules of the CPB?[33] These rules – minimize the average cost of production and price products at marginal cost – are used by producers in a perfectly competitive market, but it is the drive for profit which makes such producers follow these rules, and the profit motive is supposed to be absent from the LT system. However, Buchanan fails to see that the problem with getting the managers to follow these rules is at least as much epistemological as motivational. These are rules that apply in the static model of perfect competition where there is perfect knowledge; no matter

[32] SCT, pp. 196–98.
[33] Buchanan, p. 112.

how much the managers *want* to follow these rules, they face the problem that these rules are empty in the real world of divided knowledge and continual and continuous change. For example, in order for the rule that price equals marginal cost to have content, one has to figure out the minimum total cost necessary to produce various quantities of a certain good (marginal cost is the cost of producing an extra unit on that curve), and *that* involves knowing all the possible production functions[34] and the prices of the factors of production. No manager (or anyone else for that matter) knows all the production functions, and the prices of the factors depend on what happens in the future. (E.g., the price of a machine per year depends on how it is discounted over time.)[35]

I have shown that both of Buchanan's arguments in defense of the LT model fail. The relevant comparison is not between the informational needs of an individual producer on the market and the CPB; rather, it is between the fixed prices of the CPB and the nonrigid producer prices on the market. Hayek's point is that the former cannot contain as much or as up-to-date information as the latter, since a sytem of *fixed* producer prices cannot reflect and disseminate information about constantly changing conditions that is scattered throughout the economic system. And though it is true that the CPB's trial-and-error method is analogous to trial and error in perfect competition, it is irrelevant, as Hayek was comparing trial-and-error methods in real markets with trial and error in the LT model. The latter eliminates price competition and reduces product competition – the very mechanisms which move producers towards producing at the cheapest discoverable cost.

III. PARETO-OPTIMALITY AND PLAN COORDINATION

Hayek's argument, as I have presented it, is that market capitalism has better processes or mechanisms than the LT model for handling the problems of the division of knowledge and continual and continuous change. This argument appears to have a rather tenuous relationship to the conclusion that market capitalism is more *efficient* than the LT version of market socialism. The usual standard is that efficiency is taken to be Pareto-optimality, and a perfectly competitive market in equilibrium is Pareto-optimal. But we've already seen that Hayek is not comparing perfectly competitive markets in equilibrium to the LT model. Perhaps, then, Hayek's point is that real markets approximate the conditions of perfect markets

---

[34] A production function is a technical relationship, defined for a given state of technical knowledge, which sets out the maximum output capable of being produced by each and every set of specified inputs. Any standard introductory economic text will explain how given knowledge of production functions and factor prices, one can determine when price equals marginal cost.

[35] SCT, pp. 196–99, PSD, pp. 226–29, CDS, p. 185.

more than does the LT model. At times Buchanan seems to argue or suggest that Hayek thought that real markets approximated the conditions of perfect markets.[36] But Hayek does not say this, and it cannot be supported. What sense does it make to say that a market characterized by a division of knowledge *approximates* perfect knowledge, or that a market characterized by price and product competition *approximates* one that lacks these? Lack of information is not an approximation of perfect knowledge, and price and product competition is the *opposite* of the absence of such competition. The model of perfect competition is a static model; it describes *a state of affairs* which logically must eventuate in an equlibrium. Hayek's model of competition describes a *process* which does not yield an end-state that can be described as an equilibrium; given scattered information and continual and continuous change, real markets are always in disequilibrium. A market process which is always in disequilibrium can hardly be called an approximation of a static market in equilibrium.

Although real markets do not approximate perfect markets, and though a perfectly competitive market in equilibrium is Pareto-optimal, it doesn't, strictly speaking, *follow* that real markets do not approximate Pareto-optimality. Perhaps, then, Hayek's argument was that real markets approximate Pareto-optimality to a greater extent than the LT model. Indeed, at one point Hayek seems to argue that real markets approximate Pareto-optimality:

> It must not be forgotten that in this respect the market brings about an approach towards some point on that n-dimensional surface, by which pure economic theory represents the horizon of all possibilities to which the production of any one proportional combination of commodities and services could conceivably be carried.... This competitive game, at the price of leaving the share of each individual in some measure to accident, ensures that the real equivalent of whatever his share turns out to be is as large as we know how to make it. The game is ... one through which, by playing it according to the rules, the pool to be shared is enlarged, leaving individual shares in the pool in a great measure to chance. A mind knowing all the facts could select any point he liked on the surface and distribute this product in the manner he thought right. But the only point on, or tolerably near, the horizon of possiblities which we know how to reach is the one at which we shall arrive if we leave its determination to the market. The so-called "maximum" which we thus reach naturally cannot be defined as a sum of particular things, but only in terms of the chances it offers to unknown people to get as

[36] Buchanan, pp. 15–16.

large a real equivalent as possible for their relative shares, which will be determined partly by accident.[37]

The horizon of possibilities Hayek refers to is, perhaps, the Pareto-optimal frontier, so perhaps Hayek is claiming that real markets approach that frontier.[38] This claim cannot be substantiated. Strictly speaking, Pareto-optimality is an all-or-nothing affair; a state of affairs is Pareto-optimal or not. We can, perhaps, speak of approaching Pareto-optimality if, at a certain time, there are a variety of Pareto-superior improvements available – that is, ways of making someone better off without making anyone worse off – and it is clear which of these improvements gets us closest to the Pareto-optimality frontier. However, in the real world economic systems over time will always produce changes that make at least someone worse off; thus to evaluate such changes one needs to make interpersonal comparisons of utility – and the main attraction of the Pareto-optimality standard of efficiency is that it avoids such comparisons.[39]

Now Hayek does not talk about Pareto-superior improvements, so these criticisms may seem beside the point. But Hayek's emphasis on comparing the probability that unknown persons will obtain as large a real equivalent for their relative shares as is possible runs into the same problem. The reference to unknown persons indicates that Hayek is aware that, for his proposed standard of efficiency to be plausible, we have to focus on a variety of (presumably randomly selected) persons and see what the chances are that they will achieve as large a real equivalent for their relative share as possible. But since some of these persons will do better in changing from one system to another, while others will do worse, then we once again have to make interpersonal utility comparisons. And even if we could avoid this problem (perhaps if there was some defensible notion of a representative person), we would run into the problem that, in different economic systems, people have significantly different preferences and interests. Since a person's well-being

---

[37] CDS, pp. 185–86. This is the *only* passage I am aware of where Hayek seems to say that real markets tend towards Pareto-optimality.

[38] A referee for this journal thinks that the horizon of possibilities that Hayek is referring to is not the Pareto-optimality frontier. Two points seem to support the referee's interpretation: Hayek seems to refer to all the possible ways of producing goods, which is a different notion than Pareto-optimality (since utility or welfare is affected by distribution and production), and he refers to markets increasing the general pool, also a different notion than Pareto-optimality (since increasing the general pool may make some worse off). However, the evidence is mixed. Hayek also says that markets increase the chances that unknown people will get as large a real equivalent for their relative shares as possible; since he does not refer to the chance that markets may decrease certain people's real shares, a natural interpretation is that Hayek does not believe that real markets will make some better off while making others worse off. In any event, my aim in the text below is merely to show that *if* one thought that Hayek's criticism of the LT model rested on the claim that real markets approach or approximate Pareto-optimality, then Hayek's argument falls apart.

[39] Buchanan, pp. 42–44.

or welfare is constituted by one's preferences or interests, then what constitutes one's welfare or well-being may dramatically shift in a change from one society to another. In such a case, evaluating whether one person is better off than another person in changing from one society to another may be functionally equivalent to making interpersonal utility comparisons.[40]

If Hayek's (apparent) claim that real markets approximate Pareto-optimality cannot be maintained, and if he does not claim that real markets approximate perfect competition, then in what sense can he plausibly argue that real markets are more efficient than the LT model? Some economists who follow Hayek's approach have suggested that Hayek's critique of the model of perfect competition also requires a different conception of efficiency. Israel Kirzner, for example, proposes the standard of plan coordination. Intuitively, the idea is this.[41] Where an opportunity for a mutually beneficial exchange between A and B exists, but A and B fail to exchange, this can be described as an absence of coordination. Scattered information and continual and continuous change can produce such failures of coordination; A and B may fail to exchange because they don't know about the existence of the other, or because they mistakenly believe that the other doesn't want to exchange, or because the information they based their plans on has changed. Given Hayek's view that economic problems arise, in large part, because of scattered information and continual and continuous change, and given his view that market capitalism is superior to the LT system in the way it accumulates and disseminates scattered information about continuously and continually changing conditions, it seems reasonable to conclude that Hayek's argument can be interpreted as the claim that market capitalism is more efficient than the LT system, in that the former has coordinating processes or mechanisms which the latter cripples.[42]

[40] Buchanan, p. 41.

[41] *Entrepreneurship and Competition* (Chicago: University of Chicago Press), pp. 215–17. Hayek seems to suggest something like the plan coordination standard in CDS, p. 184. A number of Kirzner's essays on Hayek and issues arising out of the socialist calculation debate can be found in *Perception, Opportunity and Profit* (Chicago: University of Chicago Press, 1979).

[42] The relationship between the plan-coordination standard and Pareto-optimality seems to be something like the following. One way to explain the sense in which a perfectly competitive market in equilibrium is Pareto-optimal is that there are no unexploited opportunities for mutual gain anywhere in the system. One important reason why real markets are never Pareto-optimal is that given scattered information and continual and continuous change, there are always unexploited opportunities for mutual gain. The plan-coordination standard of efficiency thus focuses on some of the salient reasons why real markets cannot be Pareto-optimal. However, unlike the Pareto-optimal standard, it does not use the situation where there are no unexploited gains from trade (e.g., a perfectly competitive market) as its benchmark by which to judge the efficiency of systems. Rather, the plan-coordination standard takes as a given that there is scattered information and continuous change – and accordingly unexploited gains from trade – and evaluates the processes or mechanisms a system has for coordinating the constantly changing scattered information.

REVIVING THE SOCIALIST CALCULATION DEBATE

Another reason to believe that the standard of plan coordination is a good reconstruction of Hayek's notion of efficiency is that it is connected with his analysis of equilibrium – and economists' conceptions of efficiency and equilibrium tend to be linked.[43] In a paper called "Economics and Knowledge,"[44] Hayek defined equilibrium (for more than one person) as the mutual compatibility of plans (and plans seem to be defined in terms of expectations and intentions). A society is in equilibrium at a certain time if the world is such that at a later time all its members' plans could be carried out. Now in order for equilibrium to *continue* in a society where one person's plans depend upon other persons' plans, the foresight of the different members of the society "must be correct in the sense that every person's plan is based on the expectation of just those actions of other people which those other people intend to perform . . . so that under certain conditions nobody will have any reason to change his plans. Correct foresight . . . is the defining characteristic of a state of equilibrium."[45,46]

Since we don't have correct foresight, equilibrium never comes about, nor would it persist through time if it did; people's plans must continually be revised. But those processes and mechanisms which help to coordinate people's plans, despite scattered knowledge and continual and continuous changes, can, given the Hayekian view of equilibrium, be viewed as equilibrating processes. So Hayek's view of the nature of economic problems, the plan-coordination standard of efficiency, and the Hayekian notion of equilibrium appear to be linked together in a theoretically satisfying way. Scattered knowledge and continual and continuous change produce discoordination: these conditions prevent the satisfaction of everyone's plans. Equilibrium – that is, perfect plan coordination – occurs when there is perfect foresight, so we can also view scattered knowledge and continual and

[43] There are (at least) two reasons for this. First, it is desirable if an efficient system can be shown to be in equilibrium, e.g., shown to be stable, or at least to have equilibrating tendencies. Second, assuming that considerations of welfare or well-being count for something, there is a *prima facie* reason to promote and maintain an efficient system; and an understanding of those conditions which help to stabilize an efficient system can aid us in helping to bring about that system.

[44] *Individualism and the Economic Order*, pp. 33–56.

[45] *ibid.*, p. 42.

[46] Gerald O'Driscoll and Mario Rizzo, in *The Economics of Time and Ignorance* (New York: Basil Blackwell, 1985), p. 84, argue that Hayek's notion of equilibrium is mistaken since, under certain circumstances, correct foresight will prevent any equilibrium. They use an example, borrowed from Oskar Morgenstern, of Sherlock Holmes being pursued by his opponent Moriarty. If each perfectly anticipates what the other will do, this will lead to an endless series of plans, revisions of those plans, new plans, etc., and so no stability will ever occur. However, this example does not provide any problem for Hayek's analysis of equilibrium. Hayek says that, in order for any equilibrium to exist at a certain time, there must be a state of the world at a later time in which all the parties' plans could be carried out. Since Holmes and Moriarty's plans were mutually incompatible – the achievement of one of their plans requires the thwarting of the other's plan – in the first place, their plans couldn't be in equilibrium no matter what degree of knowledge they had. Thus Holmes and Moriarty's perfect foresight does not *prevent* an equilibrium.

continuous change as producing disequilibrium. Given Hayek's view that economic problems are largely defined in terms of the existence of scattered knowledge and continual and continuous change, then it is reasonable to evaluate and compare systems in terms of their coordinating or equilibrating processes. The plan-coordination standard thus seems to capture reasonably well Hayek's argument that real market capitalism is more efficient than the LT system.

Despite the fact that the plan-coordination standard seems to fit well with and explain Hayek's criticisms of the LT model, one might wonder whether it really should be considered a conception of *efficiency*, for plan coordination, unlike Pareto-optimality, is not defined in terms of welfare or well-being. As Buchanan notes,[47] standards of efficiency interest us because efficient systems are supposed to serve the well-being or interests of individuals, so a conception of efficiency which has no nontrivial connection with welfare is seriously deficient. However, though plan coordination is not *defined* in terms of welfare or well-being, it has obvious connections with welfare. If there is an opportunity for a mutually beneficial exchange between *A* and *B* and such an exchange does not occur because of ignorance, etc., then the lack of coordination between *A* and *B* has made them both worse off than they otherwise might have been. To the extent that an economic system has processes or mechanisms which help to coordinate economic activity, then, all other things being equal, individuals are better off. The "all other things being equal" clause is necessary, since other factors can make people worse off even if there is successful coordination: the lack of congruence between preferences as expressed on the market and well-being, the alleged failure of the market to produce a sufficient amount of certain public goods, discoordination that may be a side-effect of successful coordination, etc.

As there is only a probabilistic or *prima facie* connection between successful coordination and welfare, this suggests a way that a defender of the LT system might reply to Hayek's arguments that market capitalism has coordinating or equilibrating processes which the LT system cripples. Perhaps it can be shown that the LT system has compensating benefits which make up for its efficiency losses. It is to this type of reply that we now turn.

IV. REPLIES AND CONCLUSION

Hayek's argument that the CPB's planning will produce more discoordination than markets is something that a socialist or Marxist has to take seriously. Part of the traditional Marxist and socialist critique of capitalism is criticism about capitalism's anarchy of production, its wastefulness and destructive business cycles, and the like. These criticisms can reasonably be

---

[47] Buchanan, p. 5.

translated into a complaint about capitalism producing a significant amount of discoordination; as such, any socialist or Marxist should be bothered by any argument that shows the relative superiority of markets in this regard.

What the socialist or Marxist can say in response to Hayek's arguments is that, even if Hayek is right, what welfare or well-being we lose by way of discoordination produced by planning is made up for by a gain in welfare produced by getting rid of capitalism.[48] In this section, I shall show that it is difficult for those who defend the LT system to make this sort of rebuttal. To see why, consider the ways in which a socialist or Marxist might attempt to show that efficiency losses produced by planning are made up for by gains produced by other features of socialism.

One possible gain might be this. Marxists have often argued that people's preferences on the market diverge significantly from what is truly in their interest or what truly promotes their welfare or well-being. Thus, even if there are real losses in well-being which occur because of the discoordination produced by planning, these are made up by the fact that in socialism people's true needs are addressed, rather than their preferences on the market. An advocate of *market* socialism, like Lange, cannot seriously make this reply. His system presupposes markets in consumer goods and in labor, so there is no compensating gain in this system, unless one could somehow show that the abolition of markets in producer goods makes people's preferences in labor and consumer markets reflect or be in rough accordance with their genuine well-being.[49]

A second reply the defender of the LT system might make focuses on the alleged gain in welfare that results from the abolition of the capitalist-worker conflict. From a Marxist or socialist point of view, it would appear that capitalists and workers are involved in a zero-sum game; that is, their interests are such that one group's gain is the other's loss, and vice versa. (E.g., capitalist income and wealth results from the extraction of surplus value from the workers, and the capitalist mode of production cripples the workers' creative abilities and makes work alienating, etc.) In the last section I argued that *all other things being equal*, coordinative processes make people better off, but when people's interests or preferences are in fundamental conflict, all other things aren't equal. If one person's plans involve the frustration of another's plan and vice versa, then a process which tends to coordinate information, such that people are more likely to achieve their plans, can hardly make the people with the opposed plans better off.[50] Thus the

---

[48] Such a reply will involve interpersonal utility comparisons. For the sake of the argument in this section, I will assume that there is no problem with making such comparisons.

[49] Lange does provide an analysis of a socialist system with no markets in consumer goods and labor, but he does not favor such a system. See Lange, pp. 90–95.

[50] Of course, it doesn't follow that a coordinating process makes them *worse* off.

advocate of the LT system might argue that under capitalism, with its worker–capitalist conflict of interest, the coordinative processes of the market does not make people better off. Furthermore, while the discoordination produced by planning does make people worse off, this is counterbalanced by the gains produced by the abolition of the producer goods market, and thus the abolition of the capitalist class. So we have the following two claims: first, the efficiency gains produced by coordinative process in capitalism cannot be shown, given the worker–capitalist conflict; second, the efficiency losses produced by planning in the LT system are made up by the gains produced by the abolition of the capitalist class. Thus, in a rough (and vague) way, the LT system is no less efficient than market capitalism.

Both of the above claims cannot be made out. Let us first turn our attention to the claim that the Marxist or socialist views the worker–capitalist relations as purely a zero-sum game.

A Marxist or socialist views capitalism as a vast improvement over feudalism. This is compatible with viewing the worker–capitalist conflict as zero-sum if and only if the sense in which capitalism is a far better system than feudalism is *completely* independent of the production relations between workers and capitalists. This independence cannot be shown. It is uncontroversial that, for a Marxist or socialist, capitalism is a vast improvement over feudalism because it produces an enormous growth in productive power. If we set aside the view that capitalism produces the progressive impoverishment of the working class, which I take it no Marxist or socialist could now hold, the growth in productivity also leads to a rise in real wages and a better standard of living. This growth in productive power could not be achieved, in the long run, by slaves or serfs, so capitalism requires the abolition of slavery and serfdom. Capitalism's search for new markets bring about greater interdependence and more of a world market, thus helping to break down parochial attitudes, "rural idiocy,"[51] and the like. An increase in real wages, the abolition of slavery and serfdom, and the elimination or reduction of parochialism are obviously in the workers' interests. That socialism or communism would or could promote these interests in a more humane, non-alienating manner and without the existence of the capitalist class does not detract from this point.

Turning to the other claim in the second reply – that the efficiency losses produced by planning are made up by gains produced by the abolition of the capitalist class – it runs into the following problem: although capitalists do not exist in the LT system, virtually everything else remains the same from the point of view of the workers. There is no explicit provision for, or even

---

[51] "The bourgeoisie ... has rescued a considerable part of the population from the idiocy of rural life." Karl Marx and Friedrich Engels, *The Communist Manifesto*, chapter II.

mention of, worker control of the means of production in the LT model.[52] Indeed, since the CPB, not the workers, plans investment and fixes producer prices, there could at best be an extremely attenuated form of worker control in the LT system.

To see why, suppose the workers in the various plants hire and fire the managers of the plants, rather than the CPB choosing them.[53] Suppose further that the workers wish to have effective control over pay scales and differentials, worker relations and conditions, and so forth. The myriad of choices that they can make on these matters will affect the amount and type of products they wish to produce. But as I noted in Section II, with prices fixed, the managers – now we substitute "workers" for "managers" – can't induce suppliers to supply more or different inputs or purchasers to purchase more or different outputs by changing prices. Yet it is just such alterations in quantity and quality of inputs and outputs that are needed if the workers are to have some significant effect on the type and amount of products they wish to produce. Worker "control" which purports to control how work is paid and organized, but which has little control over the quality and quantity of what is produced, is pseudo-control, since genuine control of the former requires control of the latter. Or, to put matters another way, since the workers' control over the quality and quantity of what is produced is crippled by the CPB's price-fixing, then their control over the pay and organization of work will be crippled as well.

Thus, from a Marxist or socialist point of view, the gains in the LT system from the abolition of the capitalist class do not appear that great, and so it is dubious that the defender of the LT system could show that the gains from the elimination of the capitalist class cancel out the losses produced by planning.

A third possible gain that a defender of the LT system might mention is the abolition of business cycles. In order for an advocate of the LT system to make this reply, he would have to show that it is the existence of markets in producer goods, rather than markets *per se*, which cause such cycles (and its attendant phenomena, such as unemployment). In fact, Lange made just this argument.[54] Such an argument cannot be taken lightly, since Hayek's

[52] This is one of the primary differences between the LT model and more modern models of market socialism, wherein the economy largely consists of worker controlled firms. The workers in these firms hire and fire managers and have control over pay scales and differentials, worker relations, conditions in the firm, etc. The other principal difference between the LT model and more modern market socialist models is that, in the latter, there is no CPB which fixes producers' prices. There is a full-blown market for producer goods; the role of the state is largely limited to planning new investment. For a representative sample of models of modern market socialism, see David Schweickart, *Capitalism or Worker Control?* (New York: Praeger Publishers, 1980).

[53] Lange's sole comment on this issue is that the managers are "public officials" (p. 74). This doesn't tell us who chooses them.

[54] See Lange, pp. 103, 105–6.

argument rules out the claim that markets coordinate economic activity perfectly, and business cycles involve systemic discoordination.[55] Nevertheless, without delving into business-cycle theory which would take us too far afield, we can provide a good reason to be skeptical of Lange's claim.

If producer markets cause systemic discoordination, this must presumably be due to or constituted by a large number of economic agents' mistaken anticipations about other economic agents' plans, as well as there being no mechanism which has quick enough feedback regarding these errors. In order for the LT system to eliminate or significantly reduce such discoordination, there has to be a mechanism which can discover these mistakes that are scattered throughout the system, and quickly correct them shortly after (or before) they occur. This is precisely what the LT system *lacks*. The small group of persons that makes up the CPB cannot possess all the information scattered throughout the system; nor can they quickly correct mistakes, since its system of price-fixing precludes constant adaptation to changes in local conditions. When Lange says that the advantage of the CPB is that mistakes can be localized in his system, this assumes that the CPB has access to the local knowledge or information scattered throughout the system, and given the division of knowledge, this is precisely what is *not* true.[56] If we are to be persuaded that the LT system gets rid of business cycles, we need to see why Hayek's arguments against the CPB's price fixing do not count against the claim that the CPB can somehow have the information necessary to spot and quickly eliminate systemic discoordination.

I cannot here go into all the possible ways in which a defender of the LT system might argue that it produces gains which compensate for or outweigh losses stemming from discoordination produced by the abolition of producer markets. I have said enough, though, to make it clear why Hayek's arguments, plus the fact that the LT system is one of *market* socialism, place Lange on the defensive. Some of the efficiency gains that a socialist might claim compensate for or outweigh the losses produced by planning are gains that are allegedly produced by the absence of markets *per se*; a market

[55] In fact, on Hayek's view, business cycles arise from problems in producer markets, though the ultimate cause is the monetary policy of central banks. Hayek's business cycle theory is discussed in Gerald P. O'Driscoll, *Economics As a Coordination Problem: The Contributions of Fredrich A. Hayek* (Kansas City: Sheed Andrews and McMeel, Inc., 1974).

[56] *ibid.*, p. 106. When Lange said that mistakes can be localized in his system, perhaps what he meant was simply that there would be less mistakes in his system, since there would be less markets. The abolition of producer markets does not, however, mean that there will be less mistakes in the system. The mistakes in question concern mistaken beliefs or hunches about changing economic conditions, and the replacement of producer markets by CPB price-fixing does not mean that in capital, natural resources, the relation of inputs to outputs, etc., will cease or slow down. That decisions about producer goods will be made less often and by fewer people in the LT system as compared to market capitalism does not show that the amount or complexity of these decisions will diminish.

socialist cannot refer to such gains. Other gains are those allegedly produced by the abolition of producer markets and the capitalist class. However, gains brought about the abolition of the capitalist class are not that high in the LT system, since one of the main benefits that is supposed to occur under socialism – worker control of the means of production – is absent. And Hayek's point that economic problems arise in large part because of the division of knowledge and continual and continuous change counts against the view that a centralized, relatively rigid system could produce efficiency gains that would make up for the efficiency losses produced by planning. Whatever problems there are that are inherent in producer markets in capitalism, solving them will involve obtaining and rapidly disseminating scattered information about constantly changing conditions, and the LT system is worse than market capitalism in this respect.

Summarizing my main conclusions, I have argued that Hayek's dispute with Lange and Taylor has been misunderstood. Hayek was not using the model of perfect competition nor the Pareto-optimality standard of efficiency as the basis for his criticism of the LT system. Instead, he argued that real markets had coordinating mechanisms or processes – that is, mechanisms which, despite scattered information and constant change, tended to bring about the satisfaction of mutually compatible plans – which the LT system crippled. Hayek can be faulted for not making explicit that his conception of efficiency was plan coordination, not Pareto-optimality, but once we realize that this was his standard, his argument seems plausible and strong enough to sustain the charge of relative inefficiency that he leveled against the LT system.

Philosophy, West Virginia University

MARX, CENTRAL PLANNING, AND
UTOPIAN SOCIALISM*

By N. Scott Arnold

Marx believed that what most clearly distinguished him and Engels from the nineteenth-century French socialists was that their version (or vision) of socialism was "scientific" while the latters' was utopian. What he intended by this contrast is roughly the following: French socialists such as Proudhon and Fourier constructed elaborate visions of a future socialist society without an adequate understanding of existing capitalist society. For Marx, on the other hand, socialism was not an idea or an ideal to be realized, but a natural outgrowth of the existing capitalist order. Marx's historical materialism is a systematic attempt to discover the laws governing the inner dynamics of capitalism and class societies generally. Although this theory issues in a prediction of the ultimate triumph of socialism, it is a commonplace that Marx had little to say about the details of post-capitalist society. Nevertheless, some of its features can be discerned from his critical analysis of capitalism and what its replacement entails.

Despite a recent revival of interest in Marx, there has been little discussion of the basic form of economic organization that will characterize post-capitalist society. I shall argue that Marx's view was that post-capitalist society would have a centrally planned economy. If this is right, it should be a matter of some embarrassment or consternation to twentieth-century Marxists. Experience with central planning in this century has not been encouraging, to put it mildly. Gross waste, inefficiency, and general impoverishment (as well as occasional famine) have characterized serious attempts to institute central planning. Furthermore, it has been argued at a variety of levels of abstraction that the Soviet economy, perhaps the historical paradigm of a centrally planned economy, has profound structural problems. That is, its problems are attributable to central planning itself and are not explainable by the usual excuses, e.g., peculiarities of Russian history,

* I should like to thank Peter Cloyes, Harold Kincaid, Danny Shapiro, William Shaw, and th editors of *Social Philosophy and Policy* for helpful comments on earlier drafts of this essay.

capitalist encirclement, or seventy straight years of bad weather.[1] Finally, and perhaps most importantly, central planning does not seem to be on the agenda for the developed and the developing countries today; some combination of markets and noncomprehensive planning seems to be the preferred alternative. No charge is more damaging to a Marxist than one of irrelevance.

How can Marx's commitment to central planning be dealt with by Marx's defenders? Two strategies suggest themselves. One is to argue that Marx need not have committed himself to central planning as the form of economic organization for post-capitalist society. That is, central planning – and the absence of markets it entails – is not crucial to Marx's vision of socialism. The other alternative is to take a harder line and challenge the arguments alluded to above, i.e., deny that central planning necessarily results in gross waste, inefficiency, and poverty. Actual historical phenomena are always deter-mined by a complex of circumstances and conditions. The manifest failure of central planning in, e.g., the Soviet Union and Cuba could perhaps be accounted for by factors external to central planning itself. It could be argued that the latter will work if conditions and circumstances are right – and, so far, they just have not been right.

One of the main purposes of this essay is to show that neither alternative is acceptable. The discussion divides naturally into two main parts: the first part (Sections I and II) documents and provides the motivation for Marx's commitment to the proposition that post-capitalist society will have a centrally planned economy. Section I argues that, despite the apparent paucity of textual evidence, Marx is clearly committed to central planning as the form of economic organization for post-capitalist society. Section II shows that this commitment runs fairly deep in Marx, in that it is motivated by key critical and explanatory elements of his analysis of capitalist society. More specifically, I argue that, according to Marx, alienation is endemic to market systems. If post-capitalist society is to be non-alienating, it cannot have a market system. As Section I demonstrates, central planning is the only alternative (in a complex industrialized society) to some kind of a market system. At the end of Section II, I shall briefly suggest some additional motivations for this commitment. If the argument of Section II succeeds, Marx's commitment to central planning cannot be brushed aside as superficial or inconsequential.

The second part of this essay (Sections III and IV) explores the normative

---

[1] See, for example, Trygve J.B. Hoff, *Economic Calculation in the Socialist Society* (London: Armamento, 1949), and Don Lavoie, *Rivalry or Central Planning?* (Cambridge: Cambridge University Press, 1986). For less abstract, yet highly illuminating, discussions of the Soviet experience, see Alec Nove, *The Economics of Feasible Socialism* (Cambridge: Cambridge University Press, 1983), Part 2 and Peter Rutland, *The Myth of the Plan* (La Salle: Open Court, 1985).

and theoretical problems this commitment creates for Marx and his defenders. Section III is a reconstruction of the argument (first offered in 1919 by Ludwig von Mises) that socialism with a central planned economy has deep-seated structural inefficiencies. This argument provides a relatively abstract and powerful explanation for the failures of existing centrally planned economies; it has the further implication that central planning cannot perform as advertised, given some fairly weak assumptions about the natural and social world in which it operates. Furthermore, these structural inefficiencies are serious enough to raise questions about what would sustain the workers' commitment to Marxian socialism, assuming the latter had been instituted. Section IV considers some ways Marxists might try to avoid the implications of von Mises's argument and raises further questions about the stability of Marxian socialism. If the main argument of Sections III and IV succeeds, it renders Marx's prediction – that his vision of socialism would persist as a stable social form – highly improbable. Finally, it calls into question, in a rather fundamental way, Marx's radical critique of capitalism. If there really is no plausible alternative to some kind of market system, then, to the extent that Marx's complaints about capitalism are directed at the market, Marx turns out to be as utopian as his French predecessors.

I. MARX'S COMMITMENT TO CENTRAL PLANNING

Marx's view on the nature of the economic organization that will characterize post-capitalist society has been the subject of some dispute. Part of the problem is that Marx did not have very much to say about the matter. In addition, partisans of competing visions of post-capitalist society have claimed to find support for those visions in Marx's writings.[2] However, I suspect that one of the main reasons this has been a contentious issue is that those who are in basic sympathy with Marx are reluctant to identify him with any existing non-capitalist economic system. None of these – especially central planning – has performed very well in the twentieth century, and his followers are understandably unwilling to admit that the problem might lie in the master's teaching. Nevertheless, independently of these motivations, the interpretive issue is not straightforward; the attribution of any economic system to Marx's vision of future society requires argumentation and textual support.

Before proceeding to the textual evidence, it would be helpful to construct an analytical framework within which alternative economic systems can be located. Marx's own taxonomy provides a useful point of departure. For Marx, there is a fundamental distinction between systems of production for

[2] For conflicting evidence, see John E. Elliot, "Marx and Contemporary Models of Socialist Economy," *History of Political Economy*, vol. 8 (Summer 1976), pp. 151–84; see especially 175–77

exchange (what he sometimes calls "commodity production") and systems of production for use. In the former, the purpose of production is to get exchange value in the market. (What makes something a commodity is that it is produced for exchange.) The distinguishing feature of a market economy is that there are autonomous and independent producers or production units whose activity is guided by market phenomena. Prices for factors of production and finished goods shape the structure of production in that goods are produced only if (at least) the price of the product covers its cost. Marx claims that the only historically significant system of production for exchange is capitalism.[3]

By contrast, in a system of production for use, products are produced with their ultimate use in view. In primitive, non-exchange economies, the producer either is the consumer or is part of the relatively small social group to which the consumer belongs (e.g., the family, the feudal manor). Production decisions are guided by the need for what Marx calls "use values" (i.e., consumer goods), though of course not always use values that meet the needs of the producers themselves.

All pre-capitalist societies have been systems of production for use. For Marx, this includes primitive communism, Oriental despotism, slavery, and feudalism. This is not to deny that commodity production and market exchange took place in such societies. Indeed, Marx emphasizes that commodity production was present in all pre-capitalist societies, except possibly primitive communism. However, in no case was commodity production the predominant form of production. That is, market phenomena did not determine most of what was produced, nor could the operation of market forces explain the main lines of the division of labor, to the extent that there was such.

What about central planning? From an economic point of view, the ultimate goal of production under a regime of central planning is the production of certain quantities of consumer goods and perhaps a certain rate of growth in the quantity of means of production; the latter makes sense only in the light of the future consumer goods that will flow from them. Thus central planning can be considered a system of production for use. The plan informs production by assigning certain quantities of inputs and certain production targets (outputs) to various production units. Both inputs and outputs are expressed in material terms and not monetary or value terms. A

---

[3] Marx does discuss a system of production for exchange in which the workers control the means of production; he calls this 'simple commodity production'. However, he never maintains that this is an actual, stable historical form of social organization. (See G. Catephores and M. Morishima, "Is There An Historical 'Transformation Problem'?", *The Economic Journal*, vol. 85 (June 1975), pp. 314–15.) This system of simple commodity production is a hypothetical abstraction used to illustrate some points about the economics of commodity production.

steel plant is told to produce certain quantities of various grades of steel instead of being directed to generate a certain monetary volume of sales. Indeed, in a centrally planned economy, there are no sales, since buying and selling entail the mutual alienation of owned objects. Production units in a centrally planned economy do not individually own their means of production or the products they produce. The means of production may be owned by the "associated producers" as a whole, or by the state, or perhaps even by an absolute ruler. (Stalin seems to have conflated all three of these.) The crucial point, however, is that central planning is incompatible with independent and autonomous control of the production of individual production units. Central planning, however much it may be informed by democratic procedures, cannot allow genuine independence for individual production units, at least about what and how much to produce, as well as what shall be done with the products (in the case of raw materials and producer goods). These things must be determined by the plan. Indeed, the whole point of central planning is to eliminate the "anarchy of production" that results from decentralized control and decision-making.

Markets and central planning are alternative ways of solving a problem that arises only at a certain level of complexity in the economic life of a community: the problem of production coordination. Consumer goods in the modern age are rarely produced directly from original factors of production (natural resources and labor). Not only are there many stages involved in the production of finished goods from natural resources, but many raw materials and semi-finished products go into a multitude of production lines. Any complex economic system must solve the problem of coordinating the various lines and branches of production. Competitive markets and central planning are alternative ways of solving this problem. A comparative evaluation of how well they solve this problem will be given in Section III of this essay.

Developments in the twentieth century may seem to have blurred this distinction between planning and markets. Capitalist societies are not pure market economies, and socialist societies have employed markets more or less extensively. However, to say that a society has a market economy (i.e., is a system of production for exchange) does not imply that there is no production for use; it only means that the predominant method of production coordination is exchange on the market. Under capitalism, much of education and national defense have been the result of production for use. In a similar vein, the Soviet Union, perhaps the historical paradigm of a centrally planned economy, has for many years allowed some markets in agriculture and personal services. It has also produced some goods for exchange on the international market. However, these examples of production for the market do not individually or collectively predominate in

Soviet society. It is not misleading to say that the Soviet Union does not have a market economy.

On the other hand, socialist countries that rely extensively on markets (e.g., Yugoslavia) are systems of production for exchange, i.e., market economies. Although the state controls most new investment, as well as the rate of growth, production is still for the market. Production units are autonomous; they buy their inputs from whatever firms they can come to an agreement with and, in a similar manner, sell their output to firms, consumers, or the state. What makes these systems not centrally planned is that the production of certain quantities of products is not mandated by a comprehensive plan. The firms may be state-owned or owned by the workers themselves. In either case, however, since products are sold, profit and loss considerations guide production (subject to selective state interference, but that is true under capitalism as well).

Although it is at least logically possible for a complex society to have no predominant method of production coordination, this does not seem to be empirically possible. It is possible for a market socialist society to have a state sector that is nearly the same size as (or even larger than) the private or worker-controlled sector, but in such cases the state sector will contain many firms producing for the market. Although it may not be possible to prove it outright, I suspect that a system which had a market sector and a planned, production-for-use sector of roughly equal size (so that the system in question could not be called a centrally planned economy or a market economy) would be inherently unstable because of coordination problems. Given the highly interdependent character of production in a complex economic system, the planners would be continually frustrated by the actions of independent production units not subject to their directives. Assuming they had the power of the state on their side, they would have an obvious incentive to bring the so-called private sector under their control, or they might decide to withdraw from active direction of the entire economy, perhaps to concentrate on a few key sectors. That withdrawal would mean that they would defer to market forces for the rest of the economy (subject of course, to selective and irregular interference, such as one finds in capitalism).

It has become fashionable to talk about a mix of plan and market as a third way between capitalism and centrally planned socialism; such a system may be viable,[4] but my point here is that, whatever its virtues and defects, it is a market economy, since the predominant micro-level coordination mechanism is the market. On the other hand, if planning is the primary coordinator of production among the various production units, then it is a centrally

[4] I have argued elsewhere that market socialism, as it is usually conceived, would probably degenerate into capitalism or non-democratic state socialism. See my "Marx and Disequilibrium in Market Socialist Relations of Production," *Economics and Philosophy*, vol. 3 (Spring 1987), pp. 23–47.

planned economy. In such a system, if markets exist, either they are insignificant, or they are merely pseudo-markets. Vague talk about combining plan and market does not specify a coordinating mechanism. Most of those who have thought through the implications of market socialism envision the use of markets as the micro-level coordinating mechanism.[5]

As an aside, it seems that the popularity of vague talk about combining plan and market can be traced in part to contemporary economic thought, which (at least until recently) has been dominated by static equilibrium models. The conception of economic systems that underlies the arguments of this article is much more dynamic. If one is asking how production is coordinated, one is asking for the specification of a mechanism, a dynamic *process*, instead of an account of static *states* of systems. That centrally planned economies, or models thereof, have certain structural similarities to market economies (e.g., both have equilibrium states) obscures the fact that they are activated by very different mechanisms. To repeat, this is not to deny that an actually existing centrally planned economy can allow for some production for exchange in the market, and, similarly, market economies can have some production for direct use, but it is hard to see how an economic system could persist if neither method of production coordination predominated.

Are there any other possible coordinating mechanisms? In the post-feudal world, the answer would seem to be "No." Before the advent of capitalism, production was not a significant problem, since the structure of production was relatively simple. Not only were many fewer kinds of products produced, but the production of most use values was a relatively simple affair. By contrast, in a modern economic system a vast number of different kinds of use values are produced. Perhaps more importantly, the production of nearly everything today is astonishingly complicated. Compare, for example, the steps involved in getting from sowing wheat to eating bread in the context of the feudal manor to the steps involved in the comparable production-consumption sequence in a contemporary (market or centrally planned) economy.

In pre-capitalist economic systems, the highly conservative forces of custom and tradition informed the production of use values and determined whatever division of labor existed. Clearly, however, custom and tradition are inadequate at a certain level of economic complexity and technological change. Although it cannot be proven outright that there is no alternative to central planning or markets as a coordination mechanism for a complex economy, it is hard to imagine what that alternative would look like.

---

[5] See, for example, David Schweickart, *Capitalism or Worker Control?* (New York: Praeger Publishers, 1980); Branko Horvat, *The Political Economy of Socialism* (Armonk: M.E. Sharpe, 1982); Jaroslav Vanek, *The General Theory of Labor-Managed Economies* (Ithaca: Cornell University Press, 1970).

If the above arguments are sound, they establish that (in the post-feudal world, at least) the categories of market economy and centrally planned economy, *as they have been defined here*, are effectively mutually exclusive and collectively exhaustive (which is not to say that there are not important differences between different kinds of market economies or, for that matter, centrally planned economies). The following table summarizes the results:

	PRODUCTION FOR USE	PRODUCTION FOR EXCHANGE
Pre-Modern (simple) **Societies**	primitive communism, Oriental despotism, slavery, feudalism	(simple commodity production)[6]
Modern (complex) **Societies**	central planning	capitalism, market socialism

With this analytical scheme in hand, it is now possible to address the question of Marx's views about the economic system that will characterize post-capitalist society. One factor that might appear to complicate this question is that, in the *Critique of the Gotha Program*, Marx clearly envisages two separate states of post-capitalist society, which have been anachronistically designated as 'socialism' and 'communism'.[7] There are two main differences between them: 1) In the first phase, distribution of the products of labor to the workers is directly proportional to the quantity of labor expended. In the higher phase, the operative principal is "From each according to his abilities, to each according to his needs." 2) Socialism, the immediate successor to capitalism, is characterized by the dictatorship of the proletariat. That is, the state survives as an instrument of the ruling class – this time, the working class. It is used to keep class enemies in line, notably the former bourgeoisie. The state "withers away" after a time, however. The reason for this is that post-capitalist society is a classless society, and without classes, there is little (and eventually nothing) for the state to do. When the state has withered away, communism has arrived.[8]

Despite these important differences, both are classless societies in that the workers control the means of production, and all able-bodied adults are workers. However, by itself this does not imply central planning, since market socialism also involves worker control of the means of production.

[6] See note 3.
[7] This designation of the two stages of post-capitalist society seems to have been first made explicit by Lenin. See his *State and Revolution* (Moscow: Progress Publishers, 1971), ch. V.
[8] Karl Marx, *Critique of the Gotha Programme* (Moscow: Progress Publishers, 1971), pp. 14–18, 26.

Nonetheless, Marx clearly states that the first stage of post-capitalist society will not have a market economy:

> With the co-operative society based on common ownership of the means of production, the producers do not exchange their products.[9]

This passage seems quite strange if one thinks of exchange as a physical phenomenon. It is, however, a social phenomenon, involving mutual transfer of ownership rights among autonomous individuals or production units. What this passage means is that there is no exchange in the sphere of production. That is, production units will not buy and sell raw materials and producer goods from one another. And, if they do not buy and sell from one another, markets cannot coordinate their production.

On the other hand, there will be exchange in the sphere of distribution, since the operative distributive principle is "To each according to his labor contribution." Marx envisages workers receiving labor certificates for the quantity of labor expended (less various deductions for social spending); these certificates are then exchanged for consumer goods. That is, consumers buy products, but Marx insists that what they use is not money, since it does not circulate. That is, it cannot be used as capital. It's not as if there is no exchange in the first phase of post-capitalist society, but there is no *production for* exchange because market phenomena do not guide production. Since there is no suggestion that exchange in the sphere of production will be reintroduced in the second or higher phase of post-capitalist society, it is fair to say that both stages will be systems of production for use. This implies that market socialism is not an option for Marx.

Although the above establishes that Marx believed that post-capitalist society (for ease of exposition, hereafter both stages will be designated indifferently as "socialism") would not have a market economy, it does not prove that he believed that it would have a centrally planned economy; perhaps he did not think about it enough to have any definite views about how production would be organized once markets had been abolished. Though detailed discussion is hard to find, there are some passages in which Marx seems clearly committed to central planning:

> The national centralization of the means of production will become the natural base for a society which will consist of an association of free and equal producers acting consciously according to a general and rational plan.[10]

---

[9] *ibid.*, p. 16.

[10] Karl Marx, *Sochineniia* vol. XIII (Moscow, n.d.), pp. 241–42; as cited in Peter Wiles, *The Political Economy of Communism* (Cambridge: Harvard University Press, 1962), p. 358.

In *Socialism : Utopian and Scientific*, Engels describes the results of proletarian revolution as follows:

> State interference becomes, in one domain after another, superflu-
> ous, and then dies out of itself; the government of persons is
> replaced by the administration of things ... Socialised production
> upon a predetermined plan becomes henceforth possible. ... In
> proportion as anarchy in production vanishes, the political authority
> of the state dies out.[11]

Engel's *Socialism : Utopian and Scientific* is a shortened version of one section of *Anti-Dühring*. Elsewhere in the latter, he is even more explicit in his commitment to central planning:

> The seizure of the means of production by society puts an end to
> commodity production [i.e., production for exchange] and therewith
> to the domination of the product over the producer. Anarchy in
> social production is replaced by conscious organization on a planned
> basis.[12]

Both of these passages seem to indicate Marx's and Engel's commitment to central planning. Market socialists who claim a Marxist heritage might object that, at most, these passages indicate a commitment to planning of some sort, but not necessarily highly detailed and centralized planning. A national strategic plan which leaves room for the limited operation of market forces is not explicitly ruled out by these passages. However, this reading of Marx and Engels is strained and implausible in light of Marx's explicit rejection of markets in the third previous quotation from the *Critique of the Gotha Program* and Engel's rejection of commodity production in the quotation from *Anti-Dühring* just cited. If markets do not coordinate production, then planning must do so; there is no suggestion in Marx or any other writer of any other alternative in a complex economic system. Marx and Engels may well not have thought through the implications of his commitment to central planning – indeed, much of the rest of this paper indicates that they did not – but there cannot be any serious doubt that this is what they believed.

This commitment takes on added significance when we consider what motivates it. The next section investigates one such motivation in Marx's radical critique of capitalism. I shall argue that, according to Marx, one of the most important defects of capitalist society – alienation – is due to the fact that capitalism is a system of production of exchange. If socialism is to be a system in which alienation has been effectively eliminated, this requires the

---

[11] Frederick Engels, *Socialism: Utopian and Scientific* (Moscow: International Publishers, 1985), pp. 70, 75.
[12] Frederick Engels, *Anti-Dühring* (New York: International Publishers, 1939), p. 309.

elimination of commodity production (production for the market) and, by implication, the institution of central planning.

II. MARX'S MOTIVATIONS FOR CENTRAL PLANNING

Alienation is a prominent topic in Marx's early writings, notably in the *1844 Manuscripts*. In the later writings (e.g., *Capital* and *Critique of the Gotha Program*), it is less prominent. This fact, among others, has led to speculation that there are "two Marxes," an early Marx and a later Marx. This is a dispute into which we need not be drawn for the purposes of this essay. It is sufficient to point out that Marx never repudiates the early discussion of the phenomenon, and, as I shall show, the resources made available by the later, more strictly economic writings can be brought to bear to explain in a more detailed way the nature and consequences of the phenomenon. In particular, I shall argue that Marx's explanation of alienation appeals to necessary features of any society in which commodity production predominates.

Commodity production is inherently alienating in a number of respects. Particular, concrete labor becomes "abstract" labor when it takes the form of exchange value. This is a loss for the worker since control over (the product of) his labor belongs to another (under capitalism, the capitalist) and passes to yet another through market exchange. Even if the workers were to control the means of production in a system of commodity production, they would still lose control of the product of their labor at the point of exchange. Secondly, the activity of production – laboring – is itself alienating under a regime of commodity production. It is not intrinsically

> the satisfaction of a need; it is merely a *means* to satisfy needs external to it. Its alien character emerges clearly in the fact that as soon as no physical or other compulsion exists, labor is shunned like the plague. ... As a result, therefore, man (the worker) only feels himself freely active in his animal functions – eating, drinking ... in his human functions he no longer feels himself to be anything but an animal. What is animal becomes human and what is human becomes animal.[13]

This passage says quite a bit about Marx's conception of human nature and its connection to labor; our interest, however, is in the light it sheds on the inherently alienating nature of commodity production. Marx thought of (unalienated) labor as a form of self-creation and as inherently satisfying. Man has an original need that is satisfied by the activity of laboring. However, in commodity production man is not producing to meet this need; instead, he

---

[13] Karl Marx, *Economic and Philosophic Manuscripts of 1844* (Moscow: Progress Publishers, 1974), p. 66.

is producing for exchange in a double sense: the creation of exchange value is the aim of production. Secondly, for the laborer himself, the ultimate goal is not the creation of the product; rather, it is wages. Labor is a mere means, not an end in itself. In consequence, the laborer becomes a mere means to a mere means. By contrast, in a system of production for use, the goal of production is the creation of use values. In such a system, labor is fulfilling its "natural" function or purpose.

Alienation under commodity production has a social dimension as well. Under a regime of production for exchange,

> Each of us sees in his product only his own objectified self-interest and in the product of another person, another self-interest which is independent, alien and objectified. . . . My social relationship with you and my labor for your want is just plain deception . . . Mutual pillaging is at its base.[14]

This is a rather remarkable passage in that Marx seems to be suggesting that exchange is necessarily mutually exploitative, though not in his technical sense of the term. Others' wants and needs are levers that we manipulate in satisfying our selfish desires. This stands in sharp contrast to the more standard (i.e., bourgeois) conception of exchange as mutually beneficial. Which view is correct? Perhaps both are, and a skillful application of the dialectical method is needed to reconcile them. In any case, there is an element of truth in what Marx says.

In the mutual alienation of owned objects that constitutes exchange, there is an inherent conflict of interests: there is always a more favorable alternative for each side which can be achieved only at the other's expense – to wit, the price could be less (at the limit, zero). The inherently conflictive nature of exchange fosters the kind of egoism and individualism for which capitalism has been condemned since its inception. In addition, where exchange value is king, everything from human bodies to good will has a price. It is Marx's insight that these attitudes are rooted in the basic principle that organizes production: exchange in the market. Furthermore, the harmony of interests achieved by competitive markets is a kind of forced harmony resulting from the exploitation of comparative advantage by market participants. Marx views production in its "natural state" (i.e., production for use) as inherently cooperative and directed towards the fabrication of use values. The fact that commodity production is not like this makes it, by its very nature, perverse or pathological.

---

[14] Karl Marx, *Excerpt-Notes of 1844*, quoted in Allen Buchanan, *Marx and Justice* (Totowa: Rowman and Allenheld, 1982), p. 39.

The social character of alienation receives its most elaborate treatment in Marx's famous discussion of the fetishism of commodities in *Capital* I.

> A commodity is therefore a mysterious thing, simply because in it the social character of men's labor appears to them as an objective character stamped on the product of that labor; because the relation of the producers to the sum total of their own labor is presented to them as a social relation, existing not between themselves but between the products of their labor.[15]

The upshot of this passage is that relations among producers masquerade as relations among products of labor. This follows directly from the labor theory of value and the nature of commodity production. According to the former the (exchange) value of a commodity is identical with the quantity of socially necessary labor "congealed" in the product. When objects are produced as commodities (i.e., for exchange), they seem to have value in and of themselves. The exchange value of commodities appears to be an autonomous phenomenon, but it is in fact a reified and distorted expression of relations among producers.

Many commentators on Marx stop here in their exposition of commodity fetishism and do not press on to ask the obvious question: "What is so bad about commodity fetishism?" It is true, if Marx is right, that things are not as they appear in the social world. But physics teaches that this is true of the natural world. For example, a table appears solid, but contemporary physics tells us that it is mostly empty space. The fact that appearance and reality diverge cannot by itself constitute grounds for criticism. To see what the problem is, it is necessary to examine the forces unleashed when commodity production becomes widespread.

In a system of widespread commodity production, market forces – notably competition – shape the structure of production.[16] Things do not get produced for long unless there is a profit to be made; firms that do not show a profit are driven out of business by those that do. These forces can be controlled and moderated to some extent. Capitalists are notorious for trying to get the State to protect them from the rigors of competition. However, as

---

[15] Marx, *Capital* I (Moscow: Progress Publishers, 1977), p. 77.

[16] It might be thought that a regime of petty producers who both own their own means of production but produce for a non-competitive market would be a counterexample to this claim. Marx does discuss such a system under the heading of 'simple commodity production'. However, as noted above (see note 3), he never maintains that such a system ever actually existed. Indeed, at least under conditions of moderate scarcity, it is hard even to conceive of a system of commodity production in which competitive forces do not have a major role. It is worth noting that Engels excoriates Rodbertus for failing to recognize the functional necessity of competition for market economies. See Frederick Engels, "Preface to the Second German Edition," in Karl Marx, *The Poverty of Philosophy* (New York: Intenational Publishers, 1963), p. 16ff.

long as the purpose of production is to get exchange value in the market, competitive forces will operate to favor some individuals and firms over others. This virtually guarantees serious problems for some of the losers. For example, the meager skills of a workman can be rendered useless by the technological advances fostered by competition. In addition, since a regime of commodity production is guided by no overall plan, coordination among independent producers can and does break down, leading to massive unemployment.[17]

The role that fetishism plays in all these phenomena is that it allows the true nature of the problem to be obscured. Market forces are experienced as alien and impersonal; they can and do crush firms as well as individual workers. The root of the problem is, of course, commodity production itself, but the latter produces the illusion that these problems are somehow rooted in the nature of things and are trans-historical in their incidence. That is, it is not evident that they are peculiar to a particular, historically transitory mode of production. The hired flacks of the bourgeoisie, notably the vulgar political economists, bend their efforts to perpetuating these myths. This, as Marxists are fond of saying, is no accident. Fetishism thus prevents the worker from recognizing the true nature of his problem, which is commodity production.

One consequence of Marx's account of the fetishism of commodities is that the mystification produced by commodity production can be dispelled only by eliminating the latter[18] and replacing it with a consciously organized system of production for use. For example, if technological advances render some skills obsolete, the associated producers can consciously decide to withhold the application of this technology; even if they do not, this will be the result of a conscious decision and not something that just "happens," as is the case under a regime of commodity production. Under a system of production for use, social life has a kind of transparency that is lacking under a regime of commodity production.

Marx admits on a number of occasions that commodity production is not

[17] Some economists (e.g., F.A. Hayek) have argued that commodity production is not inherently crisis-prone, and that state intervention in the economy is primarily responsible for the business cycle. Even if this is true, it may be that capitalism is crisis-prone, if state intervention in the economy is endogenous to the latter. In any case, it is clear that Marx and nearly all Marxists believe that capitalism is inherently prone to economic crisis and that the "anarchy of production" is a contributory cause.

[18] Although it is clear that the elimination of commodity production is a sufficient condition for eliminating the mystification it causes, it is less clear that it is a necessary condition as well. For Marx, the false beliefs induced by commodity production are like mirages, which do not "go away" even if their explanation is known. Why Marx thought this is a complicated story which cannot be adequately discussed here. For an excellent discussion, see G.A. Cohen, *Karl Marx's Theory of History: A Defence* (Princeton: Princeton University Press, 1979), pp. 115–33; pp. 326–38.

unique to capitalism; it can be found in all class societies. Only primitive communism and post-capitalist society are without it. To the extent that there has been commodity production in pre-capitalist societies, there has also been alienation as described above. However, only capitalism is characterized by extensive or widespread commodity production. That is, only under capitalism is commodity production the organizing principle by which production is coordinated. In consequence, only under capitalism does alienation become widespread and virulent.

It follows from these considerations that a progressive and revolutionary transformation of society which eliminates alienation requires the virtual elimination of commodity production. It should be clear how this motivates Marx's commitment to central planning. As I have argued in Section I, it is a short step from the wholesale rejection of markets to central planning: recall that without commodity production (and, by implication, market prices), production must be guided and coordinated by some other mechanism. The complexities of any post-feudal society, together with the considerable interdependence that is fostered, make central planning the only genuine alternative way to coordinate production. It is, I think, uncharitable to maintain that Marx was unaware of this relatively immediate implication of this central aspect of his radical critique of capitalist society.

Not all the ills of capitalism are traceable to commodity production. Some, such as exploitation, are due to the class structure that gives control over the means of production to non-workers. In fact, the class structure may be casually related to feelings of alienation among the workers (as many twentieth century writers have stressed) that arise from their powerlessness vis-à-vis the internal structure of the firm. However, all of the other ills associated with alienation are directly traceable to commodity production.

The relation between commodity production and alienation in Marx's writings has been partially obscured by the fact that these topics commanded his attention at different times in his career. In the early writings, where alienation is a prominent topic, he had not clearly identified commodity production as the key to understanding capitalism. In the *German Ideology*, for example, private property and the division of labor are accorded greater significance; both presuppose commodity production, though Marx did not seem to be aware of this at the time (of if he was, he did not make much of it). This is understandable in light of Marx's belief that capitalism is the only historically significant system of production for exchange. Commodity production first gets extensive treatment in the *Grundrisse* and *Capital*. By that time, alienation was not as prominent in Marx's critique of capitalist society. Instead, exploitation (and the associated class struggle) had taken center stage. However, the earlier account of alienation is never repudiated, and, as I have argued above, the later writings (notably the material on commodity fetishism) serve to augment the earlier discussion of alienation.

There are, I think, other motivations for Marx's belief that commodity production cannot characterize socialist society. Elsewhere I have argued[19] that Marx's explanation of the genesis of the capitalist class structure assigns a key causal role to commodity production. If lawlike statements of social causation are construed as tendency claims, and if Marx believes that there really are laws of social development, he would be committed to the view that any society that made widespread use of markets would have a tendency to degenerate into capitalism. Consequently, if socialism is to be a stable form of social organization, it cannot have a market economy.

Furthermore, as noted above, class societies tend to go together with some measure of commodity production. This, I suspect, is no accident. A case can be made that there is a causal connection between commodity production and class societies generally, though I am aware of no place where Marx himself explicitly advances this argument: when products are produced for the market, especially efficient production units have a competitive advantage. That is, comparative advantage (in Adam Smith's sense) yields competitive advantage, at least insofar as there are markets. The accumulation of exchange value that results from success in the marketplace gives those who control these means of production disproportionate social and economic power. Insofar as this disproportionality manifests itself in differential control over the means of production (e.g., by growth of successful enterprises), social classes, in Marx's sense, exist. In other words, production for the market tends to give some producers (or those who control the means of production) social and economic power at the expense of their less advantaged rivals. If production for exchange is not widespread, capitalism may not result; indeed, it did not in pre-capitalist societies, which had some production for exchange. My claim here is only that wherever commodity production occurs, there is some reason to think it will contribute to the formation and/or maintenance of a class society.

How can this problem be dealt with? The comparative advantage that some producers enjoy over others cannot be systematically eliminated. For example, some national and ethnic groups work harder than others, the fertility of land and fisheries varies, energy sources are more abundant in some places than others, etc. On the other hand, competitive advantage can be eliminated, but the only systematic way to do it is to eliminate competition itself, at least as a guiding principle of economic life. That, of course, requires

---

[19] Arnold, "Marx and Disequilibrium ...," Section II.

the virtual elimination of markets. If all this is true, it means that a necessary condition for a classless society is a non-market economic system.

* * * * * * * *

The fact that Marx's vision of socialism, which includes central planning, does not seem to be on the horizon for the developed and developing countries of the First and Third World may be compatible with his prediction of the ultimate triumph of that vision. If the laws of historical change Marx thought that he had discovered are conceived of as tendencies, those tendencies may well still be at work. And the predictive upshot of even strong tendencies can be hard to specify with exactitude. Historical accident and minor counter-tendencies can slow the working-out of dominant trends. It seems to be open to Marxists to claim that (world-wide) socialism is coming; it is just taking longer than Marx thought. After all, capitalism, as a world-wide phenomenon, is still quite vibrant. In the argot of the technological interpretation of historical materialism, there may yet be room for development of the forces of production within capitalist relations of production; the latter may not yet constitute a significant fetter on the former. It might be that the inner dynamics of (world) capitalism were correctly diagnosed by Marx, and its internal contradictions will yet lead to its replacement by socialism.

There is some dispute about Marx's position on how capitalism will meet its demise. Breakdown theorists interpret Marx as saying that capitalism is headed for economic collapse and that socialism will rise to take its place. Others, such as G.A. Cohen,[20] interpret Marx as saying that, although there is no economically legislated final breakdown, the forces of production will grow to the point where capitalist relations of production are significant fetters on the former. Recurrent crises, though not ultimate collapse, will eventually lead to capitalism's replacement by socialism.

One of the main challenges for Marxist theoreticians in the twentieth century has been to deal with the *apparent* failure of Marx's prediction of recurrent and increasingly severe crises for capitalism and the concomitant immiseration of the proletariat in advanced capitalist countries. This might be called "the problem of the transition": how will capitalism, especially in advanced countries, be transformed into socialism? Focus on this question makes the politics of social change (i.e., the transition to socialism) the central issue.

Because attention has been focused on this problem, an equally important question has been neglected, *viz.*, assuming that it can be instituted, can

[20] Cohen, pp. 201–4.

socialism, as Marx conceived it, persist as a stable social form? Perhaps this problem has not seemed so pressing because socialism is usually described (or is it 'defined'?) in such a way that no one would have an incentive to undermine it, at least once the former bourgeoisie have been taken care of in one way or another. But this ignores the possibility that an invisible-hand mechanism might undermine it. In addition, it is possible to describe socialism in a relatively non-normative manner, which allows the evaluative chips to fall where they may. For Marx, socialism, like any other historical form, can be characterized in terms of its relations of production: the workers and only the workers control the means of production, and they do not sell their labor power. For reasons outlined in this section and the last, Marx also maintained that socialism would have a centrally planned economy.[21]

The arguments of the next two sections are addressed to the question of the stability of Marxian socialism. My intent is to raise serious doubts about its viability or stability. Section III argues that central planning faces profound structural problems of economic efficiency. Section IV argues that this and some related difficulties provide good reason to believe that Marxian socialism cannot persist as a stable social form. That is, Marxian socialism is "utopian."

III. INHERENT IRRATIONALITIES OF A CENTRALLY PLANNED ECONOMY

The argument of this section has, by contemporary standards, a long and somewhat checkered history. It was first stated in 1919 when the economist Ludwig von Mises published a paper[22] in which he argued that rational economic calculation in a centrally planned economy is impossible. Since Marxian socialism (hereafter, just "socialism") has a centrally planned economy, it follows that rational economic calculation under socialism is impossible. Exactly what this claim amounts to will take some unraveling, but first some historical background would be in order.

Von Mises's paper inaugurated what came to be known as the "socialist calculation debate."[23] His challenge to socialism was taken seriously by some

[21] It is unclear whether central planning is a logically necessary condition for socialism as Marx conceived it. Although one can be reasonably confident that there are some logically necessary features (e.g., those that specify the relations of production), any attempt to construct a list of jointly sufficient conditions is probably indicative of an unhealthy preoccupation with the analytic/synthetic distinction; in any case, it is foreign to the spirit of Marx. Throughout this essay, I use the term "Marxian socialism" to refer to a system of socialist relations of production with a centrally planned economy.

[22] Ludwig von Mises, "Economic Calculation in the Socialist Commonwealth," reprinted in *Collectivist Economic Planning*, ed. F.A. Hayek (London: Routledge and Kegan Paul), pp. 87–130.

[23] For a useful analysis and summary of the debate, see Don Lavoie, "A Critique of the Standard Account of the Socialist Calculation Debate", *Journal of Libertarian Studies*, vol. 5 (Winter 1981), pp. 41–87. Lavoie's article contains the most complete citation of sources on the debate to date.

economists with socialist sympathies. The textbook account of the debate has it that these economists, notably Oskar Lange (in his "On the Economic Theory of Socialism") and Fred M. Taylor (in his "The Guidance of Production in a Socialist State"[24]), decisively refuted von Mises. It is also commonly held that an argument similar to von Mises's, advanced by F.A. Hayek, was also defeated by the Lange-Taylor argument. A host of other figures took sides in the debate, but the consensus is that von Mises and Hayek were decisively defeated. Despite this convergence of opinion (or conventional wisdom), we know that debates of this sort are not settled by a show of hands.

Great and long-lasting debates almost always involve some misunderstandings on both sides about exactly what is at issue. This one is an outstanding case in point. More than his proponents are willing to admit, von Mises himself was responsible for much of the misinterpretation of his position by the neoclassical economists who opposed him. He often stated that he proved the impossibility of socialism, and he seems to have regarded his proof as *a priori*. On the face of it, neither of these claims seems plausible. However, there is a core argument that has not yet been touched by von Mises's neoclassical critics. In what follows, I should like to reconstruct this argument and explain why it is basically sound.

Von Mises's challenge can best be understood by considering the problem of production coordination. Unless one supposes a pre-established harmony that rivals that of Leibniz, the various branches of production will have to be coordinated in some manner. Since the rise of capitalism, consumer goods have rarely been produced directly from original factors of production (labor and natural resources). Often, many stages of production are required, and many non-specific factors go into a variety of production lines. Basically, this is an allocation problem – how limited resources (i.e., specific and non-specific factors of production, including labor power) are to be allocated to various firms and industries to meet the ultimate goals of production. Let us consider briefly von Mises's vision of how capitalism solves this problem (according to its own lights).

The consumers transmit their needs and wants to the capitalists by their acts of buying and abstentions from buying. The retailer, the wholesaler, the manufacturer, the supplier of capital goods, and the owners of the original factors of production all get information from the marketplace in terms of prices and costs. The existence of pure or entrepreneurial profit is an indication that the existing productive structure is not meeting the needs and wants of the consumers as satisfactorily as possible. In consequence, capital flows into those lines where demand is not being adequately met, and the

---

[24] Both are reprinted in *On the Economic Theory of Socialism*, ed. B.E. Lippincott (New York: McGraw Hill, 1964).

system becomes better coordinated relative to consumer wants and needs as expressed by their dollar "votes." Entrepreneurial profit is not to be confused with the capitalists' return on investment (*qua* capitalist).[25] The fact that most entrepreneurs are also capitalists can obscure this fact. Entrepreneurial profit is the residual left over after all the productive factors (including means of production) have been paid for at their market price. Let us call a decision "entrepreneurial" if it is a decision to initiate, maintain, expand, contract, or terminate a line of production (however one defines the latter). Functionally defined, the entrepreneur is *not* an owner of a factor of production. As a production organizer – and not as a manager – he sets the parameters (if not the details) on what and how much to produce, i.e., the product line and the production quota. Price information is clearly central to this process, though the distinctively entrepreneurial act consists of noticing the right combination of information.[26]

Critics of capitalism have long challenged basic elements of consequences of this story: the demand for consumer goods is manipulated (some say controlled) by the owners of the means of production or their minions; the distribution of income significantly shapes what gets produced and how much it costs; in consequence, the relatively important needs of some go unmet, while the relatively unimportant – or even frivolous – wants of others are met; monopolies distort allocations in favor of certain firms, and so on. In addition, neo-Marxist economists have recently charged that the distribution of income can, in part, be explained by the ruling classes' use of economic and political power.[27] But even if these (essentially normative) points are well-taken, they are consistent with the central claim in the above story: that resource allocation and production coordination is achieved by entrepreneurial decisions based on prices and motivated by the desire for profits. (There is no price theory based on the use of economic and political power.)

To be sure, capitalism operates according to no overall plan. Entrepreneurs are as myopic (and only as myopic) as their personal plans require. This is true even if there is some better way production plans can be coordinated. But, according to von Mises, if markets and market prices are abolished, there will be no adequate data by which to make rational entrepreneurial (i.e., allocational) decisions for the production of consumer goods and producer goods. Those making allocational decisions will be inevitably and forever "in the dark." We have yet to detail exactly why he thinks that this must be the

---

[25] For a discussion of the contribution of the capitalist *qua* capitalist, see my "Capitalists and the Ethics of Contribution," *Canadian Journal of Philosophy*, vol. 15 (March 1985), pp. 87–102.

[26] On all this, see I.M. Kirzner, *Competition and Entrepreneurship* (Chicago: University of Chicago Press, 1973), pp. 154–81.

[27] This approach was inspired by the work of Piero Sraffa. See his *Production of Commodities by Means of Commodities* (Cambridge: Cambridge University Press, 1963). See also Ian Steedman, *Marx After Sraffa* (London: New Left Books, 1977).

case. Before turning to his argument, let us look briefly at two ways the problem might be avoided.

The existence of a problem about production coordination for socialism presupposes that the workers *care* about the extent to which their products fit into some larger scheme. One way to render this problem inconsequential is to drop this assumption. For example, if what is most important to workers is to have satisfying and interesting jobs (in Marx's terminology, labor has become life's chief want), then production coordination will not be very important; dislocations in production that arise because of shortages and surpluses (as well as inappropriate production of consumer goods) will not be viewed as inefficient but as the inevitable accompaniments of a more satisfactory work environment. After all, what counts as efficient depends on what one's ultimate goals are. It is myopic to believe that the goals of production will be the same under socialism as they are under capitalism.

Unfortunately, this approach does not satisfactorily avoid the problem of production coordination. Although the internal organization of productive processes may be very important, it will not have infinite value. Clearly, if the workers are faced with the choice between starvation and more onerous working conditions, they will choose the latter. Labor may become "life's chief want," but it is not the only one. These observations are obvious enough, but they point to some facts about production which have been insufficiently appreciated by Marx and his followers:

(i) Economic or productive efficiency (i.e., efficiency considered in abstraction from the intrinsic value of labor) is not completely determined by the physical productivity of the productive process. Efficiency claims make sense only relative to some goal. Under socialism, the goal of production is the creation of use values. If a steel mill produces ten thousand tons of steel, half of which rusts unused in the yard, it – or the economy of which it is a part – is grossly inefficient, irrespective of the physical productivity of the manufacturing process.[28] Production coordination has significant instrumental value whether the ultimate goal of production is profit or use. It is preposterous or perhaps even logically impossible for a system of production for use, rationally controlled by the workers, to be indifferent to efficiency considerations generated by the problem of coordinating production.

(ii) The human condition is such that people cannot have everything they want – or even everything that it would be good for them to have,

---

[28] This also suggests that physical output figures may be an inaccurate guide to growth in the forces of production. Unused, rusting steel is not a force of *production*.

however the latter is defined.[29] There is no reason to believe that there would be a pre-established harmony between what the workers would most prefer with regard to the nature and organization of work in the production unit and what would satisfy productive efficiency demands imposed by coordination requirements of the plan. Indeed, if this harmony did exist, capitalism would not have many of the problems it has; choices have costs in terms of foregone opportunities, and rationality requires calculation on the margin. For example, some productive efficiency can be sacrificed for better working conditions, but at some point the (productive efficiency) costs become too high. In a system of production for use, these conflicts must be systematically and rationally adjudicated. In short, production coordination poses problems that cannot be ignored.

The general problem underlying these considerations is that scarcity, in the economic sense, will not disappear: there will be competing demands on limited resources. Marx's utopian vision of a world of superabundance notwithstanding, scarcity is a feature of the human condition for the simple reason that some projects must be foregone if others are to be seen through – and there are always useful projects that can be done. If these opportunity costs are to be calculable, and if competing demands on limited resources are to be rationally adjudicated, resources, including labor power, must be rendered commensurable as to their scarcity value. Calculation, as opposed to mere guesswork, requires that this value be expressible in units of something. In short, productive resources must have prices. (We do not here consider the question of whether or how consumer goods should be priced.)

This poses an obvious and immediate problem for central planning as it has traditionally been understood. Central planning proceeds by what Peter Rutland[30] has called the method of material balances. The plan assigns firms a certain quantity of inputs and calls for a certain quantity of outputs. Both inputs and targeted outputs are expressed in physical terms, not value terms. This is appropriate in a system of production for use, since decisions to produce use values (i.e., consumer goods) determine the production of producer goods in such a system. If rational economic calculation requires prices which reflect relative scarcity values, then von Mises's claim that rational economic calculation is impossible in a centrally planned economy seems sustained, simply because central planning uses the method of material balances and makes no significant use of prices.

[29] For the purposes of this essay, nothing hangs on distinguishing wants and needs. Nor does the argument depend on any account of the difference between legitimate or undistorted needs and wants and illegitimate or distorted needs and wants. That would require a large theory of human nature. Marx's conception of what counts as a need is fairly generous, since he believes that needs are historically determined.

[30] Rutland, pp. 114–17.

However, it is at least possible for central planning to use prices as expressions of relative scarcity, so as to calibrate the value of inputs and outputs. But they cannot be *market* prices, i.e., prices set by individual autonomous firms whose purpose is to get exchange value in the market; in this case, the system is one of commodity production. Instead, prices must be set by some non-market mechanism. And the method of material balances must continue to be used if central planning is to be a genuinely centralized system in which decisions to produce use values guides production (i.e., a system of production for use). What role would there be for prices? The non-market prices of a centrally planned economy could serve to inform the planning process on the question of relative costs, even if such prices do not determine what and how much gets produced. For example, the planners may not want to shut down a large factory that is operating at a loss, but they would want to know that it is operating at a loss, and they would want to have some idea of the extent of those losses. Pricing the factors of production is a necessary condition for knowing either of these.

Marxian socialists might agree that the problem of relative scarcities cannot be ignored and must be solved by pricing the factors of production. However, they might maintain that this problem really has already been solved. After all, socialism does not come onto the scene *ex nihilo*; it replaces capitalism. The workers can and will take over the existing productive apparatus of society. The coordination achieved under capitalism by market mechanisms can, with minor adjustments, be maintained by the new social order. Unfortunately this method of calculation will not be rational in an economic system whose purpose is to meet human wants and needs. The reason for this fact is, in a word, *change*.

If the workers, through their central planning committee, are to use the means of production efficiently to meet human wants and needs, they must take into account five broad categories of change:[31]

1. *Change in the physical world.* Soil becomes exhausted, minerals and petroleum are consumed, weather and climate change. Many environmentally conscious socialists envision a world almost totally dependent on renewable resources.[32] It is pertinent to wonder whether this presupposes a technological *deus ex machina* that rivals that of the most fanatical advocates of growth. However, even if it does not, and a decent standard of living can be achieved by an almost complete reliance on renewable resources, the problems involved in dealing with

---

[31] See Ludwig von Mises, *Socialism: An Economic and Sociological Analysis* (New Haven: Yale University Press, 1951), pp. 196–208.

[32] See, e.g., Schweickart, pp. 219–20.

changes in the physical world remain formidable. Mutually adjusting changes that bring an ecosystem into balance can dramatically alter those features of the natural world that humans happen to find valuable. It is also likely that the manner in which resources can be renewed will change over time. An acre of fertile land can be kept at a constant level of fertility almost indefinitely, provided that one is willing to devote sufficient resources to keeping it that way. For the renewal of these resources to be rational, opportunity costs must be calculable.

2. *Changes in population.* The absolute number and demographic profile of a population will change over time. The rough outlines of some of these changes can be predicted, but this does not alter the fact that change will occur and must be dealt with.

3. *Changes in means of production.* Machinery and tools wear out. Assuming that the relevant raw materials and consumer needs remain constant (an enormous assumption), the means of production will have to be replaced. Furthermore, new means of production must be produced if social welfare is to be increased or even redistributed.

4. *Technological changes.* New techniques of production will be discovered and decisions must be made about whether and how they are to be used. Not all technological change counts as an improvement vis-à-vis the task of meeting the goals of production. Suppose that a change in a chemical plant can produce greater output with the same raw material input. Is the plant more efficient? Not necessarily. If the process requires more labor or more highly skilled labor (that could be better used elsewhere), it might not be. It also might be less efficient if the machinery wears out more quickly. Technical change, like all other change, ramifies in ways that require new decisions.

5. *Changes in consumer preference.* Marx reminds us that human needs are historically determined. It is an impoverished socialist vision which assumes that human needs in the future will differ in only minor ways from human needs under capitalism.

Change is inherently disruptive to the productive apparatus of any society, but it is an economically significant fact of life. In the words of G.L.S. Shackle, we live in a kaleidic world.[33] Continual *and* continuous change require that entrepreneurial decisions be made all the time. Schumpeter partially recognized the importance of entrepreneurial decisions under

---

[33] "It will be a kaleidic society, interspersing its moments or intervals of order, assurance, and beauty with sudden disintegration and a cascade into a new pattern. ... It invites the analyst to consider the society as consisting of a skein of *potentiae* and to ask himself not what *will* be its course, but what the course is capable of being in case of the ascendency of this or that ambition entertained by this or that interest." G.L.S. Shackle, *Epistemics and Economics* (Cambridge: Cambridge University Press, 1972), p. 76.

capitalism in his discussion of the "creative destruction" of the innovator-entrepreneur.[34] The vision of von Mises that has been sketched here views entrepreneurial activity in a market economy as much more pervasive and basic than Schumpeter imagined. Entrepreneurial activity is not limited to the application of major technological innovation. Entrepreneurship consists of marshalling resources to meet changing conditions, and conditions are changing all the time. Even the decision to continue to produce a given product in the same quantity is speculative and entrepreneurial in a kaleidic world. In a world of no change (in the five broad categories of change outlined above), there would be no entrepreneurial activity.

What this discussion of change shows is that the price structure of a socialist economic community must change to reflect changing economic realities if the productive apparatus is to be tolerably coordinated to meet human wants and needs. To put it another way, rational economic calculation requires changes in the valuations of the various factors of production.[35] The nature of the challenge von Mises poses for socialism should now be fairly clear. What is not yet clear is why it cannot be met.

To get a handle on this, it is necessary to clarify how market prices are used – and, in particular, how changes in market prices are used – to coordinate production in a market system. It is at this juncture that Hayek's contribution to the debate takes center stage.[36] Hayek's central insight is that market prices are fraught with epistemological significance. The price at which someone is willing to buy or sell tends to reflect his plans for the money or the object he would get in exchange *and* his knowledge of alternatives. The prevailing market price (if there is just one price) amalgamates the knowledge and plans of (some of) the participants. Changes in prices reflect changes in those plans or beliefs about alternatives. Let us consider an example. Suppose that a new use for tin is discovered or an existing source of tin dries up unexpectedly. All the users of tin should be informed that it should be used more sparingly. A rise in the price of tin indicates this. These firms and individuals do not know why tin should be used more sparingly, but for their purposes, they don't have to know. The rise in price simply says, "Use less tin." The height of the rise gives them some indication of how much less should be used. The actual drop-off in demand cannot be predicted very

[34] Joseph Schumpeter, *Capitalism, Socialism, and Democracy* (New York: Harper and Row, 1942), pp. 81–86.

[35] This assumes that no one can foresee all changes or their effects, i.e., that no one is omniscient in this connection. Of course, to the extent that the effects of change can be foreseen, they will be reflected in current factor prices. More on this below.

[36] F.A. Hayek, "The Uses of Knowledge in Society," *American Economic Review*, vol. 35 (September 1945), p. 524; reprinted in F.A. Hayek, *Individualism and Economic Order* (London: Routledge and Kegan Paul, 1949).

well, since how much less will be demanded at the new price will depend on the plans of the users and the knowledge of alternatives open to them.

A further consequence of the rise in price is that the production of substitutes will increase, as will (eventually) the production of substitutes for substitutes, and so on. Of course, what counts as a substitute will vary from one individual or group to another, depending on the uses for which they have plans. Some uses of tin will no longer be economical, and production of those items will cease. Exploration for new sources of supply may increase. In short, the structure of production will undergo a number of changes which may be more or less significant. That is, production has been recoordinated to meet changes in the underlying economic realities (here a drop in supply or an increase in demand for tin). No one person or committee had to make all of these decisions. Prices transmit the necessary information from the owners of the tin mines to those who wanted and needed to know. Entrepreneurial profit (or loss) comes from being among the first (or last) to notice, either through luck or foresight, that people's plans are not as well-coordinated as they might be relative to the underlying economic realities. By the actions they take in response to changing realities, they signify to others to follow suit. For example, if a speculator learns of an ecological disaster in the cranberry bogs of eastern Massachusetts (where most of the world's cranberries are grown), he immediately begins buying up all the cranberries on hand that he can. Competition tends to wipe out entrepreneurial gains as time passes and more speculators enter the field.[37] What causes the price to go up is the fact that some owner of cranberries sees a profit opportunity and raises his prices to speculators. Other owners soon follow suit. It is an obvious but important truth that people, and not "the market," raise the price. The Mises–Hayek insight is that *all* profit is essentially speculative. The desire for profits makes the knowledge provided by previous or existing prices *effective* knowledge, since those affected have a strong incentive to act on the perceived discrepancy between actual prices and prospective prices. In a market system, present prices tend to reflect present and past economic realities; price changes represent changed estimates about future realities. Since the number of different possible combinations of productive factors is enormous, successful entrepreneurship is usually a matter of reshuffling a number of different resources to meet changing realities.

The entrepreneur does not upset equilibrium as Schumpeter believed; rather, the quest for entrepreneurial profit moves the system *towards* equilibrium, insofar as entrepreneurs are successful. Equilibrium exists if and

---

[37] Von Mises and Hayek do not presuppose perfect competition in the neoclassical sense. Under "perfect competition," there are no entrepreneurial profits at all. Everyone is a "price-taker," and all factors receive their marginal value.

only if everyone's plans are perfectly coordinated.[38] To put it another way, the potential for entrepreneurial profit will exist as long as the plans of individuals and firms are not perfectly coordinated. As long as some factor of production (specific or non-specific) is or could be used in some undertaking somewhere to generate a (pure) profit, coordination will not be perfect, and the system will not be in equilibrium. It is of considerable importance to see why this will *always* be the case.

Part of the answer should already be obvious. Changes in the underlying economic realities can disrupt coordination among various branches of production. However, the occurrence of change is not a sufficient condition for the possibility of entrepreneurial profit. After all, if all relevant changes could be foreseen by those people and groups that are affected, those changes would already be reflected in factor prices and no profit opportunities would exist. A necessary condition for entrepreneurial profit is ignorance on the part of some market participants about these underlying realities. The attempt to capture entrepreneurial profit consists in the attempted exploitation of (what the entrepreneur believes to be) the ignorance of others.

One might wonder why ignorance is so widespread in a market economy. Actually, it is not; the knowledge exists, but it is socially scattered. Everyone possesses or comes to possess economically significant knowledge of a very particular nature. For example, the farmer knows that his tractor cannot make it one more season and that he will need to buy a new one before next year; the tin mine operator learns that his deposits are not as extensive as he had thought; the peach orchard owners know of a local killing frost; a Marxist pamphleteer knows he will need the services of a printer to get out his latest warning about the plans of the multi-national corporations. The "economic problem" is to transmit that knowledge to others who need to know about it – and it must be transmitted in a way that is effective for action. According to Hayek, the economic problem is *not*, as standard neoclassical economics maintains, merely a question of how to allocate given scarce resources among given competing ends. Rather, Hayek (and von Mises) see the problem as one of how dispersed and fragmented knowledge not given to any one mind can be socially mobilized. Though market systems are never perfectly efficient (in the sense that everyone's plans are perfectly coordinated), they possess a mechanism that allows and motivates individuals and firms to make the system more efficient when they discover uncoordinated plans arising from the ignorance of some people about present or future realities. Given the empirical fact that some people have the knack

[38] See F.A. Hayek, "Economics and Knowledge," *Economics*, vol. 4 (February 1937); reprinted in *Individualism and Economic Order*, pp. 59–61.

for becoming alert to price discrepancies (i.e., uncoordinated knowledge and plans), the market provides for a systematic way to wipe out social ignorance.

An adequate understanding of how market pricing solves the problem of production coordination helps to make clear what is required of central planning. We have seen that rational economic calculation under socialism requires the (non-market) pricing of factors of production. Although it is not irrational to have a socialist firm producing at a loss, it would be irrational for those in control to make no effort to find out the extent of those losses. Only by pricing factors of production can competing demands on scarce resources be systematically adjudicated. Von Mises never explicitly considered a pricing mechanism for central planning, because in the late nineteenth and early twentieth century advocates of central planning envisioned the abolition of money prices. However, his argument can be easily extended to cover central planning with a pricing mechanism.

Von Mises's basic insight is that the abolition of market prices creates insurmountable knowledge problems for the planners. *Given* a complete set of consumer preferences, *given* a certain level of technological development, *given* various quantities and qualities of natural resources, means of production, and labor power, marginal productivity theory yields a Pareto-optimal allocation of resources. Von Mises's most famous opponent in the "great debate," Oskar Lange, took von Mises to be denying that a Pareto-optimal allocation is possible for socialism.[39] However, the problem for von Mises has always been that the above "givens" are not given to any one mind or small group of minds. With the assumption of perfect knowledge, standard in neoclassical economics, the latter clearly begs the question against von Mises. The latter was always willing to grant the feasibility of Marxian socialism if God was the chief planner. (This is not wholly tongue-in-cheek; some Europeans, at least since the time of Hegel, have been known to regard the State as possessing some of the attributes of the Deity.)

The basic problem is that changes in the underlying economic realities are revealed directly to individuals scattered throughout the economy and not to the planners. In extending von Mises's argument, the crucial claim is that any non-market pricing mechanism in a (complex) centrally planned economy must be completely inadequate to the task of tending to reflect accurately these economically significant changes.

The argument for this claim starts from the observation that the ultimately significant changes discussed above are of a very specific nature – the mechanical integrity of a particular machine, the fertility this year of this plot of land, Farmer Brown's need for a particular constellation of farm machinery at various times, the unexpected discovery of new coal deposits of

---

[39] Lange in Lippincott, pp. 59–61.

a certain grade at a certain location, etc. These facts are not under the control
of the planners and thus are not directly known to them. Even whether or not
previous plans have been successfully carried out is not directly known to the
planners. How, then, will the planners find out about these changes?

Presumably, reports will be filed by those at the periphery (i.e., those
closest to the changes). However, those at the periphery cannot transmit to
the center everything they know (or, more accurately, everything they think
they know) that might be relevant. The relative value-significance of the
information that is revealed at the level of the individual or the firm will
always be somewhat unclear in a complicated system in which the ultimate
goal of creating use values guides all production – even production that is at
the greatest remove from the consumer. In consequence, those who gather
the information must be given guidelines (how are these to be determined?),
and their knowledge must be summarized in statistical form to be
manageable. Furthermore, as information flows up to individuals or
committees with wider and wider areas of responsibility, those who are
responsible must evaluate what information will be most significant for the
ultimate decision-makers. The problem with statistics as a basis for economic
decision-making was clearly recognized by Hayek nearly forty years
ago:

> The statistics which such a central authority would have to use
> would have to be arrived at precisely by abstracting from minor
> differences between things, by lumping together as resources of one
> kind, items which differ as regards location, quality, and other
> particulars, in a way which may be very significant for the specific
> decision. It follows from this that central planning based on
> statistical information by its very nature cannot take direct account
> of these circumstances of time and place.[40]

Those who view aggregates (e.g., price levels, GNP figures, various indexes)
as the basic economic realities often miss this point; much economically
significant knowledge will always remain beyond the comprehension of any
one mind or even a small group of minds. Given that the ultimate
determinants of relative scarcity value are continually changing and highly
particular facts, the farther removed the price setters are from the periphery,
the more blind they must become as economically significant information
gets screened out. As the above quotation from Hayek implies, pricing
decisions will reflect misleading and inappropriate aggregations.

There is also a serious incentive problem facing a centrally planned
economy. Traditionally, critics of socialism have argued that people just

---

[40] Hayek, "The Uses of Knowledge in Society," p. 524.

won't put forth the required effort for the greater good. This has been a genuine difficulty for existing centrally planned economies, and a variety of schemes have been devised to overcome it. However, this is *not* the problem I am calling attention to here. Rather, the problem is how to design institutional mechanisms which will give those at the periphery the incentive to report the relevant information accurately. If success for a production unit is defined in terms of fulfilling the stated goals of the plan (and in a centrally planned economy, it is hard to see how else it could be defined), it would seem that there will be strong incentives for the workers or their representatives to underestimate plant capacity, to hoard means of production and labor power, and to overstate actual production. (Nor need all of this be intentional.)

Indeed, production coordination may well have the characteristics of a public good, in Mancur Olson's sense. The benefits are non-excludable in that they are provided to many non-contributors (e.g., the public at large), providing this good is usually a cost for a given individual, and the contribution one person can make will usually be negligible. As Olson has argued,[41] even an altruist will find it rational not to contribute when these general conditions are met. In consequence, it is likely that the institutional structures which emerge will have to rely on coercion (the classic solution to a public goods problem) to secure the good in question (production coordination). It is at least suggestive that the problem sketched above – and the coercive solution – have characterized existing centrally planned economies such as the Soviet Union.

It might be objected that pricing decisions for factors of production could be left to the discretion of individual firms as a way of giving the planners access to new information about the state of the economy. They could let their planning be guided (though not completely determined by) this information. In other words, the problems described above arise only if those making production decisions also have to set producer prices. Let us assume, then, that individuals and firms are given the authority to set prices for the factors of production they produce.

The difficulty with this solution becomes apparent when one asks what guides those who make these pricing decisions. Certainly they cannot be aiming at maximizing exchange value for the firm; by definition, they are not producing for exchange. Nor can they use the neoclassical economists' equilibrium rule, "Let price = marginal cost," for two reasons. First, this rule is appropriate only if costs are equilibrium costs, which, as Hayek has shown, is never achieved in the real world. More importantly, the actual (as opposed to hypothetical) marginal cost of a product depends on which

---

[41] Mancur Olson, *The Logic of Collective Action* (New York: Schocken Books, 1965), chs. I and II.

constellation of inputs a producer chooses and what kind of deal can be arranged with suppliers. If individual production units are allowed to decide these questions for themselves, then the plan is no longer affecting production coordination by determining what is going to be produced and in what quantities. In short, central planning has been abandoned. This is production for the market, whatever the legal fictions are.

Firms in a market economy do not know the best price to charge, either. They have to guess, but competition (including competitively-determined cost prices) provides the feedback mechanism to let them know how they are doing. By contrast, in a centrally planned economy which leaves pricing decisions to the firm, there is no direct feedback mechanism to inform those who make pricing decisions about how well they are doing. They could try to make their prices bring supply and demand into balance – where what is supplied and what is demanded is set by the plan. Then, however, prices are not providing the planners with new information about underlying economic realities; instead, they are needlessly duplicating information contained in the plan.

If prices are to reflect relative scarcities, and yet if prices do not determine what actually gets produced in what quantities, it is hard to see how success can be distinguished from failure. The planners are supposed to be getting information from the price-setters, and neither the former nor the latter has any independent way (in the absence of markets) to determine whether their estimates are even roughly accurate. Paper losses may indicate faulty pricing or poor planning; there seems to be no way to know which. Plant managers (who, presumably, would set prices) can be and are evaluated, but success for them is defined in terms of fulfilling the target set by the plan. If firms have price-setting autonomy and ordinary financial criteria determine production, then the system has regressed to one of production for exchange.

Successful human action requires knowledge and will. By separating production decisions (will) from pricing decisions (knowledge), this version of central planning lapses into incoherence. A system in which the planners make pricing decisions is like a market system in one important respect: those who make the pricing decisions are the same as those who make the production decisions. Unfortunately, the former kind of system is overwhelmed by the epistemological problems outlined earlier.

Thus far, the argument has proceeded on the tacit assumption that the planners know what consumer goods are to be produced and in what quantities. The Mises–Hayek argument is powerful enough to grant this (wildly implausible) assumption. But, in the real world, central planning must face this problem. Undoubtedly it will begin with historical data, though socialist thought invariably envisions a resetting of priorities in this area. The problems facing central planning in the production of consumer goods are basically the same as those encountered with producer goods.

In another context, Oskar Lange has suggested[42] that the planners could be guided by shortages and surpluses in setting consumer prices. If there is a shortage of a product, its price could be raised; if there is a surplus, it could be lowered. There are a number of obvious difficulties with this approach. First, it makes prices reflect what happened in the past instead of a speculative guess about future conditions. It assumes that people's buying habits are constant, which, in general, is not true. Perhaps more importantly, it specifies no mechanism for innovation or valid product differentiation. The relevant information must be gathered through other means; the problems detailed above for producer goods will apply, *mutatis mutandis*, to the consumer goods sector.

There is a suggestive parallel to these problems in ethical theory; the so-called paradox of happiness is that happiness is best achieved not by aiming at it directly but by aiming at things that cause it or accompany it. In a similar vein, producing things that meet the wants and needs of the consumers is best achieved not by planning directly for the production of use values. Instead, the most efficient procedure is for producers to produce for exchange value.

Von Mises's claim about the inefficiency of Marxian socialism is an empirical one. His argument does not amount to an *a priori* proof, though he sometimes seems to have thought so. Perhaps the reason for this is that the empirical assumptions the argument makes are extraordinarily weak. Given a moderately complex economy, given that economically significant change happens continuously, and given that knowledge of these changes is widely scattered, the constraints imposed by a system of central planning create significant barriers to the effective use of this knowledge for the purposes of coordinating production.

IV. Doubts About the Viability of Marxian Socialism

The exact significance of Mises's argument for Marxian socialism is not immediately evident. It does show that central planning has important inherent irrationalities ("contradictions"). If the problem is serious enough, it becomes hard to explain why the associated producers would retain it, especially since post-capitalist society is not a class society. Perhaps the ultimate significance of the argument can be best appreciated by examining some strategies Marxists might adopt[43] to defeat it, or at least to take the sting out of its conclusions.

[42] Lange in Lippincott, pp. 86ff.
[43] I say "might adopt" because, as far as I am able to determine, few Marxists are even aware of this problem; among those that are, none has dealt with it at a theoretical level without retreating to some form of market socialism.

It might be objected that the epistemological problems caused by the elimination of market prices can be satisfactorily solved by the extensive use of computers. Because computers are able to process quickly huge quantities of information, the hope is that the pricing mechanism in a centrally planned economy could be automated to the extent that the epistemological problems facing central planning would be significantly ameliorated.

There are four difficulties with this objection. First, the quantity of information that would have to be processed for computers to make a real difference is simply staggering. In the Soviet Union, for example, it has been estimated that the planning apparatus currently can process only 3 billion out of 120 to 170 billion bits of information.[44] Given that unforeseen but economically significant change is happening continuously, it is hard to see how computers could do what needs to be done in a timely manner. More importantly, the information generated only provides a picture of what has happened in the past. A simple projection of this data into the future would be as irrational as driving a car by watching the rear-view mirror. If the data include estimates from the periphery about impending changes in the relevant information, then inconsistent estimates have to be resolved and unforeseen changes must be ignored. It is hard to see how a systematic solution to these problems can emerge without decentralizing actual decision-making.

Another problem concerns how information is categorized or aggregated for the purposes of planning and pricing. As the above quotation from Hayek suggests, aggregation must be very fine-grained to be useful. It is not enough for the planners to know how much steel there is in the country; they need to know, e.g., what grades are available, what its condition is, etc. Ideally, two things would be of the same kind if and only if they are substitutes for one another. The problem is that "a" is a substitute for "b" only relative to some purpose. For example, two grades of coal are substitutes for one another relative to one purpose (e.g., power generation in a low-pollution environment) but are not substitutes for one another relative to some other purpose (e.g., power generation in a high-pollution environment).

The real problem here is not that this (ideal) level of aggregation is unachievable (though that is probably true); after all, no system is perfect. Rather, the problem is one of determining how fine-grained the distinctions should be. To assume that some sort of cost-benefit analysis can resolve this difficulty is to assume that there is a reliable pricing mechanism already in place; that, of course, is just what is at issue. Indeed, an entrepreneur in a market system (whether capitalist or market socialist) can rationally decide to remain ignorant of certain information if the costs of gathering and

---

[44] Rutland, p. 192.

processing information are too high relative to prospective benefits. This rational ignorance presupposes that the cost prices of information tend to be relatively accurate reflections of scarcity value. Since posted prices under central planning would not tend to be relatively accurate, central planning has a kind of second-order irrationality in that the planners cannot have any clear idea about when it is rational to seek or not to seek more information.

The third problem is that some economists have argued[45] that successful entrepreneurship in a market economy requires a "sense of the situation" that cannot be articulated. That is, it requires tacit knowledge that cannot be expressed in propositional form. If computers are to simulate successful entrepreneurship through the pricing mechanism, the prospects for computerizing this process are not promising.[46]

Finally, a more profound difficulty becomes evident if we grant that, eventually, computers can satisfactorily solve the epistemological problem. It is one thing to maintain, as Marx does, that different relations of production are appropriate to different levels of development of the forces of production. Marx adduces some relatively deep reasons why there are such correlations. However, if the success of socialism crucially depends on the development of one particular technology (the digital computer), that success would be very fragile indeed.

A second approach to mitigating the problem of production coordination in a centrally planned economy would be to simplify the structure of production. If the pathways from original factors of production to consumer goods were fewer and shorter, central planning might be more adequate to the task. This objection is hard to evaluate because of its vagueness. However, there is some reason to think that it won't do.

Two factors primarily determine the level of complexity in an economic system:[47] the variety of consumer goods that the system ultimately produces, and the number of alternative pathways from the original factors of production to the consumer goods. The latter factor is largely determined by technology and the current state of scientific knowledge. As technology develops, the number of alternatives grows. Furthermore, technological advances can make what were once relatively specific factors of production relatively unspecific; finally, technology brings new factors of production

[45] See Don Lavoie, *National Economic Planning: What is Left?* (Washington: The Cato Institute, 1985), pp. 76–87.

[46] There have been some efforts to program computers to simulate abilities of this sort in expert systems research. Results thus far have been disappointing. For some principled objections to this program, see the revised edition of Hubert Dreyfus, *What Computers Can't Do* (New York: Harper and Row, 1979).

[47] A third factor is the absolute size of the population served by the economy in question. How large this population is depends in part on how "economies" are individuated. At this time, it is unclear to me how much absolute population size is responsible for complexity in the structure of production. Pre-capitalist economic systems were composed of relatively small autarchic units; their small size was surely a factor in making a system of production for use feasible.

into existence. This obviously makes production coordination more complicated and difficult. Socialists clearly do not envision regression in the level of technological development. What about consumer goods? Probably there would be less product differentiation than under capitalism, but it is by no means clear there would be appreciably fewer kinds of consumer products. Socialists in general, and those inspired by Marx in particular, conceive of socialism as the "realm of (positive) freedom" in which each person's individuality could be expressed and/or realized. As previously exploited and oppressed peoples' individuality and creative potential are unleashed, the challenges to the economic system will increase, not decrease.

The objections discussed above attempt to argue that the epistemological problems posed by the need for production coordination could be manageable under central planning. However, even if these objections were well-taken, they do not address the parallel motivational problems. Recall that this is *not* the problem of how to get people to work hard under a different distributional system. Rather, it is how to motivate those at the periphery to report accurately changes in economically significant information, e.g., the extent to which past production targets have been met, the quantity and condition of labor power and means of production on hand, etc. A coercive solution to this problem is contrary to the other socialist ideals and inefficient to boot. I leave it to Marxists to articulate a non-coercive solution to this problem.

A more promising strategy for dealing with the Mises-Hayek argument would be to grant its conclusion about the productive inefficiency of central planning, but argue that this problem would not be so serious that the associated producers would reject Marxian socialism.[48] Suppose that there is a socialist revolution; the workers seize control of the means of production and proceed to "organize production consciously on a planned basis." As priorities are reordered, discoordination will probably increase, but it is not evident that utter chaos would result. Eventually, the economy might stabilize and plug along at a lower level of productive efficiency. Growth might occur over a long period, so progressive immiseration is not a worry.

Although this is abstractly possible,[49] the problem with this scenario is that it runs up against one of the more plausible theses of Marx's theory of

[48] Indeed, there is an instructive parallel here with the development of socialist thought since Marx. Originally, socialists, including Marx and Engels, argued that the superiority of socialism lay in its huge potential for creating wealth – wealth to meet human wants and needs, and not wealth for its own sake. When actually existing socialist regimes failed in this mission, socialism was advocated on other, "non-economic" grounds.

[49] It might be thought that existing centrally planned economies would provide a model for this scenario. However, they have access to prices on the world market to use as a rough guide to scarcity values. If world-wide socialist revolution resulted in one centrally planned world economy or a number of relatively autarchic centrally planned economies, the planners would be significantly worse off than existing central planners are, since there would be no market prices anywhere to serve as guides to scarcity values.

history, *viz.*, that fettering of the forces of production[50] is causally related to instability in the dominant pattern of ownership relations. Marxian socialism is supposed to replace capitalism in part because capitalist relations of production fetter the development of the forces of production. Perhaps Marxian socialism will face the same problem. To assess this objection, it is necessary to clarify Marx's notion of fettering. G.A. Cohen provides a useful explication:

> Existing forces are fettered when, for example, capitalist depression makes plant and labor power idle. But fettering also occurs when relations block the formation and/or entry into the productive sphere of new forces.[51]

If the Mises-Hayek argument shows anything, it shows that central planning will fetter the development of the forces of production in both ways. The poor production coordination that characterizes central planning manifests itself in widespread shortages, supply bottlenecks, and the overproduction of inappropriate and unusable producer goods.[52] In addition, there is systemic resistance to innovation under central planning because of the disruption the former occasions. Those who would benefit from innovation (e.g., consumers) are unorganized, unaware of impending developments, and usually stand to benefit only modestly. On the other hand, those who would be hurt by innovation will usually be more seriously affected; those whose lives will be made considerably more difficult or complicated will tend to have the knowledge, power, and incentive to block important changes. Existing forces are therefore fettered and the development of new forces is frustrated.

What makes this problem pressing is that Marxian socialism is a "transparent society" in which nothing comparable to commodity fetishism operates. In a market economy, workers may suffer from the illusory belief that their problems result from ineradicable features of the human condition. But, under Marxian socialism, this won't happen. The sources of economic difficulty will not be mysterious; in existing centrally-planned economies the structural nature of the problem is widely known, even if the deeper explanation for it is not. For the most part, only those blinded by ideology (and their numbers decrease over time) deny that central planning is at the root of their economic difficulties. That illusion can exert its power only over those who disproportionately benefit from the system.

---

[50] "Forces of production" is a technical term for Marx whose extension includes means of production, labor power, and scientific and technical knowledge, etc. Cohen (pp. 31–55) has painstakingly delimited the intensional and extensional boundaries of this term as Marx uses it.

[51] Cohen, p. 177.

[52] See Rutland, pp. 131–33; 146–49.

It is undoubtedly oversimplified and inaccurate to say that these difficulties will lead to the abandonment of central planning by the associated producers. For one thing, it will take some consciousness-raising for workers to see that some kind of market system is in their best interests. However, a classless society not blinded by ideological illusions induced by the economic system is likely to be more responsive to pervasive economic difficulties than class societies have been. The fettering of the forces of production cramps the expansion of positive freedom. This fettering – or its evident consequences – provides some motivation for the associated producers to abandon central planning. If, on the contrary, Marxian socialism is to persist, it must do so for other reasons. What might those reasons be?

The most obvious move for Marxists to make is to argue that, despite the fettering of the forces of production, central planning will result in other benefits to the workers; chief among these is the absence of alienation. As Section II of this essay makes clear, one of Marx's main complaints against capitalism is that, *qua* market system, it is responsible for widespread alienation. Marxists could argue that the abolition of markets would lead to the virtual elimination of alienation, and that this would provide sufficient motivation for the associated producers to retain central planning.

To evaluate this objection, recall the respects in which market systems are alienating:[53]

1. The workers necessarily lose control of the product at the point of exchange (i.e., when it is sold).
2. The goal of production is not use but the creation of exchange value.
3. The goal of the worker is wages, not the production of use values.
4. There is an inherent conflict of interests in the exchange relationship; this results in men and women being alienated from each other. Production is conflictive instead of cooperative.
5. Large-scale social forces not under anyone's conscious control (alien forces) shape and destroy people's life chances.

Let us consider each of these in turn. It is true that, under central planning, the producers do not exchange their products. However, in such a system it is not plausible to maintain that the producers control the product, at least if the economic system is large and complex. Even if central planning is informed by democratic procedures, there is no question of voting on the micro-level decisions that aim at integrating production. At most, workers will have a say on broad policy questions, or, more likely, they will vote for individuals who have a say on these questions. The length and complexity of production in a

[53] It can be granted that subjective alienation relating to the organization of the workplace under capitalism would disappear under Marxian socialism, since the latter envisions democratic self-governance in production units.

modern economy makes genuine control of the product by those who produce it impossible. By contrast, such control is possible in small-scale economies with simple structures of production. The wish to return to such a system can only be characterized as utopian and far from anything envisioned by Marx.

Under commodity production, the fact that the goal of production is the creation of exchange value (and not use values) is supposed to explain in part why work is experienced as meaningless. Production for use is supposed to give work a point and purpose that is lacking when exchange value drives production. But is this really so in a centrally planned economy? Although the production of use values ultimately informs production in central planning, what guides production is the plan (the output target). There is no reason to think that work will be seen as more meaningful when production is driven by an output target instead of profits. Indeed, it may seem less meaningful, given the inherent irrationalities of central planning.

Wage labor, of course, is abolished under Marxian socialism. But what does this really amount to? In the first phase of post-capitalist society, the distribution of consumer goods is proportional to the amount of labor performed. This is because, in Marx's "obstetrical metaphor" (to use Cohen's phrase), the society is "still stamped with the birth marks of the old society from whose womb it emerges."[54] It is at best unclear how working for labor certificates differs from working for exchange value. Certainly the incentive principle that drives each system is basically the same. Of course, in the higher phase of communist society, distribution proceeds according to the principle, "From each according to his ability, to each according to his needs." A demonstration of the incoherence or unworkability of this principle goes beyond the scope of his essay; suffice it to say that it presupposes a level of development in the forces of production incompatible with the permanent fettering of those forces which is the inevitable accompaniment of central planning.

The inherent conflicts of interest that characterize an exchange society will not disappear with the abolition of production for exchange. In a complex network of production, life can always be made easier for some at the expense of others. As noted above, in a centrally planned economy production units will find it in their interests to understate plant capacity, hoard means of production and labor power, overstate output, etc. After all, the harm done to others will usually be slight and the benefits significant. The "public goods" nature of this problem makes it resistant to facile assumptions about changes in human nature. Furthermore, conflicts of

---

[54] Marx, *Critique of the Gotha Programme*, p. 16. The irony of Marx's metaphor is that most birthmarks are permanent!

interests are inevitable as long as there is scarcity, in the sense that not all useful projects can be pursued.

The abolition of markets that accompanies central planning will eliminate one kind of large-scale social force not under anyone's conscious control: market forces. It is less clear that other such forces will not then come into play. There is the possibility, which cannot be pursued here, that central planning requires the concentration of political and economic power in the hands of a few. The worry then is that there are large-scale social forces that are *not* beyond someone's power to control. Even if that problem can be avoided, there is the very real danger that the plan itself will be viewed by individual workers and production units as an alien force imposed on them from without, because the plan cannot be the collective design of all producers, nor can it satisfy everyone. Even if the planning process is informed by democratic procedures, there is no guarantee that the workers won't feel as alienated from the process or its results (the plan) as voters in a democracy feel from their governments or its policies.

The upshot is that there is good reason to believe that central planning will be about as alienating as capitalism. Given that, and given that central planning necessarily faces serious economic problems, the motivation for the associated producers to retain Marxian socialism remains elusive.

* * * * * * * *

This last section has attempted to show that there are serious motivational problems facing the workers who have abolished capitalism. What would sustain the commitment to Marxian socialism once the realities of central planning have taken hold? For the purposes of this essay, the most important consequence of von Mises's argument is that it shows that central planning will seriously fetter the development of the forces of production. The argument proceeds at a high level of abstraction, presupposing only a post-feudal level of complexity in the economic system and scarcity in the economic sense. In this section, I have argued that the most promising attempts to avoid this conclusion will not succeed. Given that the development of the forces of production is a necessary condition for the expansion of positive freedom for the workers, it is at best unclear how or why Marxian socialism will persist. For a system to be stable and enduring, it must generate the sources of its own support. Ideology can help, but the benefits must be more direct and tangible *if* the ruling class is the proletariat or if the society is genuinely classless. In addition, not only does central planning result in the permanent fettering of the forces of production, it probably will not significantly ameliorate alienation. If the associated producers are to retain Marxian socialism, it must be for some other reasons.

The arguments of this essay go some way towards showing that the

Marxian vision of socialism is truly utopian in the sense of being unrealizable. To clinch the case for this would require that all other feasible motivations be explored. Obviously, that requires much more than can be accomplished here. What this essay allows us to conclude is that there is as yet no good reason to believe that Marxian socialism can persist as a stable socioeconomic system and there is some reason to believe that it will not. David Hume advises that "A wise man proportions his belief to the evidence." On this advice, it seems that a wise man would incline towards believing that a dictatorship of the proletariat, or a truly classless society with a centrally planned economy, is unlikely to become an actor on the stage of world history; at most, it could be a bit player who holds the stage only for a brief scene.

Finally, it is worth pondering the significance of Marx's commitment to central planning. How much would be lost for Marxists by admitting the force of the Mises-Hayek argument as well as the observations about alienation and central planning? Actually, quite a bit. From the point of view of Marx's theory of history, an important prediction would be falsified. (How this affects the central claims of historical materialism is unclear to me at this time.) If socialism does replace capitalism, its economic system will be dramatically different from what Marx thought it would be – if it is to persist as a stable socioeconomic form. In addition, if the economic system is different, it may be that the relations of production would have to be different as well.[55] Also, Marx's radical normative critique of capitalism would be revealed as seriously defective. Recall that one of the major defects of capitalist society – alienation – is traced to the commodity character of production. If socialists admit (as many have) that production for the market is an indispensable condition for economic growth and prosperity, one of Marx's chief complaints against capitalism looks utopian. Given a commitment to markets, and given a certain level of size and complexity of the economy (however economies are individuated), alienation is likely to be a permanent feature of the modern human condition. Of course, its ill effects may be ameliorated, but this obvious fact is something non-radical, reformist critics of capitalism have been emphasizing for two centuries. Without the promise of the virtual elimination of alienation, Marx's radical critique of capitalism loses much of its force and interest. Without the promise of a substantial increase in positive freedom made possible by the rapid development of the forces of production under socialism, Marxian socialism loses much of its appeal.

Philosophy, University of Alabama at Birmingham

[55] See note 4.

MARKETS, SOCIALISM, AND INFORMATION:
A REFORMULATION OF A MARXIAN OBJECTION TO
THE MARKET*

BY JOHN O'NEILL

One of the paradoxes of recent political and economic theory is that, in spite of a period of extended economic difficulty, there has been a growing consensus concerning the virtues of the market economy. In particular, there has been a trend in socialist theory to argue that not only are socialism and the market not incompatible, but that some version of market socialism is the only feasible, practicable, and ethically and politically desirable form of socialism. Notable proponents of this view with whom this paper will be particularly concerned are Selucky, Nove and Hodgson.[1] I will not, in this paper, address the question of whether the market and socialism are necessarily incompatible.[2] Neither will I examine the whole gamut of political and ethical issues surrounding the relation of the market to democracy, freedom, individual rights, and so on – not because they are unimportant, but because they require more extended attention than I could give here. My concern will rather be with some of the economic arguments to which defenders of market socialism have appealed.

The project of defending a form of market socialism has involved both an implicit and explicit acceptance of some of the main claims of traditional liberal defenses of the market – in particular, those of the Austrian school of economics of Menger, von Mises, Hayek, *et al*. While the Austrian school's defense of the free market is criticized in its details, the general account of the

* An earlier version of this paper was read to a philosophy seminar at Lancaster University during which several helpful comments were made: I would particularly like to thank Russell Keat for his detailed critical remarks. I would also like to thank Ric Best, Shanti Chakravarty, and Andrew Collier for their conversations and critical comments on an earlier draft of this paper. I am also grateful to the journal's editorial board and referees for their comments.

[1] See Radoslav Selucky, *Marxism, Socialism, Freedom* (London: MacMillan, 1979), Alec Nove, *The Economics of Feasible Socialism* (London: Allen and Unwin, 1983), and Geoffrey Hodgson, *The Democratic Economy* (Harmondsworth: Penguin, 1984). Other notable expositions are those of David Miller, "Socialism and the Market," *Political Theory*, 1977, pp. 473–90 and "Marx, Communism and Markets," *Political Theory*, 1987, pp. 182–204, and Raymond Plant, *Equality, Markets and the State* (London: Fabian Society, 1984); the view has attained wider influence – see, for example, Roy Hattersley, *Choose Freedom* (London: Michael Joseph, 1987).
[2] For a recent argument that they are incompatible, see Adam Buick and John Crump, *State Capitalism* (London: MacMillan, 1986).

market as a mechanism for communicating information has been accepted. The market is presented as a self-regulating economic homeostat, providing the informational feedback between consumers and producers necessary for the mutual adjustment of their activities. The market may not be perfect, but it is the most efficient social device we could have to enable production and consumption to grow and contract in the appropriate places. This acceptance of the Austrian model of the market has been coupled with a rejection of Marx's account of the nature of economic crises in capitalism. The economic problems with the market are not problems with the market, *per se*, but problems that arise in any complex, changing, and innovative economic system.

In this paper, I will argue that both the acceptance of the Austrian model of the market and the rejection of Marx's critique of the market are mistaken. I will show that Marx's account of the economic crises of capitalism is misrepresented by recent defenders of market socialism, and I will reformulate what I take to be its main point through criticism of the Austrian model of the market as it is formulated by Hayek.

I. Marx's Critique of the Market: Some Recent Criticisms

In recent work on market socialism, Marx's critique of the market is standardly presented in terms of a distinction between *ex ante* and *ex post* economic mechanisms for the allocation of resources. The market is subject to crises because it always blindly responds to demand, allocating resources *ex post*. Within socialism, the problem of economic crises is solved by replacing *ex post* regulation with planned regulation of resources *ex ante*; production is able to anticipate demand rather than anarchically respond to it.[3] Thus presented, Marx's analysis is clearly untenable. On the one hand, the idea that one could rely completely on *ex ante* economic regulation, that one could plan production in such a way that future demand is always anticipated, has plausibility only in the context of a static and simple economy. In the context of a complex, changing economy, there exists inevitable uncertainty about future demands and resources. Hence one needs some *ex post* economic regulator, some feedback mechanism, which will allow the adjustment of plans in the light of unforeseen economic changes.[4] On the other hand, it is a myth that in a market economy actors merely respond, *ex post*, to economic changes. Within a free market, a firm will constantly plan

[3] See Selucky, *Marxism, Socialism, Freedom* (London: MacMillan, 1979), p. 6ff., and Nove, *The Economics of Feasible Socialism* (London: Allen and Unwin, 1983), p. 39ff.
[4] See Nove, *The Economics of Feasible Socialism* (London: Allen and Unwin, 1983), p. 40ff., and Hodgson, *The Democratic Economy* (Harmondsworth: Penguin, 1984), p. 115ff.

its production to anticipate (and even shape) future demand. The market economy is not an economy without plans.[5]

If Marx's analysis of the nature of economic crises in market economies, and his proposed solution to them in socialism, relies on this distinction between *ex post* and *ex ante* economic regulation, then it should be rejected. The criticisms outlined above are conclusive. However, this account of Marx's position does not do justice to his arguments. It is true that the reliance of economic actions in the market on prior demand reflected by price, together with the existence of a temporal gap between the production of goods and their sale on the market, plays a role in Marx's analysis.[6] However, as I show in Section III, it would be a mistake to take the point of this analysis to be that, in the market, productive resources are allocated *ex post* in response to demand.

An important feature of this presentation and critique of Marx's attack on the market is that it implies that the economic problems of the market are not a consequence of any specific feature of the market. They are problems of informational uncertainty that result from economic complexity and change. Hence, they are incidental to the market. They are problems that the modern market economies have in virtue of being complex and changing, not in virtue of any special properties they have as market economies. As such, they are unavoidable. Any dynamic economic system will face problems involving the use of information to draw up plans *ex ante* and adjusting those plans *ex post* in the light of unforeseen economic change.

In the rest of this paper, I will reject this picture of the problems of the market economy: crises in market economies are not simply problems of complexity and change. I will reformulate Marx's arguments with a view to showing that there are specific problems with market economies that are the basis of their crises. I will argue that the problems with market economies are not problems of *ex post* economic regulation, but problems of the coordination of the actions of independent producers. This claim lends itself to an explication by way of a critique of Hayek's defense of the market economy. The central point of Hayek's defense of the market is precisely that the

[5] See Nove, *The Economics of Feasible Socialism* (London: Allen and Unwin, 1983), p. 40. Hayek makes this point in a number of places; for example, see F. A. Hayek, *The Road to Serfdom* (London: Routledge and Sons, 1944), pp. 24–26, and F. A. Hayek, "The Use of Knowledge in Society," F. A. Hayek, *Individualism and Economic Order* (London: Routledge and Kegan Paul, 1949), pp. 78–79.
[6] These elements in Marx's analysis are developed at length in his most systematic discussion of crises in Karl Marx, *Theories of Surplus Value: Part II* (London: Lawrence and Wishart, 1969), chapter XVII, especially sections 8 to 11; see also Karl Marx, *Capital* (London: Lawrence and Wishart, 1974), vol. 1, chapter III, section 1. The thrust of Marx's argument here is as follows: the possibility of crises in the market economy is a consequence of the spatial and temporal gap between the processes of production and sale of commodities; this possibility becomes a reality in the capitalist market in virtue of its additional features of being a competitive social order in which the production and sale of commodities is undertaken with the purpose of increasing the value of capital.

market is a successful mechanism for the coordination of the actions of economic actors – the price system serves as a means of communicating between economic actors the information that is relevant to the coordination of their actions.

II. HAYEK'S DEFENSE OF THE MARKET: INFORMATION AND THE PRICE MECHANISM

Hayek's defense of the market starts from the observation that economic problems in part stem from the division of knowledge in society.

> There is . . . a problem of the division of knowledge which is quite analogous to, and as least as important as, the problem of the division of labour.[7]

The problem is that of communicating between independent economic actors information dispersed amongst them that is relevant to the coordination of their actions. One needs a mechanism which will "convey to each agent the information he must possess in order to effectively adjust his decisions to those of others."[8]

The price mechanism is presented by Hayek as a solution to this problem of the division of knowledge in society. By serving as a numerical index of changes in the relation between the supply and demand for goods, it communicates between independent actors the information that is relevant to the coordination of their economic activities. And, Hayek claims, information of such changes is all that is relevant to actors for them to be able to adjust their activities appropriately.

His claim is illustrated nicely by the following example. Assume a new use of tin is discovered or a source of tin is eliminated: tin becomes more scarce, supply falls relative to existing demand, and the price of tin rises. This change in price provides *all* the information about the change in the supply of tin that is relevant to enable actors to suitably adjust their plans. Consumers do not, for example, need to know why the tin has become more scarce; all they need to know is

> that some of the tin they used to consume is now more profitably employed elsewhere and that, in consequence, they must economise tin. There is no need for the great majority of them to even know where the more urgent need has arisen, or in favour of what other needs they ought to husband supply. If only some of them know directly of the new demand, and switch resources over to it, and if

[7] F. A. Hayek, "Economics and Knowledge," Hayek, *Individualism and Economic Order* (London: Routledge and Kegan Paul, 1949), p. 50.
[8] Hayek, *The Road to Serfdom* (London: Routledge and Sons, 1944), p. 36.

the people that are aware of the new gap thus created in turn fill it from still other sources, the effect will rapidly spread throughout the whole economic system and influence not only all the uses of tin but also its substitutes and the substitute of these substitutes, the supply of all things made of tin, and their substitutes and so on; and all this without the great majority of those instrumental in bringing about these substitutions knowing anything about the original causes of these changes. The whole acts as one market, not because any of its members survey the whole field, but because their limited individual fields overlap so that through many intermediaries the relevant information is communicated to all.[9]

The price system, then, in communicating all relevant information, acts "to coordinate the separate actions of different people."[10] The effect of the mechanism is that the whole of society acts in the way it would have acted, had it been consciously directed by a single mind possessing all the information dispersed throughout the economy. A planned economy is less efficient because no actual mind could possess such information: this kind of economy effectively reduces the amount of information available in society. However, the market already acts in the way that defenders of a consciously planned economy believe it would act, if it could be directed by a single suitably-informed body.

It must be granted that Hayek's account of the market is not without foundation. The market clearly does communicate information to independent economic actors about changes in the relative scarcity of different resources, and consumers and producers do respond to these changes by altering their planned production and consumption of these. The question to be asked is: does the information so communicated in fact lead to the coordination of the activities of independent actors? There are two aspects to this question:

1. Does the price mechanism communicate all the information that is relevant for the coordination of actions?
2. Is the communication of relevant information not only a necessary, but also a sufficient, condition for the coordination of actions?

I will argue that the answer to both of these questions is no. Hayek is mistaken in his assertion that the price mechanism provides all the information that is

[9] Hayek, "The Use of Knowledge in Society," Hayek, *Individualism and Economic Order* (London: Routledge and Kegan Paul, 1949), pp. 85–86.
[10] *ibid.*, p. 85.

relevant to the coordination of the actions of economic actors.[11] And the assumption in his arguments that the communication of relevant information is sufficient to achieve coordination is likewise false.

III. THE MARXIAN CRITIQUE OF THE MARKET: A REFORMULATION

1. There is, in any competitive economic system, a disincentive to communicate information between actors who are in competition. Put simply, if producers A and B are in competition, and A informs B of his or her activities and B does not reciprocate, then B is in a position to adjust his or her behavior in order to compete more effectively than A. In this situation, standard game theory applies. While cooperation through mutual communication might be beneficial to both parties, if one cooperates and the other does not the non-cooperating party benefits. Given that both parties are self-interested, the rational strategy is to act non-cooperatively. Non-communication is the competitively stable strategy.

However, the existence of this general disincentive to communicate information does not itself imply a problem of coordination. One must show that the information that the market fails to communicate is information that is relevant to the coordination of actions. The question is more specific: does the market fail to communicate information that is relevant to the coordination of the plans and activities of independent actors?

There are at least two kinds of information that competitors will attempt to keep from being communicated: (1) technical and scientific information, and (2) information of their plans. It is the second of these that is most clearly relevant to the problems of coordination. It is information that actors need to coordinate their actions. Furthermore, the way that it is relevant provides a useful way of reformulating a Marxian analysis of economic crises in the market.[12]

[11] Hayek's positive discussion of the notion of relevant information is a major weakness in his defense of the market. *Cf.* Hayek, *Individualism and Economic Order* (London: Routledge and Kegan Paul, 1949), p. 50ff and p. 84ff for Hayek's analysis. Hayek cites as irrelevant information that is concerned with *why* a particular item has become more or less scarce, and suggests that all that is relevant is how much more or less scarce it has become. However, the relative scarcity of items and the reasons for that scarcity hardly exhaust the full gamut of information that is distributed throughout society which might be relevant to the coordination of economic activities and plans.

[12] The technical and scientific information relevant to the production and marketing of goods that is actively kept non-public I do not consider here for two reasons. First, there exist within the framework of the market economy solutions to this problem, notably the maintenance of a domain of public knowledge. It is an interesting and important question if and to what extent the market necessarily requires basic technical and scientific information to be kept public, and, vice versa, what the consequences would be if all information were treated as a commodity to be bought and sold like any other. Space will not allow me to pursue the question here. Second, it is not clear to me that this information is relevant to the coordination of the plans and activities of independent economic actors. It might impede the general economic development of different producers by blocking the distribution of significant information, but it does not thereby lead to a coordination problem in Hayek's sense.

206   JOHN O'NEILL

When actors at some point in time make plans concerning future production, they are planning not with respect of demand at the present moment t_0, but with respect to expected demand at some future moment t_1 when their products reach the market. The information the price mechanism provides is that of the relation of supply and demand at t_0.[13] While this information is relevant to the actors' plans, it is not *all* the information that is relevant in order that actors' plans are coordinated with those of other actors. The information that is relevant is that which will enable the actor to predict demand at t_1. A major component of the information required for such a prediction is that of the plans of other producers which respond to that demand. This is information that the market, as a competitive system, fails to distribute.

This point is at the basis of Marx's analyses of economic crises in the market. A major element of his account of why the market is subject to booms and slumps runs as follows: where there is an increase in demand against supply for some good at t_0, producers and consumers respond by increasing production and decreasing consumption. Each responds to the same signal – the change in price. However, each agent acts independently of the response of other producers and consumers. The result is that, at t_1, when the plans of different actors are realized, there is an overproduction of goods in relation to effective demand for them. Goods cannot be sold. There is a realization crisis: producers cannot realize the value of their products. Given this overproduction, demand falls against supply. There is a slump. This eventually leads to a rise in demand against supply, production expands leading to another boom, and so on.[14] It should be noted here that the

[13] The price of a commodity does not, of course, simply reflect the relation of supply and demand at t_0. It is also modified by the beliefs of consumers at t_0 concerning future states of the relation of supply and demand. However, what the market necessarily fails to distribute is information concerning producer plans in response to demand, and this information is relevant for coordination. The market's failure to distribute this information leads to overproduction for the reasons outlined.

[14] The main points of this element of the Marxian analysis are economically stated by Engels thus:

The law of competition is that demand and supply always strive to complement each other, and therefore never do so. The two sides are torn apart again and transformed into flat opposition. Supply always follows close on demand without ever covering it. It is either too big or too small, never corresponding to demand, because in this unconscious condition of mankind no one knows how big supply and demand is. If demand is greater than supply the price rises and, as a result, supply is to a certain degree stimulated. As soon as it comes onto the market, prices fall; and if it becomes greater than demand, then the fall in prices is so significant that demand is once again stimulated. So it goes on unending – a permanently unhealthy state of affairs – a constant alternation of overstimulation and collapse which precludes all advance – a state of perpetual fluctuation perpetually unresolved.

Friedrich Engels, "A Critique of Political Economy," Karl Marx, *Economic and Philosophical Manuscripts* (London: Lawrence and Wishart, 1970).

This articulation of the theory also has the virtue, in this context, of highlighting the two elements involved in my reformulation – knowledge and competition.

problem is not one of economic agents making a number of unrelated mistakes in the prediction of future demand. Rather, it is that the market imparts the same information to affected agents, and this information is such that the rational strategy for each agent is to expand production or contract consumption, while it is not rational for all agents to act in this manner collectively. In a competitive economy, the simultaneous distribution of information about supply and demand at t_0 and the suppression of the mutual exchange of information concerning planned responses leads to overproduction.[15]

These local booms and slumps in production of the kind outlined are then amplified into general crises precisely through the interconnections in the market that Hayek highlights in his example of the production and consumption of tin. The demand by industrial producers for goods such as machinery or raw materials such as tin are at any point in time based on their expectations concerning demand for their products at some future point in time t_1. To the extent that these are mistaken (for reasons concerning constraints on information flow noted) the price mechanism succeeds in communicating, not information to the producers of primary goods for industrial production, but misinformation. The effects of the failure in coordination in one area are thereby distributed throughout the system. A localized slump becomes a generalized crisis, paradoxically just

[15] Hayek appears to suggest in places that information about the planned responses of producers in competition is indirectly distributed by changes in interest rates: the planned increase in production by separate producers is reflected in an increased demand for credit, and hence a rise in interest rates; this lowers anticipated profits and dampens the expansion. See F. A. Hayek, *Prices and Production* (London: Routledge and Sons, 1931), and F. A. Hayek, *Monetary Theory and the Trade Cycle* (London: Jonathan Cape, 1933). The credit system, if it is working satisfactorily, will communicate the relevant information. This is one of the reasons why Hayek holds that the explanation of the business cycle must lie in features of the credit system which result in its failure to perform this function. However, this argument is flawed. It is not clear that the *relevant* information is communicated by changes in interest rates. The problem is this. The information about which a producer needs to be informed if over-expansion in the production of some good is to be avoided is not the general level of demand for credit, but the level of demand amongst competitors. However, interest rates reflect the general aggregate demand for credit in an economy, not the relative demands in different industries. An increase in the planned production of some good by a group of competitors will be reflected in a proportional change in interest rates only if the change in demand for credit by that group is identical with that found in the whole economy, i.e., if rates of change in the demand for credit are even throughout an economy. However, there is no reason to suppose such an assumption is true, given the different production cycles of different industries. Assuming uneven changes in the demand for credit, it is quite possible for overproduction to occur even if the credit system is working 'satisfactorily'. The credit system does not communicate the *relevant* information. For this reason, it is not the case that we must look to a departure from an ideal credit system to explain the business cycle.

because the market does connect producers in the way that Hayek highlights.[16]

2. This analysis of the problems that follow from the competitive nature of the market is also of relevance to the second question concerning Hayek's position raised at the end of the last section. In Hayek's defense of the market, there is an assumption that the communication of relevant information in the market is not only a necessary condition for the achievement of coordination, but also a sufficient condition. He treats the solution of the problem of information distribution as *ipso facto* a solution to the problem of coordination. The two are, however, distinct. The possession of information about the plans and actions of others does not of itself enable one to act so that one's actions are coordinated with those of others. For example, producers possessing information that the demands for the goods they produce is falling relative to supply are not in a position thereby to ensure that their actions are coordinated with those of consumers and other producers. The problem is not simply that of the lack of relevant information noted above. Even given this information, the problem of coordination is not thereby solved. Where plans are inappropriately coordinated, a mechanism is required to adjust those plans. For example, knowledge that (given planned consumption and production of some good) production will exceed demand is of no use to a producer who aims to achieve coordination. Even given mutual knowledge of projected discoordination, no adjustment by any particular actor of his or her own actions will necessarily lead to coordination. There must be some mechanism whereby producers can mutually adjust plans in order that activities be coordinated.

The market, as a competitive order, has no such mechanism for mutual adjustment, for the same reason that it blocks the movement of information. While mutual adjustment might benefit all parties, if one or more cooperates

---

[16] Indeed, Hayek exploits this feature of his model of the market in his own account of the business cycle, according to which manufacturers over-expand in response to misinformation distributed by the price mechanism where this results in over-investment in capital goods. See Hayek, *Prices and Production* (London: Routledge and Sons, 1931), and Hayek, *Monetary Theory and the Trade Cycle* (London: Jonathan Cape, 1933). There is, at this level, much in common between Marx's and Hayek's analyses. The significant difference lies in the explanation of the original source of the misinformation distributed from manufacturers of consumer goods to manufacturers of capital goods. Hayek assumes that, *ceteris paribus*, the price system does distribute all information that is relevant to the coordination of plans. Misinformation enters through the *disturbance* of the price system by the expansion of credit or money which artificially alters the relative prices of goods. The Marxian view I present here rejects the assumption that, in the absence of 'disturbances', the price system does distribute all information relevant to coordination. The market, in virtue of its competitive nature, fails to distribute all relevant information. This, for the reasons outlined, leads to over-expansion in some part of the economy. This, in turn, imparts false information to the producers of capital goods via the price mechanism. The extent to which local overproduction will lead to a general slump depends on the degree of interconnectivity between that part of the economy in which initial overproduction occurs and other parts of the economy.

while another does not, *ceteris paribus*, the non-cooperating party will benefit. Given that all parties are self-interested, the competitively stable strategy is non-cooperation: the market inhibits the mutual adjustment of plans. Eventual adjustments of actions are achieved in the market rather via sudden dislocations in economic life, in which overproduction of certain goods leads to the disappearance of certain competing producers, underproduction to an uncontrolled and excessive movement of productive resources to supply demand.

Marx's analysis of the problems of the market can, then, be reformulated in terms of a criticism of Hayek's defense of the market. To reiterate my earlier point, the problem is not simply one of *ex post* economic regulation – that producers are responding *ex post* to demand at t_0 in planning future production. It is rather that information that is relevant to economic actors, in order that they be able to coordinate their activities, is not communicated, and that no mechanism exists to achieve the mutual adjustment of plans. The market *in virtue of its competitive nature* blocks the communication of information and fails to coordinate plans for economic action. That feature of the market is specific to the market as a system of independent producers in competition with one another for the sale of goods. It is not a consequence of complexity or change.

The main aim of this paper has been to simply restate a classical account of the problem of market economies by way of criticism of Hayek's defense of the market. It is not my purpose in this paper to present a solution to the problem: in particular, I do not want to suggest that a "command economy" is a satisfactory solution.[17] However, the restatement of the problem points to the necessary conditions of a solution: if the problems we have outlined are to be avoided, economic life must be organized in such a way that separate producers are able to inform each other of their plans and act in order that their activities be coordinated. The solution lies in a cooperative economy with some mechanism for distributing information that is relevant in order to coordinate plans, and a mechanism for mutual adjustment of plans given this information. It requires a mechanism that does the job that Hayek falsely claims the price mechanism performs.

These problems of cooperation are not answered by defenders of market socialism. In particular, the problems of coordination that arise in market

---

[17] The debate on the market tends to be dominated by an assumption that there exist just two alternatives: a centralized economic system in which all information is distributed by the state, or a decentralized economy in which information is distributed by the market. This assumption is one that I do not accept. A predominantly decentralized yet cooperative economy is not an impossibility. As to the mechanism for distributing economic information, the answer I believe lies somewhere in the direction of Neurath's 'economy in kind'. See Otto Neurath, *Empiricism and Sociology*, eds. Marie Neurath and Robert Cohen (Dordrecht: Reidel, 1973), ch. 5.

economies are not solved by transforming privately owned enterprises into workers' cooperatives. Cooperation *within* enterprises does not entail and, in the context of a market economy, would not result in cooperation *between* enterprises. This failure to address the problem adequately is a consequence of their presentation of the problems of the market in terms of *ex post* economic regulation. The specific problems of the market are neither acknowledged nor solved by theories of market socialism.

Philosophy, University College of North Wales

LIBERTY OF THE PRESS UNDER SOCIALISM

BY WILLIAMSON M. EVERS

Writing in 1912, before the Bolshevik Revolution, American socialist John Spargo said that it was "inconceivable" that a democratic socialist society would ever abolish the "sacred right" of freedom of publication which had been won at so great a sacrifice. According to Spargo, "every Socialist writer of note" agreed with Karl Kautsky that the freedom of the press, and of literary production in general, is an "essential condition" of democratic socialism.[1]

But Spargo added that to "declare" that the press will be free under socialism "does not take us very far." As a "pious declaration" of his fellow socialists' hope and belief, "it is excellent," said Spargo. But, he added, such a declaration does not cast "any light" upon the practical problem. It does not provide an answer to the question that Spargo put: "How can there be freedom of the press when industry is socialized?"[2]

This article addresses one basic question in socialist political theory: is liberty of the press likely to exist in a socialist society? To answer this question, one must also examine the ingredients of a socialist society: could the general economic and organizational structures, institutions, and incentives that socialist theorists propose for socialist societies operate so as to ensure an autonomous and independent press? Could socialist theorists and policymakers devise special institutions for the press so as to ensure its freedom under socialism? Socialist theory itself stresses the institutional underpinnings of social phenomena, so it is appropriate to scrutinize the institutional setting of freedom of the press under socialism.

The existence of self-proclaimed socialist countries that have governmental policies of repression and control presents an additional problem for proponents of socialism. Robert Heilbroner, a socialist sympathetic to Marxism, writes:

> [D]emocratic liberties have not yet appeared, except fleetingly, in any nation that has declared itself to be fundamentally anticapitalist, which is to say within the self-styled "Marxist" socialist ambit. The

[1] John Spargo, *Applied Socialism* (New York: B.W. Hebsch, 1912), p. 287. For Kautsky's attitude toward liberty of the press under socialism, see Karl Kautsky, *Social Democracy versus Communism*, ed. and trans. David Shub and Joseph Shaplen (New York: Rand School Press, 1946), pp. 63, 121.

[2] Spargo, p. 287.

tendency in all these nations has been toward restrictive, usually repressive governments that have systematically compressed or extinguished political and civil liberties.[3]

Glasnost is not liberty of the press.[4] Proponents of liberty of the press under socialism are premature if they are already congratulating themselves over the current Soviet situation. For example, in May 1988 the authorities arrested and briefly jailed the editor of the unofficial and nonsocialist journal *Glasnost* for his political activities. The police confiscated the journal's typesetting equipment and destroyed its manuscripts and files.[5]

In Gorbachev's U.S.S.R., where can the Lockean liberal publish legally – or even the hard-line Stalinist oppositionist? In April 1988, after a Soviet newspaper published a Stalinist dissent from current reform policy, *Pravda* excoriated those who had allowed this lapse and stressed that "the Soviet press is not a private shop."[6]

Indeed, socialists must attend much more closely and thoroughly to the problem of liberty of the press than they have thus far. As radical social theorist David Selbourne has correctly stated, if it seems to the people of Western societies that the coming of socialism will bring what E. H. Carr called "the nationalization of opinion" and will impair freedom of thought, then this is, in Selbourne's words, "sufficient to halt the socialist project entirely."[7]

According to Selbourne, socialists need to examine this sort of question because one of the most difficult ideological tasks of socialists is to provide evidence, "whether drawn from 'real' socialism or anywhere else," of the existence of a "necessary connection" between socialism and liberal institutions of public life. In the absence of such evidence, according to

[3] Robert Heilbroner, *The Nature and Logic of Capitalism* (New York: Norton, 1985), p. 126.

[4] On the limits of *glasnost*, see also Bill Keller, "Soviet Cooperatives Ordered to Stay Out of Publishing World," *New York Times*, February 3, 1988; Bill Keller, "Pieces to a Soviet Puzzle," *New York Times*, May 20, 1988; Candace de Russy, "Glasnost: Constraints and Backtracking," *Resistance International Bulletin*, vol. 1, no. 2 (Fall 1987), pp. 7–9.

[5] Vera Tolz, "The USSR This Week," research report RL 203/88, May 13, 1988, p. 5, in *Radio Liberty Research Bulletin*, vol. 32, no. 20, whole no. 3485 (May 18, 1988); Keller, "Pieces," *New York Times*, May 20, 1988.

[6] "The Principles of Restructuring: The Revolutionary Nature of Thinking and Acting," editorial, *Pravda*, April 5, 1988, trans. in *Current Digest of the Soviet Press*, vol. 40, no. 14, p. 20. *Pravda* editorial in response to Nina Andreyeva, "I Cannot Forsake Principles," *Sovetkaya Rossiya*, March 13, 1988, trans. in *Current Digest of the Soviet Press*, vol. 40, no. 13 (April 27, 1988), pp. 1–5.

Pravda's words in 1988 closely parallel in language and ideology Stalin's words in 1946 (at the outset of a major campaign against artists and members of the intelligentsia): "In our country, a magazine is not a private enterprise." See "Attack on Zoshchenko, Akhmatova Recalled," *Current Digest of the Soviet Press*, vol. 40, no. 23 (July 6, 1988), p. 17.

[7] David Selbourne, *Against Socialist Illusion: A Radical Argument* (New York: Schocken Books, 1985), p. 45. Compare William E. Connolly, *Appearance and Reality in Politics* (Cambridge: Cambridge University Press, 1981), pp. 177, 178, 189; Frank Parkin, *Marxism and Class Theory* (New York: Columbia University Press, 1979), p. 177.

Selbourne, socialists will not succeed in overcoming the ideological matrix that prevails in Western societies. In this ideological matrix, personal liberty, the individual right to own property, and respect for property rights form parts of the whole.[8]

Pro-capitalist critics of socialism maintain that private property – most importantly, private property in the means of production – furnishes "a material basis for dissent from and opposition to the authorities of the day."[9] Since socialism abolishes private property in the means of production, pro-capitalist critics of socialism say that the press is unlikely to be free in a socialist society.

By socialism, I mean state ownership of the means of production, together with central planning. Because my stipulative definition of socialism distinguishes socialism from collectivist anarchism, market-syndicalism, and welfare-statism, I shall not talk about these three doctrines in this article.[10] I shall take socialism to mean what is called for in Clause IV of the constitution of the British Labour Party – namely, wholesale nationalization.

Democratic socialists who assert that liberty of the press is both possible and desirable under socialism say that political institutions and controls, rather than economic ones, are primarily responsible for the absence of liberty of the press in existing socialist societies. Sidney Hook, for instance, maintains that a socialist economy "did *not* precede" the demise of liberal democratic institutions in Russia.[11]

However, in contrast to this democratic socialist thesis of the primacy of politics in explaining the absence of liberty, the historical record shows that economic doctrine and policy have primarily determined the liberty of the press in existing socialist societies like Russia, though political controls have complemented economic ones.

In describing the controls over the press in existing socialist societies, it is wrong, for example, to speak simply of censorship. In a centrally planned economy in which the means of production have been nationalized, the

---

[8] Selbourne, p. 62.

[9] Albert O. Hirschman, *The Passions and the Interests* (Princeton: Princeton University Press, 1977), pp. 127–28. Hirschman reports this argument without evaluating it.

[10] On the analytic value of differentiating between socialist societies and redistributivist welfare-state societies, see Peter Berger, *The Capitalist Revolution* (New York: Basic Books, 1986), pp. 76, 247 n. 3; Robert L. Heilbroner, "A Reply," *Dissent*, vol. 25, no. 3, whole no. 112 (Summer 1978), p. 359. At some level of intervention and redistribution, a society becomes socialist de facto. See Berger, p. 88.

[11] Sidney Hook, *Political Power and Personal Freedom*, 2nd ed. (New York: Collier Books, 1962), pp. 401–2. Hook points to the illiberal values of the Bolsheviks and of the German National Socialists and to the undemocratic structure of their political parties as influences on governmental policy in Russia and Germany. See also Leszek Kolakowski, "The Self-Poisoning of the Open Society," *Survey*, vol. 25, no. 4, whole no. 113 (Autumn 1980), p. 8. Kolakowski calls the democratic socialist argument "a healthy rejoinder" to the classical liberal critique of socialism.

resources used by the communications media are completely under the
economic control of the government. As Paul Lendvai points out, in existing
socialist societies "literally everything" needed by the publishing industry,
from "the printing plant, working capital and newsprint" to "the typewriters,
stationery and waste paper baskets," must be provided by government
departments.[12]

Manes Sperber emphasizes the effect of economic dependency when he
writes:

> [E]verything belongs to these omnipotent regimes – the streets, the
> cities, the workshops, the factories, everything that is produced. Plus
> all printing presses, periodicals, and publishing houses. They do not
> even require censorship, for nothing can be printed that does not
> suit them.[13]

Sperber perhaps overstates the case, since some socialist governments have
found direct coercion and censorship useful as ways of double-checking. On
the other hand, the fact that the socialist government in Hungary has never
set up a formal censorship apparatus supports Sperber's point. Socialist
Romania abolished its censorship in 1977 but still controls the press.[14]

An officially approved Hungarian account of the institutions of the press
says, in effect, that because the state owns the equipment, because the state
distributes the paper supplies, and so forth, censorship by the police is not
needed:

> [T]he effective provisions of Hungarian press law do not insist on
> the submission of MS for the purpose of licensing [i.e., pre-
> publication censorship]. This is in charge of the competent
> specialized agencies or institutions of an economic character, and
> not of the police authorities. Consequently these provisions
> governing licensing are not of a policing character, and rely on [the
> fact] that the printing offices, publishing companies, etc. are in
> public ownership, and that governmental organs are in charge of
> paper or newsprint.[15]

The Bolsheviks' own analysis of the press under existing socialism focuses
on control of resources. Indeed, Trotsky said in debate in the early days after

[12] Paul Lendvai, *The Bureaucracy of Truth* (London: Burnett Books, 1981), p. 19.

[13] Manes Sperber, *Man and His Deeds*, trans. Joachim Neugroschel (New York: McGraw-Hill,
1970), p. 45. See also Milovan Djilas, *The New Class* (New York: Praeger, 1957), p. 143; Dragoljub
Jovanovic, quoted in Vojislav Kostunica and Kosta Cavoski, *Party Pluralism or Monism* (New York:
Columbia University Press, 1985) [East European Monographs, no. 189], p. 161.

[14] Lendvai, pp. 30, 119–24.

[15] Peter Schmidt, "The Citizens' Freedoms," in Imre Szabo et al., *Socialist Concept of Human Rights*
(Budapest, Akademiai Kiado, 1966) [Series in Foreign Languages of the Institute for Legal and
Administrative Sciences of the Hungarian Academy of Sciences, Nos. 1 and 2], pp. 256–57.

the October Revolution: "The attitude of Socialists on the question of freedom of the Press should be the same as their attitude toward the freedom of business."[16] In the same speech, he maintains that the Bolsheviks had long ago developed a "non-proprietorial view of press freedom."[17]

Sidney Hook says that the question of whether a society with a socialist economy can enjoy such liberties as liberty of the press is an empirical one. He says we must look at the specific historical evidence.[18] Let us do so. I maintain that the history of the press in the Soviet Union shows that, under socialism, economic structure and economic policy decide the fate of freedom of the press.[19]

During the Bolshevik-led Soviet seizure of power in late October 1917,[20] Soviet forces seized or shut down approximately twenty nonsocialist newspapers.[21] On October 27, only two days after the successful Soviet revolution, in its Decree on the Press – the first law issued by the new Council of People's Commissars – the government gave itself the authority to close down all newspapers that printed false information or promoted resistance to Soviet power. The text of the decree described these measures as temporary.[22] Some non-Bolshevik newspapers continued to publish under censorship.

Ten days later, the Central Executive Committee of the All-Russian Congress of Soviets passed a resolution confirming the government's Decree on the Press. This resolution, drafted by Trotsky and backed by the Leninist Bolsheviks, took a further step. It stated that restoring seized printing facilities to nonsocialist owners would constitute "capitulation to the will of capital" and was "indubitably counterrevolutionary." This resolution also stated that the "next measure" should be Soviet expropriation of all private printing facilities and supplies of newsprint.

On November 15, the Council of People's Commissars decreed that all

[16] John Reed, *Ten Days That Shook the World*, ed. Bertram D. Wolfe (New York: Modern Library, 1960), p. 355; John L.H. Keep, ed. and trans. *Debate on Soviet Power* (Oxford: Oxford University Press, 1979), p. 71. Compare Trotsky, speech to Grenadier Regiment, quoted in Isaac Deutscher, *The Prophet Armed* (London: Oxford University Press, 1954), p. 337 n. 4.

[17] Keep, p. 71. For a different recollection of Trotsky's remarks at this point, see Reed, p. 335.

[18] Hook, *Political Power*, p. 401.

[19] For an excellent brief discussion of why the Soviet Union is the appropriate existing socialist society on which to concentrate in considering the socialist project, see Berger, pp. 174–76.

[20] For Russian history before February 1/14, 1918, I use the Julian calendar, rather than the Gregorian one.

[21] Peter Kenez, *The Birth of the Propaganda State* (Cambridge: Cambridge University Press, 1985), p. 38; N.N. Sukhanov, *The Russian Revolution 1917*, ed. and trans. Joel Carmichael (1955; repr. Princeton: Princeton University Press, 1984), pp. 649–51; Albert Resis, "Lenin on Freedom of the Press," *Russian Review*, vol. 36, no. 3 (July 1977), pp. 285–86.

[22] James Bunyan and H.H. Fisher, eds., *The Bolshevik Revolution, 1917–1918* (Stanford: Stanford University Press, 1934), p. 220; Yuri Akhapin, ed., *First Decrees of Soviet Power* (London: Lawrence & Wishart, 1970), pp. 29–30.

paid advertising was henceforth to be a monopoly of government publications. That meant that no private advertising could appear in non-governmental newspapers.[23] But much more devastating than this advertising ban were expropriations of facilities and paper supplies and the business conditions after the October Revolution.[24]

In the years that followed came the 1918–1921 attempt (later called War Communism) to leap directly to full communism, the more liberal New Economic Policy of 1921–28, Stalinism, the Khrushchev reforms, the stagnant Brezhnev era, and now Gorbachev's *perestroika*. Government officials tightened up or loosened policy toward writers, publications, and the publishing industry at various times. The economic institutions of the press have remained fundamentally the same: state ownership or ownership by cooperatives that are creatures of the state.[25] Roy Medvedev notes that, by 1929, "there was not a single non-Party publication left, nor any privately owned publishing houses that might serve as vehicles for oppositionist views."[26]

Having looked at the history of the suppression of liberty of the press in the Soviet Union, let us turn to a consideration of *samizdat* and of the rare and brief periods under existing socialist regimes when the press is, by and large, free.

Underground *samizdat* publishers in existing socialist countries are rebelling both against censorship and against nationalization of the means of production when they secretly produce books and journals. *Samizdat* is a form of private publishing that takes place despite the fact that the state forbids private ownership of capital equipment (means of production) for the mass production of intellectual products.

[23] Bunyan and Fisher, pp. 222–23; Reed, pp. 365, 391–92; Resis, p. 292.

[24] See Kenez, p. 42.

[25] There were two exceptions:

(1) During the civil war, the Bolsheviks permitted pro-Soviet non-Bolshevik political parties and groups to operate and to publish their own newspapers under censorship.

(2) Under the liberalized conditions of the NEP, beginning in 1921, private capitalists and independent cooperatives published books. Such private ventures together with the mildness of the government's literary censorship at this time permitted a literary renaissance in the 1920s.

On literary policy during the NEP, see Kenez, pp. 239–45.

This was the time of greatest liberalism in Soviet literary policy. See Ernest J. Simmons, "Introduction: Soviet Literature and Controls," in Simmons, ed., *Through the Glass of Soviet Literature* (New York: Columbia University Press, 1953), p. 6. On the limits of freedom of expression during the NEP, see Jean Elleinstein, *The Stalin Phenomenon*, trans. Peter Latham (London: Lawrence & Wishart, 1976), p. 65; Raphael R. Abramovitch, *The Soviet Revoluton*, ed. Anatole Shub, trans. Vera Broido-Cohn and Jacob Shapiro (New York: International Universities Press, 1962), pp. 225–26; Leszek Kolakowski, *Main Currents of Marxism*, trans. P.S. Falla (Oxford: Clarendon Press, 1978), vol. 3, pp. 7, 45.

[26] R. Medvedev, "New Pages from the Political Biography of Stalin," in Robert C. Tucker, ed., *Stalinism* (New York: Norton, 1977), p. 205. See also Elleinstein, p. 87; Nicolas A. de Basily, *Russia under Soviet Rule* (London: George Allen & Unwin, 1938), pp. 431–32.

In some cases, governmental means of production are illegally used (e.g., during off hours). In the Soviet Union, operating any press equipment – from photocopier to rotary press – is against the law, unless the operator is acting on behalf of the state.[27] What usually happens is that persons illegally treat consumer goods as producer goods. They "misuse" consumption goods (typewriters, and so forth) as means of production to produce unauthorized publications. Since these underground producers can operate by using supposed consumption goods in this way, *samizdat* provides yet another illustration of Nozick's thesis that a socialist government must – in order for socialism to survive – outlaw capitalist acts between consenting individuals.[28]

Rare and brief periods of genuine liberty of the press do occur under existing socialism – for example, during the 1968 Prague Spring period in Czechoslovakia and during the 1980–81 period in which the Solidarity labor union operated publicly in Poland.[29] In Czechoslovakia, no basic changes in economic institutions took place in the communications industry during the Prague Spring. Prior censorship was first ignored, then abolished, and the censorship apparatus was dismantled.[30]

How do we think of the independence and autonomy of the press during these periods? It is probably best understood as a kind of anarcho-syndicalism that can function in existing socialist societies at times when the central political authorities are weak or in a state of collapse.[31]

But this anarcho-syndicalism – despite its popularity at the time – does not have sufficient institutional supports within the socialist system to sustain itself once normal conditions return.[32]

Why, according to the critics of existing socialism, do such societies not enjoy long-term liberty of the press? Skeptics about the liberty of the press under socialism point to two major difficulties. The first is the absence of opportunities for independent, nongovernmental employment. The second is the absence of opportunities to organize independent institutions for the gathering and dissemination of information, the creation and exhibition of cultural works, and so forth.

Let us first turn to the conditions of employment under socialism. The orthodox theorists of Marxism's Golden Age argued that genuine, full-

[27] Donald R. Shanor, *Behind the Lines* (New York: St. Martin's Press, 1985), p. 127.

[28] Nozick, *Anarchy, State, and Utopia* (New York: Basic Books, 1974), p. 163.

[29] See John Downing, *Radical Media* (Boston: South End Press, 1984), section three.

[30] Zdenek Mlynar, *Notions of Political Pluralism in the Policy of the Communist Party of Czechoslovakia in 1968* (1979) [Research Project: "Experiences of the Prague Spring 1968," Working Paper, No. 3], p. 18. For the text of the law abolishing the censorship, see *White Paper on Czechoslovakia* (Paris: International Committee for the Support of Charter 77 in Czechoslovakia, 1977), pp. 158–59.

[31] Compare Maria Hirszowicz, *Coercion and Control in Communist Society* (New York: St. Martin's Press, 1986), p. 47; Lendvai, p. 113.

[32] Compare P.J.D. Wiles, *Economic Institutions Compared* (New York: John Wiley, 1977), pp. 466–67.

fledged freedom of labor vanished along with what they maintained was the disappearance of the craftsman and independent farmer. Full freedom of labor was, according to these theorists, incompatible with organized, cooperative productive endeavors (like industrial factories or large-scale farms), whether capitalist or socialist.

Kautsky, however, writes:

> It is true that in one respect the workingman does enjoy freedom under the capitalist system. If the work does not suit him in one factory, he is free to seek work in another; he can change his employer. In a socialist community, where all means of production are in a single hand, there is but one employer; to change is impossible. In this respect the wage-earner today has a certain freedom in comparison with the worker in a socialist society. . . .[33]

But Kautsky dismisses this freedom the worker loses under socialism as merely the freedom to choose one's master.

This loss of freedom is, nonetheless, a genuine problem. After due allowance has been made for changes in Soviet labor policy since the era of War Communism, Trotsky's forceful candor remains perhaps the most eloquent acknowledgment ever made of the obey-or-starve condition of the worker that can exist under a socialist state's monopsony of employment:

> When we say to the turner Ivanov, "You are bound at once to work at the Sormovo factory; if you refuse, you will not receive your ration." . . . He cannot go to another factory, for all factories are in the hands of the State. . . .[34]

Italian socialist Bruno Rizzi contends that the worker under capitalism was subject to and dependent on the uncertainties of the market. Yet the worker under capitalism offered his services "wherever he chose." He could leave "at a moment's notice" and could go "where he liked." He had freedom of assembly, freedom of religion, and freedom of the press.[35] But, says Rizzi, under Soviet bureaucratic collectivism, this is no longer the case.[36]

John Stuart Mill argues that under state socialism – when all industries, all

---

[33] Karl Kautsky, *The Class Struggle (Erfurt Program)* (Chicago: Charles H. Kerr, 1910), pp. 149–50.

[34] Trotsky, *Terrorism and Communism* (1922; repr. Ann Arbor: University of Michigan Press, 1961), p. 167. See also Oliver Brett Esher, *A Defence of Liberty* (London: T. Fisher Unwin, 1920), p. 147.

[35] Rizzi, *The Bureaucratization of the World* (London: Tavistock Publications, 1975), p. 79. Compare Roy Medvedev's comment that under capitalism, "firms and monopolies are more or less indifferent to the religious and political persuasions of their employees." R. Medvedev, *Political Essays* (Nottingham: Spokesman Books, 1976), p. 36.

financial institutions, all transportation systems, all schools, all charitable endeavors, and all local public administrations are "branches" of the central government, when the government hires and pays the salary of everyone in every field of work, when everyone looks to the government for advancement – under such an all-absorbing system, a people can be free "in name" only. According to Mill, under such a system neither the press nor a representative legislature could check the central authorities.[37]

Let us turn now to the organization of production under socialism. In 1847, some early critics of nineteenth-century French egalitarian socialism said that those who tried to sustain liberty of the press under thoroughgoing socialism would soon face a dilemma. These early critics were the editors of *L'Atelier*, a monthly Paris publication that supported the artisan-socialist theories of Phillipe Buchez.

According to the working-class editors of *L'Atelier*, under a competitive regime submissions refused by one publisher could be offered to a different one. Under a state monopoly, however, only two choices exist: either everything is published or only some select items are published. If the first option is chosen, anyone who decides to dash things off – with the community bearing the cost – will be able to do so. The results will be published equally with all other works produced. According to the editors of *L'Atelier*, "no communist, after reflection, would accept in theory such disorganized liberty."

If the second option is chosen, then the state must make a selection. But the state is an institution made up of fallible individuals. What if an adherent of anti-socialist views asks to be a writer?[38] Of the second sort of option, Kolakowski writes:

> If ... it is the state which decides, then the greatest emancipation in history consists in a system of universal rationing.[39]

The thoroughgoing socialist who sincerely values intellectual freedom is in an awkward situation. This is clearly seen in a hypothetical question posed in

Compare also Kautsky's comment:

> In capitalist countries the masses of the people have a hundred times more opportunity for real knowledge, not mere drilled and regimented Communist talk; a hundred times more opportunity to break the educational monopoly of the ruling class than in the land of so-called "proletarian" dictatorship.

Kautsky, *Social Democracy versus Communism*, p. 92.

[36] Rizzi, pp. 51, 75–76, 79–80.

[37] Mill, *On Liberty, Collected Works*, ed. J.M. Robson (Toronto: University of Toronto, 1963–), vol. 18, p. 306.

[38] Richard Adamiak, "State and Society in Early Socialist Thought," *Survey*, vol. 26, no. 1, whole no. 114 (Winter 1982), pp. 22–23.

[39] Kolakowski, *Main Currents*, vol. 3, pp. 527–28.

a 1968 speech about the film industry by Czechoslovak socialist Antonin J. Liehm, who was political editor of the Czechoslovakian journal *Literarni Listy* during the Prague Spring: "How can we deprive the state of its power when we ourselves want cinema to be a national enterprise subsidized by the state?"[40] The same awkward situation exists in the print media.

To turn back the various challenges from skeptics and critics, socialist theorists need to show not merely that liberty of the press is possible under socialism, but that it will be a likely, usual, or even necessary consequence of socialism. To do so, they need to provide substantive arguments about incentives and institutions.

The proponents of freedom of the press under socialism are addressing a vitally important topic. Either we can imagine an institutional framework for freedom of the press under socialism, or we cannot. If we cannot, all talk of democratic socialism, liberal socialism, or socialism with a human face becomes rather unconvincing. Socialist political theorist Ralph Miliband writes that unless "adequate provision" is made in a socialist society for alternative channels of "expression and political articulation," any contentions about the existence of socialist democracy are "so much hot air."[41]

We will now examine various access arrangements proposed by socialists to see if they would be likely to provide satisfactory protection for liberty of the press under socialism. Proposals for such access arrangements come from persons who call themselves socialists, communists, Eurocommunists, social democrats, Fabian socialists, economic nationalists, and democratic socialists. Very similar proposals will often come from a communist and a democratic socialist, for example.

These proposals are efforts to ensure an independent, autonomous press in a society ruled by socialist authorities and in which socialist-controlled institutions predominate. Marx's own vision of socialism seems to include

---

[40] Antonin J. Liehm, "On Culture, Politics, Recent History, the Generations – and also on Conversations," in Liehm, ed., *The Politics of Culture* (New York: Grove Press, 1973), p. 80.
Compare the comments of George Orwell:

> If we are to have full Socialism, then clearly the writer must be State-supported, and ought to be placed among the better-paid groups. But so long as we have an economy like the present one, in which there is a great deal of State enterprise but also large areas of private capitalism, then the less truck a writer has with the State, or any other organized body, the better for him and his work. There are invariably strings tied to any kind of official patronage.

"Questionnaire: The Cost of Letters," *Horizon* [London], vol. 14, whole no. 81 (September 1946), p. 158. See also discussion of this passage in George Woodcock, "George Orwell, 19th Century Liberal," in Jeffrey Meyers, ed., *George Orwell: The Critical Heritage* (London: Routledge & Kegan Paul, 1975), p. 244.
[41] Miliband, "Lenin's *The State and Revolution*," in Ralph Miliband and John Saville, eds., *The Socialist Register, 1970* (London: Merlin Press, 1970), p. 316.

unrealistic assumptions (like harmony and absence of scarcity) that dispense with most conceivable practical problems of liberty of the press.

Whatever the relationship of each socialist theorist of the press is to the vision of socialism described by Marx himself, each of the theorists discussed here does see practical problems and does attempt to address them.

Some other proponents of socialism also propose unrealistic solutions. For example, James Yunker posits a socialist political culture in which no political official or anyone else could with impunity engage in "any intervention whatsoever" in the economy for narrowly political purposes.[42] But this simply begs the question.

In discussing the views of the critics of existing socialism, I have given their account of the effects of employment by the state and of production by the state. To parallel this discussion, I will now consider the likely effect on the press of socialists' proposals regarding income and the organization of production.

Let us turn to socialist policies on income and their effect on liberty of expression. Socialists at all times have complained that proletarians with their low incomes cannot effectively exercise liberty of expression. Some, such as Upton Sinclair, simply point to the higher income that they maintain workers will enjoy under socialism as a further assurance of freedom of expression.[43]

In addition, twentieth-century socialist theorists are aware that the authorities in existing socialist societies have not hesitated to demote or fire dissidents in order to stifle their voices.[44] C.B. Macpherson proposes a guaranteed income as one way of protecting a dissident from his or her employer – the state.[45]

Spargo, Liehm, and Hook, with somewhat different emphases, also rely on the right to work or the right to one's job as a guarantee of freedom of

---

[42] James A. Yunker, *Socialism in the Free Market* (New York: Nellen Publishing Company, 1979), pp. 199–200.

[43] Upton Sinclair, *The Brass Check* (Pasadena: The author, 1920), p. 409.

[44] See, for example, the discussion of job discrimination in existing socialist societies in R. Medvedev, *On Socialist Dissent: Interviews with Piero Ostellino* (New York: Columbia University Press, 1980), pp. 19, 22; R. Medvedev, *Political Essays*, pp. 15, 89; Zdenek Mlynar, *Relative Stabilization of the Soviet Systems in the 1970s* (Cologne: Index, 1983) [Research Project: Crises in Soviet-Type Systems, Study No. 2], pp. 6, 15; Ota Sik, *The Communist Power System*, trans. Marianne Grund Freidberg (New York: Praeger, 1981), p. 103; Berger, p. 63. Richter anticipated the problem of political job discrimination under socialism. See Eugen Richter, *Pictures of the Socialistic Future*, trans. Henry Wright (London: Swan Sonnenschein, 1893), p. 16.

[45] C.B. Macpherson, *Democratic Theory: Essays in Retrieval* (Oxford: Clarendon Press, 1973), pp. 153–54. See also Bertrand Russell, *Proposed Roads to Freedom* (New York: Henry Holt, 1919), pp. 177–78; Paul G. Chevigny, "Reflections on Civil Liberties under Socialism," *Civil Liberties Review*, vol. 2, no. 1 (Winter 1975), pp. 55–57. I am indebted to Robert Hessen for bringing Chevigny's article to my attention.

expression. Liehm envisions a right to see one's ideas realized. Hook proposes to extend the prerogatives of academic freedom to the publishing industry.[46]

Yet these policies on income seem to be either incompatible with socialist principles or not effective enough to do the task assigned them. Macpherson's guaranteed-income proposal clashes with the traditional socialist maxim (borrowed from Second Thessalonians) "who does not work, neither shall he eat." Socialists are traditionally antagonistic toward economic parasitism. But under Macpherson's proposal, persons could merely live off their guaranteed salary and refuse to work. As the numbers of such non-workers increased, general economic ruin would ensue.

The proponent of a socialist guaranteed income may counter that the income would not be available to the unproductive. The question which then arises is: may the dissidents use their worktime to compose dissident writings? If they are not allowed to do such writing as their regular work, and if the state will provide the dissidents with an income only if they do other work that its officials prescribe, then the state is, in effect, suppressing their dissident activities.

If, however, the proponent of a socialist guaranteed income asserts that the state will pay dissidents to compose anti-state writings, such an assertion still begs the question that is ultimately at issue. Why will the state do so? What incentive do the decision-makers of the socialist state face that will ensure that they will not use economic pressure to shut off dissent? It is not enough to say, as Macpherson does, that officials won't do this, but will pay dissenters instead: why will they?[47]

Hook suggests that the principles of academic freedom should be carried into the newspaper industry. He proposes that every individual, who is "qualified by talent and training," be regarded as holding a "vested interest" in his or her job. No one would be permitted to take away this vested interest as a result of acts or expressions of opinion "in any field unrelated to his [or her] specific task."[48]

There are several difficulties with Hook's proposal. The state can easily define the "specific task" of journalists and editors broadly – giving the task a political and social dimension. The state can hence include in the definition numerous limitations and prohibitions – thus considerably narrowing the

[46] Spargo, p. 227; Liehm, "On Culture, Politics, Recent History," p. 80; Sidney Hook, "Is Freedom of the Press Possible in a Planned Society? Discussion Notes," May 4, 1942, unpublished ms., Sidney Hook Papers, Hoover Institution Archives, Stanford University, p. 2; Hook, *Political Power*, p. 405.

[47] I owe this point on liberty of the press and a socialist guaranteed income to discussion with David Gordon. See Yves Guyot, *Socialist Fallacies* (New York: Macmillan, 1910), pp. 247–48, 250 for a quite similar discussion.

[48] Hook, "Is Freedom of the Press Possible?," p. 2. See also Hook, *Reason, Social Myths, and Democracy* (New York: John Day, 1940), p. 126; Hook, *Political Power*, p. 405.

protection offered. The government must at least ratify the definition of the required "talent and training" of which Hook speaks, and this governmental licensing power affords considerable opportunity for undermining, or even preventing from the start, the independence of the profession.

Moreover, in job disputes,[49] the government will have to adjudicate between the employing organization and the employee and will have tremendous leverage in that situation. Hook says he hopes for an independent judiciary in such cases. But Hook himself has provided a strong democratic socialist argument against an independent judiciary in various writings that denounce "government by judiciary" as "arbitrary" and "undemocratic."[50]

With the judiciary already part of the government and the economy run by the government, the social basis for judicial independence is slim if it exists at all. Perhaps Hook hopes the judiciary will be able to rely on public opinion or on the legal profession for support, but public opinion and the legal profession are less independent of government policy in existing socialist societies than they are in existing liberal ones.

One may also ask a rather basic question about Hook's proposal: is academic freedom itself compatible with socialism, at least in its early stages? Norman Thomas says that a socialist state, especially in the transition period, cannot be "indifferent" to what is said by teachers. Thomas contends that it is "inconceivable" that "a society with a social philosophy" will not teach it.[51]

Not only would Thomas's policy erode professional autonomy of teachers, it would also invite control of the press. The communications media, no less than the schools, educate a society.[52]

Let us now turn to socialist production policies and their consequences for freedom of expression. On the production side, some socialists advocate setting aside sites in socialist societies for the public expression of views – Hyde Parks, if you will, in public meeting places, in the press, and on broadcast programs. For example, Norman Thomas in *America's Way Out* proposes that the state set aside places for Hyde Park-like forums. He also proposes that the state aid the efforts of political parties to publicize their positions via the mails or broadcasting. Alternatively, he suggests, the socialist state should itself undertake this task: the state should provide the members of society with "intelligible accounts" of the views of the various

[49] See Yunker, p. 202.

[50] Hook, *Political Power*, pp. 34–35, 47–48, 64–65. David Gordon directed my attention to Hook's stance on judicial review.

[51] Norman M. Thomas, *America's Way Out* (New York: Macmillan, 1931), pp. 209–10. For a discussion of this point, see David Gordon, "Marxism, Dictatorship, and the Abolition of Rights," *Social Philosophy and Policy*, vol. 3, no. 2 (Spring 1986), p. 153.

[52] On the press as an educational instrument under socialism, see Harry W. Laidler, *Socializing Our Democracy* (New York: Harper and Brothers, 1935), p. 272; William Z. Foster, *Toward Soviet America* (New York: Coward-McCann, 1932), p. 317; Mitra Mitrovic-Djilas, quoted in Kostunica and Cavoski, p. 157.

political parties.[53] Some socialists favor huge subsidies to culture. Liehm, for example, wants the state to guarantee each film artist that his or her ideas will be turned into films and shown to the public.[54]

These proposals raise numerous questions. Thomas is aware of the fact that allocation decisions will have to be made about every means of expression, because he specifically says that political groups should be entitled to prime time for broadcasting their views.[55] But he does not begin to address the problems that will arise. For example, an auditorium can perhaps be used for five meetings a day. Many groups will want to use the facility, and to do so at times convenient to them. The government will have to decide who uses it, and when. Even if the government adheres formally to the requirements that Thomas proposes, it has a monopoly of the means of communication; it should therefore have no difficulty in effectively relegating to obscurity whomever and whatever it finds disagreeable.[56]

Democratic socialist Barbara Wootton acknowledges that it is possible for a socialist government to refuse to make assignments of meeting halls to groups that are out of favor. But she protests, it is "equally possible" to make resources available to all groups on the same terms.[57] The problem, however, lies not in conceiving the possibility of such an assignment policy. The problem lies in the fact that Wootton does not tell us what social structures and incentives under socialism would make such a policy (of assigning resources without favor) likely.

Liehm's proposed subsidy program (a guarantee that the state will produce and distribute films based on any idea submitted) is a program that can logically be applied to any medium of expression or communication.[58] Such a subsidy program must be considered in the light of the dilemma that the editors of L'Atelier recognized would confront a socialist society: namely, whether to subsidize the publication of everything regardless of expense, or, acknowledging scarcity, to have the authorities choose what to publish.

American democratic socialist Robert Picard and German Social Democratic leader August Bebel seem more practical than Liehm. Picard proposes a political basis on which to ration the subsidies that he says will

[53] Thomas, America's Way Out, pp. 210–11.

[54] Liehm, "On Culture, Politics, Recent History," p. 80. On the supply and demand for public assistance to culture, see Milton Friedman, Capitalism and Freedom (Chicago: University of Chicago Press, 1962), p. 18.

[55] For an example of a socialist theorist's dismissal of economic constraints as applying to cultural products in a socialist society, see Karl Kautsky, The Social Revolution (Chicago: Charles H. Kerr, 1905), pp. 181–83.

[56] See Richter, p. 85.

[57] Wootton, Freedom Under Planning (London: Allen & Unwin, 1945), p. 27.

[58] Liehm, "On Culture, Politics, Recent History," p. 83. Compare Robert Havemann, Questions Answers Questions, trans. Salvator Attanasio (Garden City: Doubleday, 1972), p. 213.

encourage diversity and independence of the press. Picard is frank in saying that the socialist state will exclude some persons from receiving subsidies on political grounds:

> Under a developed democratic socialist order ... diversity would not be the ultimate goal and the state would not be a funder or guarantor of all vehicles for expression. Since its major goal is the realization of the general will, such a moral order would ultimately deny financial assistance to media that do not promote the general will and the achievement of government by the people. After the achievement of such governance this kind of society would promote only the voices of the general will and diverse views on public matters within the general will.[59]

This does not sound like a program that will ensure the autonomy of the press.

Bebel calls for an elected panel of experts to ration the resources spent on culture. If the panel rejected a proposal, the applicant could appeal to a referendum of the citizenry.[60] But placing control over creative innovation in the hands of the Establishment is a structural guarantee of sterility and stultification. Bruce Goldberg writes:

> If we established a commission of the best physicists, say, who would decide what lines of thought subordinate physicists would be allowed to follow up, is it likely that breakthroughs in this science would be as frequent as in these past centuries of "anarchy," when each physicist has done as he wished? In other fields, to cite illustrations is virtually to close the case as far as these disciplines are concerned: who would wish that Bradley and Bosanquet – the outstanding British philosophers of their day – had been commissars of philosophy, empowered to decide whether Russell and Moore would be allowed to present their ideas to the public? Who would wish to have set Haydn in a similar way as arbiter over the young Beethoven?[61]

Bebel's proposed check (a referendum) on the panel of experts is likely to prove feeble indeed. Unless the public has an unusual interest in the subject under dispute, it is apt to rely on the governmental panel of experts and

---

[59] Robert G. Picard, *The Press and the Decline of Democracy* (Westport: Greenwood Press, 1985), p. 43.

[60] August Bebel, *Woman Under Socialism*, trans. Daniel De Leon (New York: New York Labor News Press, 1904), p. 334.

[61] Bruce Goldberg, "Skinner's Behaviorist Utopia," in Tibor R. Machan, ed., *The Libertarian Alternative* (Chicago: Nelson-Hall, 1974), p. 113.

confirm their decision. For a rejected innovative artist to get anywhere in such a referendum, he or she would need guaranteed access to the communications media or substantial campaign financing from the government for his or her campaign against the government's own decision. The social burden of Bebel's solution is now beginning to approach that of Liehm's plan.

Furthermore, there is a curious aspect to Bebel's approach to culture. He wants to have it both ways. He wants to have the many-sided post-revolutionary individual (who will hunt in the morning, fish in the afternoon, breed cattle in the evening, and engage in literary criticism after dinner) create a socialist culture. But the many-sided way of life that Bebel proposes for this new socialist individual will, in practice, annihilate professionalism and specialization of talents in culture.[62] At the same time, Bebel wants to have experts who can judge culture. But experts are specialists.

Kautsky, Edward Bellamy, Annie Besant, John Spargo, V.I. Lenin, Morris Hillquit, Upton Sinclair, George Soule, Harry W. Laidler, Sidney Hook, Norman Thomas, Irving Howe, Lewis Coser, Paul Chevigny, Robert Picard, James Yunker, and Sidney and Beatrice Webb all look to cooperatives and other nongovernment organizations (e.g., labor unions, professional associations, clubs, and political parties) to act as publishers.[63] They especially hope that pooling of funds to support cooperatives can serve more specialized interests and provide some independence from the government.[64]

No one, however, should underestimate the very considerable difficulties

[62] Bebel, pp. 289–91. See also Kautsky, *Socialist Revolution*, pp. 174–75; Sidney and Beatrice Webb, *The Consumer's Co-operative Movement* (London: Longmans, Green, 1921), p. 481. On the effect of Bebel's policy on specialization of talent, see Ludwig von Mises, *Socialism*, trans. Jacques Kahane, 2nd ed. (New Haven: Yale University Press, 1951), p. 190; Spargo, pp. 277–82; Albert Schaeffle, *The Impossibility of Social Democracy* (London: Swan Sonnenschein, 1892), pp. 161–63. In development of this point, I benefited from discussion with David Gordon.

[63] Kautsky, *Social Revolution*, pp. 178–79; Kautsky, *The Labour Revolution*, trans. H.J. Stenning (New York: Dial Press, 1925), pp. 186–87; Edward Bellamy, *Looking Backward, 2000–1887*, ed. John L. Thomas (Cambridge: Belknap Press of Harvard University Press, 1967), p. 202; Annie Besant, "Industry under Socialism," in George Bernard Shaw, ed., *Fabian Essays in Socialism* (London: George Allen and Unwin, 1931), pp. 148–49; Spargo, p. 294; Sinclair, p. 409; George Soule, *The Future of Liberty* (New York: Macmillan, 1936), pp. 175–76; Laidler, pp. 158, 283; Hook, "Is Freedom of the Press Possible?", p. 1; Hook, *Political Power*, p. 405; Chevigny, p. 58; Picard, p. 67; Yunker, p. 201; Sidney and Beatrice Webb, *A Constitution for the Socialist Commonwealth of Great Britain* (1920; reprint, London: Cambridge University Press, 1975), p. 270; Sidney and Beatrice Webb, *Consumers' Co-operative Movement*, pp. 411–13. For a contemporary critic of Bellamy's account of liberty of the press under economic nationalism whose criticism focuses on the monopsony of employment and the military discipline of labor, see Richard Michaelis, *Looking Further Backward* (London: William Reeves, [1890]), pp. 12, 19, 20, 23–24, 30, 36–37, 39.

[64] See Hillquit, in Morris Hillquit and John A. Ryan, *Socialism: Promise or Menace* (New York: Macmillan, 1914), p. 87. Compare Norman M. Thomas, *Socialism on the Defensive* (New York: Harper & Bros., 1938), p. 228; Thomas, *A Socialist's Faith* (New York: Norton, 1951), p. 219; Irving Howe and Lewis A. Coser, "Images of Socialism," in Howe, *Steady Work* (New York: Harcourt, Brace, and World, 1966), p. 289. Compare also V.I. Lenin, "Draft Resolution on Freedom of the

that would lie in the way of raising capital through subscription to a cooperative venture, rather than through investments. To begin with, will socialist citizens have enough disposable income for cooperatives to accumulate capital?[65] Such cooperatives will necessarily be modest in size. They will not be able to challenge the officially sponsored and subsidized culture.[66]

Will cooperatives and other nongovernmental organizations be actual owners of means of expression or merely editorial groups? If cooperatives and associations are simply editorial groups, they will be enormously dependent on the government.[67] They will have less basis for independence than Soviet collective farms had during the Stalin era when collective farms had some control over the land they cultivated but depended for equipment on state-owned machine tractor stations.[68] Certainly the independent Polish labor union Solidarity found it could not rely on government-owned presses to get its publications printed.[69]

Bellamy, Spargo, Lucien Deslinieres, Besant, and Russell each propose a legal rule to the effect that the state-owned printing house under socialism must print at cost everything that is submitted to it.[70] Once again the proponent of liberty of the press under socialism faces a variant of the dilemma recognized by the artisan-socialist editors of L'Atelier: publication of everything versus official selection of what to publish.

On the one hand, this plan to print everything submitted, at cost, envisions a special privilege for intellectuals. In no other industry do these theorists (who are themselves intellectuals) propose that the socialist state must produce at cost whatever supporters and financial backers of a project suggest. In addition, according to this plan, consumers are to reimburse the

---

Press," *Collected Works*, 4th ed. (Moscow: Foreign Languages Publishing House, 1960–1970), vol. 26, p. 283; Abramovitch, p. 305; Lenin, "How to Guarantee the Success of the Constituent Assembly", *Collected Works*, vol. 25, p. 378; V.I. Lenin, "Theses and Report on Bourgeois Democracy and the Dictatorship of the Proletariat," *Collected Works*, vol. 28, p. 461.

[65] Jane T. Stodddart, *The New Socialism* (New York: Hodder & Stoughton, [1909]), p. 146. See also Wiles, pp. 479, 484–85.

[66] Mises, p. 191.

[67] For example, G.D.H. Cole proposes socialized ownership of the presses, which could be rented by groups wishing to publish a newspaper. Cole, *Fabian Socialism* (London: Allen & Unwin, 1943), p. 41; see also Bellamy, pp. 199, 203.

[68] In fact, the government originally created the machine tractor stations because it did not wish to have the entire means of agricultural production solely in the hands of the collective farms. Roy A. Medvedev and Zhores A. Medvedev, *Khrushchev: The Years in Power* (New York: Columbia University Press, 1976), p. 86; Wiles, p. 141; Mikhail Heller and Aleksandr M. Nekrich, *Utopia in Power* (New York: Summit Books, 1986), p. 240.

[69] See Andrew Swidlicki, "The Struggle for the Media in Poland," *Telos*, no. 47 (Spring 1981), pp. 115, 122.

[70] Bellamy, pp. 199, 203; Spargo, p. 290; Lucian Deslinieres, *L'Application du Systeme Collectiviste* (Paris: Librairie de la Revue Socialiste, 1899), p. 359; Besant, p. 148; Russell, p. 180.

backers' start-up costs and pay a royalty besides (as Bellamy, Spargo, and Besant propose for books).[71]

On the other hand, what looks like a special privilege may easily be turned into a method of supression. The rule that newspapers and books must be printed at cost will not effectively safeguard liberty in a socialist economy. The authorities set the prices of goods and wages of labor. They assign "costs" to all activities. What incentive do the authorities face that will make them disinclined to raise "costs" to a prohibitive level in order to eliminate public dissent?[72]

Similarly, the authorities can easily distort a publish-at-cost rule in the name of needed economy measures. The authorities can distort such a rule by placing quite low ceilings on the numbers of copies of unofficial publications the state prints. Officials might authorize the state printing house to print only a handful of copies of unofficial publications because of, say, a supposed paper shortage or some other supposed emergency situation. At the same time, these officials might deem it vital to print millions of copies of works of governmental propaganda.

Finally, under socialism the state will distribute all products. It can stifle dissent through its control of the distribution network.[73]

But suppose cooperatives and associations are formally allowed to own printing presses; unless these groups truly control their own resources and can make decisions and take risks on their own, they are likely to be no more independent than Soviet collective farms after Khrushchev had them buy the tractors from the machine tractor stations.[74] The state would decide the size of the press that the group could own. The state would control the supply of newsprint and ink and the distribution of publications. The state would set work and product standards and control the prices both of inputs and of products.[75] Cooperatives did have some independence under the Soviet New Economic Policy and do have some independence under the current New Economic Mechanism in Hungary. They have not, however, possessed enough independence to put them in a position where they could publish unorthodox political publications.[76]

[71] On royalties, see Bellamy, pp. 199–200; Spargo, pp. 289, 291; Besant, p. 148.

[72] Mises, p. 191.

[73] H. G. Wells and Upton Sinclair, for example, are most emphatic that distribution must remain in the hands of the government. Wells, *New Worlds for Old* (New York: Macmillan, 1919), p. 281; Sinclair, p. 409. See also Bellamy, p. 199; G.D.H. Cole, *Fabian Socialism*, p. 41; Wiles, pp. 462, 466.

[74] Wiles suggests that the *kolkhoz* is best understood as a "queer kind of sovkhoz, maximizing plan fulfillment." See Wiles, p. 146.

[75] Spargo, pp. 131, 133.

[76] Wlodzimierz Brus, "Political Pluralism and Markets in Communist Systems," in Susan Gross Solomon, ed., *Pluralism in the Soviet Union* (New York: St. Martin's Press, 1982), pp. 112, 117, 120, 127.

Kenneth Arrow believes that as the state takes on the functions of full economic control, its growing numbers of bureaucratic agencies and departments (some of which he likens to feudal baronies) will constitute the basis on which political pluralism can exist under the socialist state, "no matter how all-encompassing."[77]

Arrow maintains that this bureaucratic pluralism can serve as the basis in socialist societies for the civil liberties found in liberal societies. But Roy Medvedev makes an important point that can be used to call Arrow's notion into question. First, Medvedev points out that liberal societies have complex social infrastructures that are in many ways independent of the state. In liberal societies, the state has a weakened influence in public affairs because private enterprises produce most goods. These private enterprises are largely indifferent to the background and political views of their employees.

In contrast, Medvedev says, Soviet society has no such complex social infrastructure. Sociological differences are not truly reflected in the institutional life of the society. Virtually "the entire economic and social life" of Soviet society is run from a single center. All social organizations, "including some sort of society for cactus, canary, or dog fanciers," operate not independently, but under the control of the political authorities.

The political and governmental authorities are responsible for the work of all economic enterprises, large and small. They also ensure the delivery of public services. The political and governmental authorities are constantly engaged in work that makes the economic and social life of the society continue, and the authorities make sure the citizens are aware of this.

The populace in existing socialist countries sees the authorities carrying out managerial and administrative activities without which the current economic system could not function. In the absence of enterprises independent of the state, who other than the authorities can set up and sustain productive endeavors, see that some enterprise or individual provides the public with desired goods and services, and plan the use of existing resources? The importance of such activities legitimates to some extent the power that the authorities hold.

An all-pervasive bureaucratic encumbrance of this sort, without any "counterweight" from a social infrastructure, severely hampers, according to Medvedev, the development of intellectual life. Medvedev hopes that liberty of the press can develop in this setting, without a fundamental change in the economic structure.[78] But from Medvedev's account, it would seem that Arrow is overly optimistic about the prospects for pluralism based on a

[77] Kenneth J. Arrow, in "Capitalism, Socialism, and Democracy: A Symposium," *Commentary*, vol. 65, no. 4 (April 1978), p. 31. See also Kenneth J. Arrow, "A Cautious Case for Socialism," *Dissent*, vol. 25, no. 4, whole no. 113 (Fall 1978), pp. 479–80.
[78] R. Medvedev, *Political Essays*, pp. 36–38.

multiplicity of governmental agencies. At a minimum, the extensive dependency of economic and social life on the authorities must end if pluralism is to prevail.

Indeed, the authorities in existing socialist societies have been able to use this economic dependency to re-establish their control following periods (the Prague Spring, for example) in which many persons – including those working in the communications industry – enjoyed liberty of an anarcho-syndicalist sort. The authorities reestablished control in part by having the police coerce dissidents. But much more important in making such "normalization" and stabilization possible is an ideology and a reality of economic dependency.

So long as a command economy remains in place, power will flow back to the authorities – even after a time of revolt and anarcho-syndical freedom – because they are the only employers and because they are the bosses of the societal coordinating mechanism that seems to make the economy run.

Proponents of democratic socialism must also face the fact that many of the institutions they propose in order to institutionalize freedom of the press under socialism have already been erected in existing socialist societies without an ensuing emancipation of the press. The Soviet Union has many municipalities and other geographical units: it has numerous large and rivalrous bureaucracies. The right to work, the right to a job, has long been constitutionally guaranteed there. The Brezhnev constitution assures Soviet citizens of their right to public forums. In the Soviet Union, newspapers and journals and books are published by cooperatives, labor unions, professional associations, clubs, and the only political party, as well as by various geographical and functional units of the government.[79] Although the Soviet Union has only one political party, other existing socialist societies (e.g., Bulgaria, China, Czechoslovakia, German Democratic Republic, Hungary, and Poland) have noncompetitive multi-party systems, in which the various parties have separate publications.[80] Despite the presence of these institutions that democratic socialists have suggested as cures to the ills of existing socialism, there is no freedom of the press.

The letter of the law on the books in the Soviet Union and other existing socialist societies guarantees freedom of the press. For example, the 1948 Czechoslovak constitution (no longer in force) even had a provision

[79] *The Soviet Mass Media: Aims and Organization, Past and Present* (Moscow: Novosti Press Agency Publishing House, 1979), pp. 12, 14; John Strachey, *The Theory and Practice of Socialism* (New York: Random House, 1936), p. 215; Laidler, pp. 158, 283; Lendvai, p. 185.

[80] Georges Marchais, Secretary-General of the French Communist Party, says this sort of non-competitive multiparty system would be the basis of political pluralism in a socialist Western Europe of the future. Leszek Kolakowski, "Eurocommunist Schism," *Dissent*, vol. 25, no. 1, whole no. 110 (Winter 1978), p. 36.

prohibiting prepublication censorship of the press.[81] Robert Havemann points out that the text of the East German constitution guarantees citizens the right to express their opinions "freely and publicly."[82] Yet the authorities do not respect these rights. But one should not stop with this observation. One must then ask why the authorities do not respect such rights. A proponent of freedom of the press under socialism might maintain that the authorities in office in existing socialist societies are corrupt, and that they need to be replaced with those whose vision of socialism and moral record are pure. Such a "puritan" perspective quite rightly holds individuals morally responsible for their deeds and recognizes the importance of having a morally honorable culture.

Nonetheless, one cannot rely on a social system that gives an important role to unknowable and changeable visions and motives. Far more trustworthy is a social system where the structures and incentives hedge power, do not permit the morally corrupt to exercise unchecked coercion, and encourage the exposure and accountability of those corrupted by power. In the absence of suitable institutional supports, even the favorable intentions of most political officeholders in a socialist society will not suffice to sustain liberty of the press over the long run.

Another proponent of liberty of the press under socialism might contend that the authorities in socialist societies will observe the laws upholding liberty of the press if the public is vigilant.[83]

But is it not likely that the public will defer to the government and that public opinion will be shaped by the government when the government is in charge of all schools (as would be the case in most models of socialism[84])? What can one expect when there is no independent press to speak out for liberty of the press and other liberties and to propagandize for them?

Yet the issue goes deeper than this. What is at issue is clearly suggested in the following remarks of Irving Howe:

---

[81] Jan F. Triska, ed., *Constitutions of the Communist Party-States* (Stanford: Hoover Institution Press, 1968), p. 402.

[82] Havemann, pp. 216, 219–20, 241.

[83] R. H. Tawney, "We Mean Freedom," *Review of Politics*, no. 8, no. 2 (April 1946), p. 237.

[84] For example, Wilhelm Liebknecht, *Socialism: What It Is and What It Seeks to Accomplish*, trans. May Wood Simmons (Chicago: Charles H. Kerr, [1897]), pp. 57–58. It might seem from Engels's criticism of a draft of the Erfurt Program of the German Social Democrats that he favored permitting private educational institutions under socialism. A passage in this piece in which Engels says that one cannot forbid religious persons from founding their own schools with "their own funds" is cited by Hunt as revealing Engels's "liberal and Victorian sense of decency." Richard N. Hunt, *The Political Ideas of Marx and Engels* (Pittsburgh: University of Pittsburgh Press, 1974–1984), vol. 2, pp. 181–82. But Engels's reference to the religious persons' "own funds" shows that he is talking about educational reform and church disestablishment in what he considered capitalist societies, not about private schooling under Marxian socialism, which from the outset of proletarian rule would have a moneyless economy.

> [W]hile there is no reason to suppose that . . . an intense political consciousness is a "normal" or even desirable feature of human life at all times, there can be no guarantee of minority rights except insofar as they are cherished in consciousness – and this is true for all societies.[85]

Howe has framed this problem as a universal one – which it is. But any conceivable democratic socialist society will depend more on such political consciousness to sustain its liberal features than a liberal capitalist society would. As Sidney Hook puts it, a democracy of the sort he desires needs "some of the enthusiasm and élan generated by war and nationalism". Hook believes that with the coming of central planning, the ideals of democracy can serve as the "moral equivalent" (in William James's sense) of war and nationalism.[86]

But to rely so heavily on democratic vigilance, intense consciousness, and enthusiasm is to reveal a weakness. Human beings have a limited number of interests they can attend to, and they have not historically sustained long-term enthusiasm without let-up.[87] The virtue of the institutions supporting a free press in a liberal society is that this freedom, as part of a structure of property rights, can continue in the face of limping public enthusiasm.

Opinion polls may show dislike of the news media and even distaste for specific applications of the Bill of Rights,[88] but freedom of the press is, by and large, still in place. Freedom of the press in liberal societies is based primarily on the social structure – most importantly, on property rights – and not on a need for perpetual enthusiasm.

Joseph Schumpeter writes:

> In capitalist society – or in a society that contains a capitalist element of decisive importance – any attack upon the intellectuals must run up against the private fortresses of bourgeois business which, or some of which, will shelter the quarry. . . . [T]he bourgeois

[85] Howe, "An Answer to Critics of American Socialism," review of *Socialism and American Life*, ed., Stow Persons and Donald Drew Egbert, *New International*, vol. 18, no. 3, whole no. 154 (May–June 1952), p. 132.

[86] See Hook, *Political Power*, p. 432.

[87] On the difficulty of everyone's maintaining the continuing, active involvement in public affairs that participatory democracy requires, see G.D.H. Cole, *The Next Ten Years in British Social and Economic Policy* (London: Macmillan, 1929), pp. 160–61; Michael Levin, "Marxism and Democratic Theory," in Graeme Duncan, ed., *Democratic Theory and Practice* (Cambridge: Cambridge University Press, 1983), pp. 92–94; Norman M. Thomas, *What Are the Answers?*, ed. Bettina Petersen and Anastasia Toufexis (New York: Ives Washburn, 1970), pp. 45–46. On the inevitable fading of revolutionary enthusiasm, see Thomas, *Democracy versus Dictatorship* (New York: League for Industrial Democracy, 1937), p. 19.

[88] See, for example, Samuel A. Stouffer, *Communism, Conformity and Civil Liberties* (Garden City: Doubleday, 1955).

stratum, however strongly disapproving some of [the intellectuals']
doings, will rally behind them [when they are under serious attack]
because the freedom it disapproves cannot be crushed without also
crushing the freedom it approves.

   . . . In defending the intellectuals as a group – not of course any
individual – the bourgeoisie defends itself and its scheme of life.
Only a government of non-bourgeois nature and non-bourgeois
creed – under modern circumstances only a socialist or fascist one –
is strong enough to discipline [the intellectuals]. In order to do that it
would have to change typically bourgeois institutions and drastically
reduce the individual freedom of all strata of the nation. And such
government is not likely – it would not even be able – to stop short of
private enterprise.[89]

As one looks back across the various proposals for the press under
socialism, it appears that they are, most often, a partial rejection of pure,
orthodox socialist principles – somehow partially exempting intellectual
work and intellectual products from the purview of state ownership and
planning. The proposals are attempts to produce some of the features of
property rights while retaining most of the subsidies and many of the controls
of pure socialism.

In these proposed exemptions and modifications of socialism, one can see
an effort by members of the intelligentsia to carve out a special sphere of
privilege for themselves under socialism. Such exemptions and modifications
are for brain workers, not hand workers.[90]

But the dynamics of actually existing socialist societies – in particular the
effects of the sociology of control over resources and the resulting sociology

[89] Schumpeter, *Capitalism, Socialism, and Democracy* (New York: Harper & Brothers, 1942), p. 150.
Compare Wiles, p. 461; Max Eastman, "Socialism and Freedom: A Critique of Sidney Hook," in
Hook, *Political Power*, pp. 410, 411, 413. For confirmation of Schumpeter's analysis by J.P. Nettl, a
sociologist sympathetic to socialism, see Nettl, "Ideas, Intellectuals, and Structures of Dissent," in
Philip Rieff, ed., *On Intellectuals* (Garden City: Doubleday, 1969), pp. 56–57. See also discussion of
Schumpeter and Nettl in Seymour Martin Lipset and Richard B. Dodson, "The Intellectual as Critic
and Rebel: With Special Reference to the United States and the Soviet Union," *Daedalus*,
Proceedings of the American Academy of Arts and Sciences, vol. 101, no. 3 (Summer 1972), p. 183.
Edgar Z. Friedenberg, a sociologist sympathetic to socialism, likewise maintains that capitalist
institutional structures protect civil liberties. See Friedenberg, "Our Class-Biased Bill of Rights,"
Civil Liberties Review, vol. 3, no. 4 (October–November 1976), pp. 67, 70, 76–77. See also Robert L.
Heilbroner, in "Capitalism, Socialism, and Democracy: A Symposium," *Commentary*, vol. 65, no. 4
(April 1978), p. 46.

[90] For at least tacit acknowledgement that such measures are deviations from a thoroughgoing
application of socialist planning principles, see Kautsky, *Social Revolution*, pp. 182–83; Bellamy, pp.
200, 204; Russell, pp. 180–81; G.D.H. Cole, *Fabian Socialism*, pp. 40–41; Spargo, p. 298; Besant, pp.
148–49; Wells, pp. 275–83; Sidney and Beatrice Webb, *Consumers' Co-operative Movement*, p. 412;
Hook, *Political Power*, pp. 403–4; Picard, p. 67; Yunker, pp. 200–201; Connolly, p. 190. Compare
Bukharin, quoted in Stephen Cohen, *Bukharin and the Bolshevik Revolution* (New York: Knopf, 1973),
p. 205.

of power – seem to overwhelm such efforts to carve out a special sphere for the press. Three interconnected phenomena block the emergence of a free and independent press: the absence of liberal institutions of private property, the privileged status of the *nomenklatura* (the Soviet political elite), and the concentration of power inherent in central planning.[91]

In sum, it could be argued that the possibilities for freedom of the press under socialism are open to grave doubts. Perhaps these doubts could be resolved by more work on such topics by socialist theorists. They could certainly be resolved by the existence of a pluralistic socialist society. Until that time, the obstacles in the way of freedom of the press under socialism will continue to look formidable.

Political Science, Emory University

---

[91] On the sociological implications of the *nomenklatura* and central planning for liberty of the press under socialism, see Williamson M. Evers, "Limits of Liberty of the Press in Political Theory from Milton to Hocking," Ph.D. dissertation, Stanford University, 1987, pp. 301–6, 324–25, 331–62.

SOCIALISM, CAPITALISM, AND THE SOVIET EXPERIENCE

By Alec Nove

What does the Soviet record tell us about the viability, effectiveness, and efficiency of socialism?

There are several questions that arise if one examines the Soviet experience, in addition to the comparative systems aspect (i.e., the comparison between capitalism and socialism). One question relates to the impact of the experience of the Soviet Union on theories of socialism, and also vice versa: the impact and relevance of socialist theory in assessing the Soviet system. Then there is the important issue of the role of specifically Soviet-*Russian* circumstances: traditions, political culture, and work ethic. A poet, Voloshin, wrote, *"Velikii Pyotr byl pervyi bolshevik"* (Peter the Great was the first bolshevik). The eminent philosopher Nikolai Berdyaev also remarked that "Peter's methods were purely bolshevik." Leftists of a Trotskyist persuasion argue that the Soviet Union under Stalin took the wrong turn, that the Soviet Union is not socialist at all, that it is "state capitalist" – run by a "new bourgeoisie," a bureaucratic ruling class—and continue to manufacture other variants on this theme. While official Soviet ideology claims that the U.S.S.R. is socialist and is following the principles laid down by Marx and Lenin, this can be questioned. One can indeed show that many aspects of the Soviet economic and political scene are at variance with the anticipations of Marx and of Lenin. But from this, one need not draw the conclusion that there was a "revolution betrayed," but rather that some of these anticipations were unreal or unrealizable.

Another approach is to see Soviet historical experience as that of a developing country, and the Stalinist model as a road to rapid industrialization. Comparisons can then be made with other countries at similar levels of development, or with alternative development strategies. This in turn directs our attention to the adequacy of the centralized "crash-program – industrialization" model, with its emphasis on heavy industry (and on the defense-industry sector in particular) to the circumstances of today, with a much more sophisticated economy and population, and so to the urgent need of reform, of which Gorbachev is speaking with great frankness. The "Stalin" model, which Oskar Lange once described as a "war economy *sui generis*," should be evaluated in terms of its own objectives, which gave high priority to the creation of the basis of a war economy in peacetime, subordinating to this aim its development strategy. A Western war-economy too was centralized (e.g., Great Britain in 1943) – subject to price control, administered allocation of materials, and rationing. It too generated many bureaucratic deformations of the type that we regard as typically "Soviet." Yet even a Chicago economist would hesitate (or would he?) before confidently pronouncing that one wages war more "efficiently" with an untrammelled free market. The question must be asked: efficiency for what?

This is not meant as a defense of Stalin's brutalities or the many crudities of the economic policies and planning mechanism of his time. One simply recalls Hegel: "all that is real is rational." By this I assume he meant that any existing system or institution serves or served some rational purpose (he would certainly have agreed that, through inertia, systems and institutions can become obsolete, or "fetters on the forces of production," as Marx would put it).

But all this presents us with a problem. It is the unanimous view of Soviet "reforming" economists that the economic system inherited from Stalin's day (and little changed since his death) *is* now obsolete, that "radical reform" is very urgently on the agenda. The pages of the Soviet press are daily filled with examples of irrationalities, waste, shortages, poor quality, hoarding, failure to match user requirements, informational distortions, lack of coordination, corruption, and so on. An easy way of writing this paper is to fill it with such quotations, and conclude that this shows the inherent inefficiencies of "socialism." But one must also ask oneself another question, about the system's "reformability." Gorbachev's advisers are engaged in trying to devise a reform package which is intended to overcome these deficiencies. Some socialist countries – e.g., Hungary and China – have already made such attempts (with admittedly rather patchy results). Are there not some very different possible models of socialism?

Finally, we must bear in mind the comparative systems aspect. In the introduction to the first edition of my textbook on the Soviet economy,[1] I warned against "comparing model with muddle," comparing the messy reality of Moscow with the *theory* of Chicago (i.e., comparing real Communism with a smoothly-functioning perfect or quasi-perfect market). I did once attend a conference at which someone drew on the blackboard a production possibilities frontier, and argued (correctly) that the Soviet planners cannot get to that frontier because their system cannot generate the necessary detailed information. Can ours? Do American or Japanese managers know the dollar-yen exchange rate in six months' time, or the price of oil at that date, or the rate of interest? "Rational expectations" serve well to

---

[1] Alec Nove, *The Soviet Economy* (London: Allen & Unwin, 1961), p. 22.

"close" formal macro-economic models, but decisions are taken about the future in a state of partial ignorance. It is highly likely that the Soviet economy is further from the (theoretical and invisible) frontier than is the U.S. economy. But the latter is also some distance inside it, given that there is unemployment of human and material resources. General-equilibrium Walrasian models (complete with the non-existent auctioneer) are totally irrelevant in the context of comparing systems. Our own theories remain deficient in understanding our own economies: "The analysis of the invisible hand in motion is still well beyond us," says Hahn.[2] "The theory of the internal economy of the firm is still in its infancy," says Radner.[3] Radner points out that "with the decentralization of decision-making is associated serious imperfections in the monitoring of individuals' information and actions."[4] Clearly, the problems of decentralization in the largest firm of all, U.S.S.R. Inc., are not unknown to us, either.

Similarly, the Soviet system can legitimately be "accused" of the proliferation of bureaucrats and controllers of all kinds, whose numbers grow fast. I have just been reading Medvedev, who says that "from 1965 to 1982 the gross social product rose 2.5 times, and administrative staffs nearly doubled in number," and this despite "the increased availability of computers, which increase the productivity of administrative labor."[5] He points to the "danger of a very rapid rise in the volume of information circulating within the planning organs. According to cybernetic theory, this volume increases to the square of the number of those employed."[6] But it so happens that on the very same day I read the following – about *our* economies: "Douglas North has argued that the progressive increase in the division of labour has produced an enormous increase in transaction costs, both by itself and because it has increased alienation and hence opportunism. He suggests that the increase has been of such an extent that transaction costs in advanced economies today account for about half of GDP; he interprets the rise in white-collar jobs in this way."[7]

Finally, on a list that could be prolonged, the short time-horizon of Soviet management is indeed worthy of critical comment. But so is the time-horizon of the very mobile American executive, with overconcentration on the short-

[2] Frank Hahn, "On Involuntary Unemployment," *Conference Papers:* supplement to *Economic Journal*, vol. 97 (1987), p. 14.

[3] Roy Radner, "The Internal Economy of Large Firms," *Conference Papers:* Supplement to *Economic Journal*, vol. 96 (1986), p. 3.

[4] *ibid.*, p. 17.

[5] Pavel Medvedev, "Ekonomiko-matematicheskie metody v plamrovanii," *Voprosy ekonomiki*, 12 (1986), p. 49.

[6] *ibid.*, p. 49.

[7] R. C. O. Matthews, "The Economics of Institutions and the Sources of Growth," *Economic Journal*, vol. 96 (December 1986), p. 907.

term bottom line. The contrast here is with the Japanese longer-term commitment and loyalty to the firm. On matters of this sort, the neo-classical paradigm is silent.

Then, of course, we must resist the temptation to attribute measurable statistical differences in factor productivity to the difference between "capitalism" and "socialism." There are also wide differences within the same systems – e.g., between West Germany and Ireland, or East Germany and Romania – due in varying degrees to history, work ethic and natural endowment, as well as matters organizational and systemic (therefore a comparison between East and West Germany might be more promising). I recall the work of Robert Campbell on the relative productivity of U.S. and Soviet coal mining. The U.S. is very far ahead, but the most important reason has to do with differences in accessibility and thickness of the coal seams. I would be the first to agree that the collective and state farms are inefficient, but evidently more reliable rainfall, better soil fertility, and a longer growing season are responsible for part of the superior U.S. agricultural performance.

Perhaps the best way of drawing morals from Soviet experience is to examine the deficiencies which the Soviet economics profession itself emphasizes, and which the reforms being introduced or considered by Gorbachev are intended to overcome. We may then see more clearly the link (if any) between these deficiencies and models of socialism (which could help explain why they arose and have not yet been corrected), and whether a modified or reformed socialism could be envisaged in which these sources of weakness and inefficiency could be removed.

I. SCALE AND COMPLEXITY

Contrary to the beliefs of Marxist founding fathers, there is no simple way in which "society" can control the economy and replace the invisible by the visible hand. Nor can computers resolve the problem. As Medvedev has pointed out, no computerized plan-program (and associated input-output tables) can handle more than above a thousand items, yet the disaggregated product mix runs to twelve million and more. To distribute operational task-orders to hundreds of thousands of production units, to ensure the allocation of the needed material supplies, to check on the veracity of information about costs and claims for inputs, and to ensure quality and conformity to the precise requirements of the users: these tasks cannot be efficiently performed. The growth of the economy tends to outpace the improvements in computational capacity. Fedorenko once quipped that a fully balanced, coherent, and disaggregated plan for next year will be ready in roughly thirty thousand years' time! Clearly, next year's plan will be ready next year, but it will not be fully balanced, coherent, and disaggregated. Particularly great strain is placed on the center's coordinating function, since the scale of the task necessarily involves devolution of decision-making to sectoral and/or territorial sub-units.

There are a number of derivative or associated defects: production for aggregate plan-fulfillment statistics (and not for the customer), concealment of production possibilities (to obtain a plan easy to fulfill), preference for quantity as against quality, risk avoidance, frustration through the unavailability of the desired material inputs, inconsistencies between different elements of the plan, the undesired rewarding of waste in the use and provision of intermediate goods and services (e.g., metal-goods plans in increments of tons encourage unnecessary weight, goods-transport plans in increments of ton-kilometers reward long journeys and penalize economy in the use of lorries, etc.). The emphasis on plan-fulfillment as a predominant success criterion results in a downgrading of profit and causes indifference to (or even inflation of) costs.

All these are consequences of the endeavor to plan centrally, to minimize the influence of what are called "commodity-money relations," i.e., the market. It used to be taken for granted by socialists (especially those of a Marxist persuasion) that the advance of socialism involves – even can be measured by – the gradual reduction of the role of purchase-and-sale and its replacement by planned distribution and allocation. On these assumptions, the defects summarized above are inherent in socialism. This, however, is what Gorbachev is challenging. No, he says, this is an incorrect view; we recognize the impossibility of micro-planning from the center. We recognize too (he and his advisers say) that past efforts to decentralize have ended in failure and in recentralization (e.g., the "reform" of 1979, which was much more centralizing than the abortive reform of 1965[8]). Not much has yet happened, and there is, as yet, no consensus about the alternative model. Some contours are emerging, however, which resemble the Hungarian reform of 1968 in general aspects. Material allocation is to be replaced by freely negotiated contracts, with a choice of supplier. The product mix is to be determined by negotiation with customers. Many or most prices should be subject to negotiation too, instead of being fixed by state authorities for decades. Investment in existing enterprises is to be financed largely out of retained profits and interest-bearing credits. Managerial incentives are to be linked with profits and detached from plan-fulfillment indicators. Instead of imposed output and cost plans, there will be long-term "normatives," linking incomes to performance. This kind of plan should stimulate cost-saving (via

[8] The so-called "Kosygin" reform of 1965 had as its declared objective the strengthening of enterprise autonomy and of the profit motive. However, Soviet economists now agree that it was half-hearted and inconsistent, and had little or no effect. The "reform" of 1979 stressed quantitative planning from above and tended to downgrade profits as a success indicator.

an incentive to increase profits); it should remove the perverse incentive to seek easy plans by concealing productive potential.

The center would be relieved of the impossible burden of detailed planning and allocation. However, it is realized that there are sectors of the economy which are centralizable, indeed, sectors where the needed information is best collected and acted upon at the center: electricity generation is an evident example, as there is an interconnected grid for the country as a whole. It is a matter generally neglected in textbooks, but our own experience clearly shows that some activities are dominated by very large firms. Presumably, an optimum decision-making structure in a socialist economy would also be a mixture of large and small units. When one speaks of devolving or decentralizing decision-making, the appropriate amount of change will vary.

Will the Soviet leadership in fact adopt a reform on the lines indicated here? It would very seriously affect the power structure in society – the role and privileges of the party "apparatchicki." Skepticism on this question, however, must be separated from the more general question of how a reformed socialist economy *could* operate – if it were reformed. In any country one must distinguish what is impossible on principle (or in theory) from what is politically impracticable in a given short-term situation. Thus the U.S. budget *could* be balanced, but will not be during the present decade. A Soviet-type economy *could* be reformed, if those in power are determined to enforce change. But it may well not be, for reasons which will not be discussed in this paper.

II. Shortages

In capitalist countries, one strives to find customers; in socialist countries, customers strive to find supplies. This tendency was already noted by Bazarov in the twenties,[9] and has been the subject of much attention from Janos Kornai, notably in his *Economics of Shortage.*[10] It is generally agreed that shortage (a sellers' market) adversely affects quality and attention to user needs, engenders take-it-or-leave-it attitudes, and encourages corruption and hoarding by enterprises and households.

No one doubts that the tendency to generate shortage is endemic in Soviet-type socialist economies. But does it have to be? What precisely is its cause? Interestingly, Kornai's analysis has been challenged – in a discussion with some Czech economists (over cups of coffee) and by Soviet critics.

---

[9] Bazarov wrote, "The tendency to relative underproduction should be recognized as inherent for our social structure, just as a tendency to overproduction is for capitalism." Vladimir Bazarov, *Kapitalisticheskiye tsikly i vosstanovitel'nyi protsess Khozyaistua SSSR* (Capitalist Cycles and the Reconstruction Process in the U.S.S.R.) (Moscow: "GIZ," 1927), p. 99.

[10] J. Kornai, *The Economics of Shortage* (Amsterdam: North Holland, 1980).

Kornai stresses the role of what he calls a "soft budget constraint." Management knows that, if it overspends, there will be a bailout – a subsidy. Monetary limits are frequently and easily exceeded. So, even if the original plan was supposed to ensure a macro-balance, additional claims on resources will materialize. There is "investment hunger," a demand for more investment which cannot be held in check by a rise in interest rates, since either the needed capital will be granted by the state, or, if the capital is borrowed, the necessary amounts needed to pay interest or repay the principal will be provided. Under conditions of full employment of material and human resources, unforeseen shortages (and errors) cannot be speedily corrected. In addition, price policy for consumers' goods, under conditions of chronic underfulfillment of plans, results in frequent mismatches between effective demand and supply at official prices. One sees the reflection of this *inter alia* in a wide gap between state prices for food and those ruling in the (legal) free market.

The system also generates imbalances for reasons which are not connected with soft budget constraint. Let me cite two examples. From 1965 to 1975, the output of fertilizer doubled. Serious shortages then emerged: shortages of bags to put the fertilizer in, storage space in which to house it, and machines with which to spread it. This is an imbalance due to uneven growth and to inadequate coordination of investments in complementary sectors. One cannot correct this by hardening budget constraints. An example nearer "home": the University of Glasgow expanded the number of telephones, thereby overloading the switchboard and making it difficult to obtain an outside line. Again, this was a physical imbalance, remediable (and remedied) with a new and larger switchboard which could carry more lines. *Must* the system necessarily engender unbalanced investment plans? The need for conscious coordination is not usually recognized in our textbooks, because – to repeat Hahn's words – "the analysis of the invisible hand in motion is still beyond us." In practice one gets informal lateral communication, or even government-sponsored collusion (e.g., M.I.T.I. in Japan, or "indicative" planning in France). Unexpected gaps can be plugged by imports. The recent Soviet reform wave does include some liberalization of foreign trade procedures, so this might help. A greater effort to ensure a balanced investment plan would also be helpful; this would have a greater chance of success if the planning organs could concentrate on it, instead of having their primary attention directed to the planning of current output and its allocation between users.

The measures now being taken to harden the budget constraint – to enhance the role of profits – are supposed to eliminate the tendency to overspend in the process of fulfilling plans "at any cost," thereby reducing the excess-demand pressures. As for consumers' goods, excess demand (both macro and for specific goods and services) can be eliminated through a mixture of realistic pricing and a direct link between retail prices and the wholesale prices paid to producing enterprises. It is pointed out that shortages and long lines of customers are rare not only in Hungary, which accepted radical reform, but also in Czechoslovakia and East Germany, which did not. So it could be argued that they are not an objective necessity even in a centralized socialist economy. Indeed, it was much easier to buy meat in the U.S.S.R. in 1965 than it is today; incomes have doubled since then, while official prices have been unaltered. It is this price policy, rather than "socialism," that can be blamed for the shortage of meat.

III. Monopoly

"Why are capitalist monopolies more efficient than socialist monopolies?" asked a Czech economist after a visit to the United States. He answered his own question as follows: "There is nothing so monopolistic as a socialist monopoly." If you are tied to one supplier and not allowed to go elsewhere, then the supplier can afford to ignore your needs and you do not dare use the legal remedies that are nominally available. A capitalist monopolist is always aware that poor service or excessive profits could attract a competitor.

The harm is minimal in such a sector as electricity, where the product is homogenous and performance (and price) can easily be monitored. It is very serious indeed in all those instances where quality and product mix matter.

Must socialism involve monopoly? Not necessarily. Thus in Moscow there are about thirty theaters, all publicly owned, which compete for spectators. This is because the spectators have a choice. If shortages can be overcome, state shops compete for customers. In some countries (e.g., Hungary and Poland), there are competing cooperative and sometimes private providers of some goods and many services. Something along these lines is envisaged for the Soviet Union, too. The trouble in Soviet industry and agriculture is the system of administered material allocation: managers are tied to *one* supplier, cannot exercise choice, and cannot go elsewhere. Many reforming economists therefore publicly advocate "trade in means of production," which, as already noted, must involve choice and therefore competition between suppliers. Once again, this may not in fact occur in the U.S.S.R. for a number of reasons. But it entitles us to question the proposition that socialism is necessarily associated with monopoly and its attendant abuses, even while the Soviet experience abundantly demonstrates what these abuses are.

IV. Full Employment

Most socialist countries do ensure that virtually everyone has a job. This can be said to be a clear advantage over capitalism. It can be pointed out that, for example, if three million are workless in Great Britain, the loss in output (and the human tragedies) must be set against the waste and inefficiencies of the Soviet centralized system. In fact, the opponents of reform in Moscow point to the dangers of unemployment which could grow swiftly if profit became the dominant criterion for management: unprofitable activities would cease, many workers would be declared redundant, and so security of employment, regarded as a major achievement of socialism, would come to an end.

On the other hand, full employment is associated with under- or mis-employment. Labor is often hoarded by enterprises for the same reason they hoard materials. Labor discipline suffers when the manager does not dare to dismiss a worker; it may be impossible to find a replacement, and it is easy to get another job.

A Soviet author, commenting on the poor performance of the farm labor force, remarked that "at one time they reasoned: why should we work, we will not be paid. Now they reason: why should we work, we will be paid anyway."[11] Incentives are weakened by a pervasive egalitarianism and by the too-frequent fact that extra earnings cannot be spent on what the wage-earner particularly wants to buy (a consequence of chronic shortages).

Full employment is also connected with the soft budget constraint: money to pay wages will be provided, even if the enterprise lacks funds. So, all in all, the student of comparative economic systems may find it difficult to identify the balance of advantage.

V. Prices

Marx had nothing to say about prices under socialism, since he imagined that, in a true socialist society, there would be no purchase-and-sale. All Soviet reforming economists agree that the price system that now exists is inefficient. Being (supposedly) cost-based, and altered at infrequent intervals, prices reflect cost and effort, not result. Many critical remarks refer to the *Zatratnaya kontseptsiya tseny*, the cost-based notion of price, which fails to reflect use-value, demand, or the alternative uses (opportunity-cost) of inputs. Any allocation decisions based on such prices, whatever the level of the decision, are necessarily unsound and lead to avoidable inefficiencies and misallocation. Of course the real prices of the real capitalist world do not conform to textbook standards of perfection. In particular, there can be no all-embracing futures market. However, most of our prices do not mislead decision-makers most of the time.

Must their prices be misleading? One recalls old debates: Mises, Hayek, Lange, and Lerner.[12] Can there be a rational "socialist" price system in the

---

[11] S. Vikulov, "Chto zavisit ot rukovodibelya", *Pravda*, February 4, 1987.

[12] See Israel M. Kirzner, "Some Ethical Implications for Capitalism of the Socialist Calculation Debate," *Social Philosophy & Policy*, vol. 6, no. 1 (Autumn 1988).

absence of private ownership of the means of production? Soviet experience certainly shows that the U.S.S.R. has so far failed to develop a price system which could be described as rational. Indeed, the system was based on the supposition that producer prices played a largely passive role, and that plans were, as far as possible, expressed in quantities. In practice, many plans (and investment choices too) inevitably used prices, e.g., output plans were expressed in gross values, or rates of return on investments were compared.

Suppose the reformers get their way, and prices are altered to reflect supply and demand, with most of them freely negotiable. Would this be effective, and would it be socialist? Of course, there are other questions too: if profitability is to serve as a guide to decision-making, who is to keep what share of the profits? What of the need for a capital market – a subject much discussed in both Hungary and China? Should enterprises be allowed to invest in other enterprises? But in legitimately criticizing the investment problems faced by reformed and unreformed socialist economies, we should not overlook the weaknesses of our own investment theories. (Hahn wrote that the whole question of investment "is deeply mysterious under perfect competition."[13] Also, while the absence of bankruptcy in socialist economies can be seen as an institutional weakness (part of the "soft budget constraint"), it should not be forgotten that bankruptcy, like divorce, is not itself a "good"; it is evidence of business or marital failure.

VI. INNOVATION

The Soviet record in the field of innovation is modest. While suitable for imposing innovation from above, the system has unintentionally discouraged initiative from below. This is due to two mutually reinforcing reasons: one is risk-aversion (risk, as such, is not rewarded; priority in performance evalution is given to the fulfillment of current plans); the other is the strict control over material allocation and finance, so that the would-be innovator is often frustrated when trying to acquire the needed resources. Various devices to counter this have hitherto been ineffective. It remains to be seen whether the proposed much greater incentive to make profits, and their freer use to finance decentralized investments, plus "trade in means of production," will be a remedy. There is no doubt as to the desire of the party leadership to modernize, to re-equip, and to encourage initiative. The unanswered question is whether, in the end, public ownership of the underlying capital assets is, in itself, a bar to innovation. Perhaps greater flexibility in prices and material rewards, plus the goad of competition, could have some positive results. After all, sub-units within large privately-owned corporations do

---

[13] Hahn, "Of Marx and Keynes and Many Things," *Oxford Economic Papers*, vol. 38 (July 1986), p. 360.

innovate, even though the individuals who initiate action are not themselves owners of the means of production.

VII. COLLECTIVE/STATE AGRICULTURE

Soviet agriculture has been the subject of many jests, both in and out of the Soviet Union. "If we collectivize the Sahara, soon we will be importing sand," is one example of many. The negative lessons are all too visible. Let us try to classify them.

One is the "original sin" of *forcible* collectivization – the act of depriving the direct producers of their land, their control over means of production, and the product, with all its consequences in terms of alienation. The process of forcing the peasants into pseudo-cooperatives in the early Thirties cost millions of lives and embittered relations with the peasants.

Another is the overestimation of the economies of scale and disregard for diseconomies of scale. Farms are too big and diverse, and have too large a labor force, for efficient management. Lack of effective labor incentives does much damage.

Then there is the habit, still encountered, of ordering farm management about. Party or state interference with routine operations (e.g., imposition of investments or crop pattern or livestock numbers) can be engineered by bureaucrats who sometimes ignore local conditions and fail to overcome the handicaps of soil and climate.

Recent attempts to modernize and to introduce new technology (as well as the increased use of fertilizers and other chemicals) has increased management's dependence on industrial inputs. Many are the complaints about poor quality of machinery, the failure to supply spare parts, and the existence of monopolist supply and service agencies which have their own plans to fulfill. The net effect has been a substantial rise in costs. The attempt to solve the problem by bureaucratic restructuring – the creation of a hierarchical "agro-industrial complex" – has done little or nothing to improve matters.

Finally, there is a notorious lack of infrastructure (roads, storage space, specialized transport, rural amenities), which causes severe losses and results in the loss of skilled workers through out-migration.

All these defects are well known and publicly debated in the U.S.S.R. Again, the question is not whether the record is negative, but whether, within a basically "socialist" structure, agriculture could function efficiently. The Hungarian model is here a guide to possibilities. Its essential features, contrasting with the Soviet model, are:

   a) No compulsory delivery quotas or (as a rule) any other imposed production plans. Prices are subject to negotiation, with producers free not to sell, or to sell in the free market.

b) Freedom to purchase material inputs (no material allocation bureaucracy), subject only to import restrictions due to currency shortage.
c) Freedom to use or not to use service agencies – to participate or not in "agro-industrial complexes," and freedom to undertake a variety of non-agricultural activities.
d) Flexible arrangements to provide incentives for collective labor, combined with greater freedom to undertake private activities, independently or as sub-contractors. (Unlike Poland, there are hardly any purely private farms, but there is a lively private sector within the collectives.)

Hungary's agriculture has been carefully studied in the U.S.S.R. and some lessons are being partially applied, such as the extension of small-group and family contract. Large sums are being expanded on infrastructure. There are still many difficulties with the supply system (they will persist unless and until they shift to "trade in means of production" with customer choice), and party officials and the "agro-industrial" bureaucracy still interfere in management. This is not the place to discuss the current problems of agricultural reform. The only point to make is that the Hungarian example does suggest that a reform could work with reasonable efficiency without de-collectivization – if the Soviet variety is radically altered in the context of a wider economic reform.

VIII. The Negative Effect of Outlawing Private Enterprise

Private, small-scale workshops providing such items as paper clips, toothbrushes, tools, and such services as cafés, repairs, and travel agencies would fill the many gaps left by official provision. The sheer scale of the planning process ensures that small items get overlooked. Private and cooperative enterprises can be very effective, and conversely the ban on such enterprises, and on private traders, imposes a cost on society. Some countries (e.g., Hungary, Poland, and China) have recognized this and have legalized such activities, subject to certain limits (e.g., on numbers of employees). The U.S.S.R. has resisted such ideas until very recently; only now is encouragement being given to cooperative enterprise, and limited private activities are being tolerated (but without the right to *employ* anyone). It appears to me that some private and cooperative enterprise could – should – be part of an effective model of socialism. It is a matter of controversy in the Soviet Union.

IX. Party Rule, Arbitrariness, and the Role of Contract

There is an inherent contradiction between economic reform, which rests upon contractual obligations, and the arbitrary powers of party officialdom.

This extends far beyond the economy. Much is now being written about local officials dictating decisions to the supposedly independent judiciary (see, for example, the devastating critique by Vaksberg).[14] In an odd way, one is reminded of the neo- (or pseudo-) Marxist views of the legal philosopher Pashukanis in the early thirties. He had argued that law and legal norms generally derive from commercial contract, and that when these are replaced by conscious planning, law will wither away. As Marx had foretold, under full socialism there will be no need for laws. Pashukanis's insight into the connection between the observance of commercial contract and the legal order as a whole has a point. Arbitrariness replaced contract, and arbitrariness also spread into the judicial process itself, with elementary human rights a casualty. Bureaucrats ignored the procedural rights which form part of the Soviet legal code, just as inter-enterprise contracts were too often not respected: "what mattered was 'orders from above'."[15]

Now, Gorbachev (a lawyer by training) is insisting on *both* the observance of contracts in the economy *and* the need for a legal order in society as a whole. Obviously, contrary to Pashukanis's view, an efficient and ethically tolerable socialism requires law: commercial, civil, and criminal. Its absence means not some unrealizable folk self-rule, but arbitrariness, unpredictability, and oppression. One of the key problems facing today's Soviet reformers is to find a way to limit the powers of *the* party and its full-time officials in what is still a one-party state. It is too soon to tell if they will find a way.

X. RANK-BASED PRIVILEGE, *NOMENKLATURA*, AND CORRUPTION

Despite some Western literature to the contrary, the U.S.S.R. is not a society as unequal as ours. The pay of quite senior officials of party and state is a fraction of that of leading executives of even a medium-sized American corporation – though many times higher than the legal minimum wage. However, a very important element of inequality exists in access to scarce goods and services. Rank in the official hierarchy, *nomenklatura* status, provides material privileges, and, of course, also power – power that can be abused. Reference to the existence of such privileges was strictly banned and did not appear in any publication for fifty years or so until an issue of *Pravda* in February 1986 raised it directly. The value of such privileges is also a function of the degree of *un*availability of particular goods and services to ordinary citizens without influence. To this extent, prices which balance supply and demand have the effect of reducing the value of privileged access to scarce goods and services. Power to allocate resources has resulted in

---

[14] Arkadi Vaksberg, "Pravda v glaza," *Literaturnaya gazeta*, no. 51 (December 1986), p. 13.
[15] V. Skvorrsova, "Dogovor . . .," *Selskaya zhizn*, (January 2, 1987), p. 3.

power to allocate to the allocators. This would not surprise Trotsky, who duly noted that whoever had such power "would never forget themselves." There is a lively controversy about whether the rulers, the *nomenklatura* officials, constitute a "new class." It should be noted that privilege is rank-based and is lost on retirement or dismissal from office. One hundred and fifty years ago, the great poet Pushkin remarked that overdependence for status on rank (and so on the Tsar) made for slavishness towards authority. A person who owes his position to personal wealth, or to aristocratic birth, can afford a greater degree of independence. Lower down the social scale, a source of income not dependent on the state sets in itself some limits on state power: thus the poet Mandelshtam, in exile in Voronezh, dreamt of owning a cow, so that it would be possible to live even if the local literary bureaucrats refused to publish any of his works.

Rank-based privilege is itself subject to rules. In the absence of a free press or an opposition party, however, these rules can be neglected, and recent publicity about corruption and abuse of power in the Soviet hierarchy shows what the consequences can be. However, we cannot ignore the fact that corruption is a disease from which any system can suffer (we need only refer to recent scandals in Wall Street and the City of London).

XI. Ecology, Externalities, the Public Good – and Methodological Individualism

Soviet *theory* emphasizes the general interest, and has been "guilty" of ignoring the individual while extolling the "collective." Western mainstream theory, by contrast, tends to concentrate on the individual, and to regard the whole as no more than the sum of its parts. Yet there are circumstances in which the pursuit of self-interest, or a deal profitable for those making it, has a positive or negative impact which is not "caught" by the profit-and-loss account. Men (and women) can sometimes worsen their position by the pursuit of individual self-interest, as compared with collaboration and collusion. If everyone tried to get to work by car in London, Paris, or New York, paralysis would ensue. The provision of a public-transport alternative (e.g., metros) everywhere requires public action, plus a subsidy. Infrastructure is usually externality-prone, yielding profits to third parties, which is why much of it is seen logically to "belong" in the public sector. Ecological considerations call for regulation, for reasons too obvious to require discussion. In my own work on "feasible socialism,"[16] I tried to identify those areas in which a decentralized profit-oriented market can be expected to yield the desired result, and those where divergence between private profit and the more general interest is likely to be large enough to warrant action by public bodies. A role for public authorities, and a recognition of the existence

---

[16] Alec Nove, *The Economics of Feasible Sosialism* (London: Allen & Unwin, 1983).

of a *common* weal, would seem to require recognition, or so socialists would argue.

This said, it must be admitted that the Soviet record in these matters is unsatisfactory. While much publicity has recently been given to ecological problems and new laws have been passed, the U.S.S.R. continues to stand high in the pollution league, as do most of her East European allies. While cheap public transport is usually provided, local town-planning authorities have had little power to deal with economic vested interests in the shape of economic ministries, and the press frequently mentions abuses in public housing allocations. It is apparent from Soviet experience that one cannot internalize *all* externalities, i.e., consider everything in the context of everything, because of informational and administrative overload. Tasks must be subdivided. The center itself becomes a loose federation of semi-autonomous ministries and departments, presenting not only major burdens of coordination but also creating administrative boundary lines. These in turn reproduce the externality problem: anything that is not within the purview of a given official or department is, for him or her, an externality. A Soviet chemical factory is just as likely to pollute a river as any capitalist factory unless forcibly prevented, since its manager is not responsible for the damage to fishing or bathing. Examples of so-called *vedomstvennost'* ("departmentalism") are legion. The effect on regional and industrial location policies is notorious: while the center may desire a move towards less developed areas, ministries strive to plan their investments in the more developed regions to save on infrastructure. The "free" medical service has been seriously underfunded and is the subject of much public criticism, not least for the bribes that have to be paid. Passing to a more general point, Soviet would-be reformers have often spoken of the need to devise a scheme by which enterprises' interests are in line with the general interest, and (not surprisingly) have not been successful. In fact there is some danger that, in reacting against excessive centralization, they could well overlook informational and technological economies of scale, and fragmentize excessively. This has surely been the case in Yugoslavia.

Should one therefore conclude that Soviet experience proves that the socialist agenda is, in these respects, irrelevant or negative? It seems reasonable to note that in *any* large economy or large firm there are questions of centralization and decentralization, and organizational dividing-lines can affect what the decision-maker might find it rational to do. Externalities exist as a problem in some form everywhere. One can argue that it is the endeavor to overcentralize that led (paradoxically) to the division of the bureaucratic apparatus and so to administrative overload, which manifests itself in neglecting the very externalities which socialist theorists had expected to be better handled when the state owns the means of production. The strengthening of the market mechanism could then leave more time for the planners to cope with their coordinating and "internalizing" task, confining attention to sectors and decisions where important external effects can be anticipated. Socialists are not wrong in stressing that the profitability criterion *can* mislead, but it must be recognized that the Soviet record in coping with externalities has seldom been impressive. Similarly, the heavy burden of current operational planning has left the center with insufficient time to devote to longer-term considerations.

CONCLUSION

One can only repeatedly stress that the Soviet experience must be seen in its historical and national context. It must be reiterated that the economic performance (and political culture) of a country is deeply influenced by its past. Thus, it would hardly be possible to assess the remarkable achievements of the Japanese economy without taking into account factors specific to the Japanese people. No explanation of Stalinism would be complete without consideration of Russia's autocratic tradition – the very large role played by the state in its economic development in past centuries. And it is only now that a serious attempt is being made to modify the centralized economic structure inherited from the Stalinist period. It is also worth recalling that the Russians have not been noted through the ages for possessing a great deal of discipline or work ethic. Not only are some institutions and practices partly explicable by "Russian" traditions and circumstances, but these same institutions can be made to work better in a more "efficient" environment, such as East Germany. The Soviet path to so-called modernization was ruthless, despotic, and centralizing. These methods were costly in human terms, and also in micro-economic allocational inefficiency. These methods came, in many people's minds in and out of the U.S.S.R., to be equated with "socialism." *The* question, not yet answered, is whether the U.S.S.R. and other Communist-ruled countries will find it possible to achieve a modernization based upon a substantial enhancement of the role of markets and prices, with competition (albeit between state-owned enterprises plus some cooperative ones), user choice, and plans based on negotiation and contract. If the answer is positive, a very different paper may have to be written in (say) five years' time. The attempt may founder. However, we may have a few problems too : mass Third World default and a collapse of the dollar could have disastrous consequences for the world economy.

Suppose the Gorbachev reforms succeed – and I again stress that it is early yet. Would such a system still qualify as "socialist"? It is a matter of definition. If by "socialism" we mean the dominance of public or cooperative ownership of the means of production, then a species of "market socialism" would not be a contradiction in terms. Soviet economists (and Gorbachev himself) have been stressing that markets are not, as such, capitalistic. Nontheless, it is true that the Marxian vision of socialism did foresee the replacement of the market by conscious allocation – by production directly for use by so-called "associated producers." The founding fathers of Marxism thought that this would be a simple matter. They could not have been more wrong. So now we are in the presence of a search for feasible combinations of plan and market. Let us not write this off in advance. Let us wait and see.

Economics, University of Glasgow